JAGUAR TOTEM

A Totem is an Animal one chooses as a Revered Symbol.

Anne LaBastille

JAGUAR TOTEM

Anne LaBastille

WEST OF THE WIND PUBLICATIONS, INC.
Westport, N.Y., U.S.A.

*Printed in the United States of America
by the Offset House, Essex VT.*

The names of certain persons in this book have been changed to protect their privacy.
Photos by Author, unless indicated.

*Book design and production: Nadine McLaughlin,
Graphics North, Jay, N.Y. 12941.
The text of this book is composed in Goudy and Korinna.
This book printed on recycled paper.
Cover design by Anne LaBastille.*

1st Edition

Credits for partial use of articles by Anne LaBastille:
National Geographic. The Quetzal, Fabulous Bird of Maya Land. January 1969.
Biological Conservation. Biology and Conservation of the Quetzal (with David G. Allen). 1969. Vol. 1 (6): 297-306.
Auk. (American Ornithologists' Union Journal). Notes on the Feather Structure and Behavior of the Quetzal. 1972. Vol. 89 (2): 339-348.
Caribbean Journal of Science. Birds and Mammals of Anegada, British Virgin Islands. 1973.
Audubon. Panama Practices the Art of the Possible. September 1973.
Audubon. India's Taj Mahal to Nature. May 1974.
Biological Conservation. Artificial Nesting of the Quetzal. 1974. Vol. 6:2.
Audubon. Heaven—Not Hell. November 1979.
E.P. Dutton Co., N.Y. Assignment: Wildlife. 1980.
Animal Kingdom. Half Moon Caye: Belize's Island Paradise. August 1982.
International Wildlife. Scotland's Strangest Landlord. July 1983.
Oceans. A Delicate Balance—Half Moon Caye. November–December 1988.

Library of Congress Catalog Card Number: 99-70821
LaBastille, Anne
Jaguar Totem, 1st ed.

ISBN 0-9632846-2-2

West of the Wind Publications, Inc., Westport, N.Y., 12993, U.S.A.

1 2 3 4 5 6 7 8 9 10

To Dr. James P. Lassoie

Chair, Department of Natural Resources

Cornell University

–my trusted colleague–

To Dr. Lawrence S. Hamilton

Cornell University

Professor Emeritus, International Conservation

–my favorite professor–

Acknowledgements

Once again I have been extremely lucky with having a great team working to produce this book. As typists, I give sincere thanks to Nancy Sherman and Sue Phillip for their excellent typing. Then, my grateful appreciation to Nadine McLaughlin of Graphics North for her expert design layout, illustration handling, and production of the book. Lastly, it is my pleasure to acknowledge Sally Matthews of The Offset House in Essex, VT, for her guidance in printing this book.

Once again I am privileged to thank my high school chum and fellow writer, Mary Jane Scott, who kindly critiqued the manuscript of this book, just as she did on **WOODSWOMAN III.**

A much-needed service was supplied by my colleague, Dr. James Lassoie, Chair, Department of Natural Resources at Cornell University, who whizzed out several e-mail messages for me to update portions of these chapters. Appreciation, likewise, goes to Dr. Lawrence S. Hamilton, Professor Emeritus, of the same Department, for updating the status of the national parks mentioned and providing the all-important quote for the back of this book.

Praise goes to the fine optometrist, Dr. Terry Walton, who keeps me reading and writing with great glasses.

And finally, heartfelt thanks goes to Dr. Dan Odell, Professor Emeritus of English at S.U.N.Y., Albany, whose vision and support made this book a reality.

Contents

Foreword

I expect that most avid readers of conservation and environmental topics harbor a deep yearning to contribute to the sustainability of the Earth's fragile natural resources through their innate, though unexpressed, abilities with the written word. Ideally, such writings would flow from professional experiences and personal insights and argue convincingly for protecting the delicate balance of nature. Better yet would be to find that by centering one's life as an indispensable part of nature, unique perspectives emerge which are lost to those contributing unabashedly to the fast pace of modern society. Add an isolated cabin with primitive amenities surrounded by an unmarred wilderness, and a vivid image of Henry David Thoreau at Walden Pond springs quickly to mind.

Today, authors focused on conservation and the environment are certainly not lacking, which perhaps is a powerful statement unto itself. Analytical and scientific tomes abound, as do personal anecdotes and passionate pleas for preservation, or at least wise stewardship, of the planet's limited environmental resources. Only a few authors, however, base their trade on scientific field research modified by a life-long personal commitment to an ecologically sustainable society. Those so talented can weave science into personal experiences to produce interesting and readable accounts which lead both the informed and the novice into the intricacies of nature and humankind's mixed relationship with it. We are fortunate that Anne LaBastille is that kind of writer.

In this book, her ninth since *Woodswoman* in 1976, Dr. LaBastille provides a chronology of conservation adventures based on her three decades of experience as an ecological consultant. Writing from her isolated cabin in the Adirondack Mountains of northern New York, she takes the reader to a variety of environmental projects in Central America, the Caribbean, and Europe.

These colorful accounts highlight her intimate involvement with wildlife and people; her long-term impact on conservation efforts; and her unique insights into herself as a scientist, ecologist, and woman. Travel with Anne from her remote cabin into the "real world" where she and her associates work through the day-by-day details and rugged field conditions that make up conservation efforts.

How hard is conservation work, and do I know enough to be effective? What is the long-term outlook for such efforts? How can one person "make a difference" when it comes to protecting the Earth's resources? What advice can I offer to all those committed to the conservation movement? The answers to these questions, and others, can be found in the chapters of this book.

As a member of Cornell's Department of Natural Resources for over 23 years, and with a keen interest in international conservation, I have watched dozens of students graduate from our program and step into the world to make meaningful contributions to the conservation of natural resources. We continually seek to broaden our instruction in international conservation and provide worthy students and professors with opportunities for foreign service to the Earth's environment. Anne was one such student. We are privileged to have her as an alumna and adjunct professor.

Protecting and conserving the Earth's limited and fragile natural resources will demand one's personal commitment, as well as scientific rigor and hard work over a sustained period of time. Reading the accounts that follow will certainly give the reader an appreciation for what is involved, in an enjoyable, exciting style. It will be up to you, and me—to all of us—to determine how to use this information in helping forge a sustainable future for modern society.

Dr. James P. Lassoie
Chair, Department of Natural Resources
Cornell University

From Author
to Reader

Yes, I'm a woodswoman—from my heart, to my soul, to my bare feet and boot bottoms. It's my personal identity and has come about naturally.

It's true I've written three books describing my life-style in a rustic log cabin with no road or electricity over the past three decades. The first in this Trilogy—Woodswoman—has sold over 160,000 copies in 22 years and continues to perform well. *Beyond Black Bear Lake,* its sequel, and the latest, *Woodswoman III,* are very popular. Apparently life in the woods appeals to many readers—both in Thoreau's time and mine.

I lecture nation-wide about the similarities and differences between Henry David Thoreau and myself in our hand-built cabins on Walden Pond and Black Bear Lake, respectively. Always I stress the strengths, benefits, and joys of our unconventional life-styles.

All of the above have given rise to certain fantasies among some fans. I smile gently when hearing questions or comments like: "Do you grow all your own food in the woods or live off the land? It must be nice to sit under a big pine and write poetry or play guitar all day. How many weeks at a stretch can you stay at your cabin without coming out? You're only five-foot, three inches? I thought you'd be an Amazon."

True or false, fantasies are fun. They're good for folks. They help soften the toughness and hurts of Life. But they also shroud the real person.

This woodswoman has a whole other life which the average reader only glimpses fleetingly. Perhaps from an article in a conservation magazine. Or from one of my other lectures dealing with a threatened animal in a foreign country. Or a small news clip about an award I received for my environmental work.

My other life is as a professional wildlife ecologist working in international conservation on all kinds of compelling jobs. It may

mean consulting for a non-government organization (NGO) about
restoring a key habitat. It can be writing and photographing an
article about an endangered species. It could be responding to a
direct request from a government conservation agency to survey a
remote ecosystem. Or, best of all, it can be being asked to set up a
protected area to save special wildlands and wildlife.

I have my former husband to thank for starting me on the path
into international conservation. We created the first eco-tourism
trips out of the USA in the early 1960s, taking our guests to
Central America and the Caribbean. Our goal was to help clients
enjoy the myriad new forms of life in the tropics *and* to convert
them into caring world conservationists. Up until then, I'd been
totally focused on the Adirondacks and helping my husband run
our rustic lodge.

After we divorced, I went back to college and obtained a doctorate from Cornell University. My most favorite course was
International Conservation, taught by my most favorite professor,
Dr. Lawrence S. Hamilton. (See his blurb on back cover.) Through
his superb teaching and a series of foreign guest lecturers, our class
was introduced to a wide range of professional possibilities. Each
student could choose a totally new challenge somewhere in the
world towards saving natural resources.

I burned with youthful determination—with a white, pure
flame—to become an international ecological consultant. After
ten years of university instruction (B.S., M.S., Ph.D.) plus two
years of teaching at Cornell, I felt ready to try this career. I based
everything at my Adirondack cabin, traveled to and from it, but
always kept one foot in the woods. I have pursued this profession
ever since and have experienced a most rewarding life.

I've shared this with you, dear Reader, to set the stage for
JAGUAR TOTEM. It is an intense, rich, colorful, and startling
story. It may be the first of another Trilogy. It reaches far beyond
academia, pure science, and modern technology. I'm portrayed as a
scientist, an artist, a writer, and a woman. Not as a woodswoman.
My goal in this book is to convert *you* into a caring and compas-
sionate conservationist.

JAGUAR TOTEM

"Our task must be to free ourselves
by widening our circle of compassion
to embrace all living creatures
and the whole of nature in its beauty."

Albert Einstein (1879–1955)

"Indian bird,
Alive in your coat of arms –
Guardian of your native soil,
May you soar higher
Than the eagle and the condor."

(Ancient Guatemalan verse.)

1

MOTHER of QUETZALS

---

ool mist was settling over the cloud forest. The steep mountainside was turning gauze white and eerie. Huge leaves fell occasionally from the trees that towered above us. In the afternoon's absolute hush, each leaf made a crashing noise like a herd of peccaries chasing after us. I was climbing, out of breath and riddled by mosquitoes, up the slopes of Volcán Atitlán in Guatemala. A barefoot Maya guide led the way. David G. Allen, bird photographer, followed. His blue workshirt was crisscrossed with cameras, and his khaki pants pockets were bulging with film. He also huffed and puffed.

We both had been leading sedentary lives back in the States. I was a graduate student for a doctorate at Cornell University, living in classrooms and libraries. David ran a photo studio from his home in Ithaca, N.Y. Our lungs and hearts were straining at this 6,000-foot elevation after being accustomed to Ithaca, N.Y., at 800 feet.

Five more Mayas walked in single file behind him, carrying tents, cooking gear, sleeping bags, photo blinds, ropes, climbing spurs, strobe lights and more bulky photographic equipment. They hiked silently, barefoot and sure, strong as mules. Bringing up the rear strode Armando, tan, fit, and well-muscled with a walkie-talkie radio and a revolver on his hip. He was used to this altitude, having lived his entire life at mile-high Lake Atitlán.

I glanced back at him. His sparkling blue eyes were alert and mischievous. His face was clean-shaven with a stubborn set to the chin, upturned full lips, and even white teeth. Nothing had changed. All the things that had first attracted me to Armando, when I began ecological fieldwork at Lake Atitlán, were still there. So, too, were his innate creativeness, self-reliance, mechanical skill, and stalwart nature.

(Well, dear reader, the story of our romance, starting the winter of 1965-66, is all set down in *Mama Poc, An Ecologist's Account of the Extinction of a Species*, 1990.)

It was March 1968 when he met David and me at the airport in Guatemala City. There stood Armando in the parking lot beside his Land Rover. He hurried into the airport. I knew he'd be right by the baggage claim when David and I emerged from Customs, ready to give us both bear hugs. The lonesome weeks and months Armando and I had to spend apart, because I was enrolled in college or writing at my log cabin, suddenly vanished. A burst of greetings and backslapping. David and Armando were fast friends ever since he'd helped the photographer obtain gorgeous pictures of the rare and flightless Giant Grebes of Lake Atitlán. *National Geographic* had sent David to Guatemala in 1967 to illustrate the article I was writing for the magazine on these endangered waterbirds.

Our baggage was quickly and efficiently loaded. I jumped joyfully onto the front seat of the jeep next to Armando. It felt just like yesterday as the three of us headed for the mountains. How fortunate that I'd been able to spend most of my first two years of studies, not at Cornell, but in Guatemala, gathering data for a thesis. Armando had become my paid assistant and supplied a rental boat, motor, and gas. We worked together easily and spent a lot of time on that magnificent lake. He taught me useful, practical skills and introduced me to a Guatemala no tourist would ever know. This assignment, however, was far different. We were headed into unknown backcountry.

It had begun when David phoned me in January. I'd answered the hall phone in my dormitory and heard, "How would you like to go back to Guatemala and write an article on the quetzal?" he asked in his gruff voice. "*National Geographic* is interested. No one has ever published a story with color photos of the national bird of Guatemala."

I started jumping up and down with excitement. "*National Geographic?*" I stammered.

"Yes. Remember when I was down there shooting the grebes? We stopped at the Museum of Natural History and met its director, Dr. Jorge Ibarra. I asked about quetzals, and he promised to find some breeding pairs. Well, he kept his promise. He's located a farm owner on Volcán Atitlán who says he has nesting quetzals in the cloud forest tract on his land. He's willing to let us work and stay there. The *Geographic* editors want me to take the photos and you to do the researching and writing."

"Oh, I'd love to do that, David," I breathed. "Anything to get out of this dorm and this miserable winter."

"It'll be tough, Anne. We'll have to go this March and April, the two driest months. Otherwise it rains the rest of the year. Hard to take good pictures in rain and mist."

"That's fine. I can take a leave of absence from Cornell. Shall I write Armando and ask him to assist us? Use his Land Rover?"

"Sure enough," was his laconic reply.

After he hung up, I whispered, "Bless you, David. I can't wait to get back in the field. *And* to see Armando."

So here we were following the complicated directions of the *fincero* (farm owner) from Guatemala City to his isolated property. Armando had driven swiftly down and around the great central volcanic chain to the Pacific coast. Then, we'd chugged and skidded in four-wheel drive on pockmarked dirt roads up the southern slopes of Volcán Atitlán. We found the farm and paid our respects to the British-Guatemalan owner. He was a dapper, cultivated tea farmer with silvery hair and a clipped British accent. We sat on his porch, sipping his brand of finest tea from Spode china cups. He offered to loan us five of his Maya laborers who spoke rudimentary Spanish (like me) to set up camp and photo blinds. He also offered clean drinking water from his mountain spring.

Armando manhandled the Land Rover with its new load of eight people up farm roads to 5,000 feet. A wall of green reaching 100 feet high blocked our way. "It's the cloud forest!" declared Armando. "Now we walk."

Everyone clambered out and took a load. We started trudging up the tortuous trail. This home of quetzals was a green and grandiose world. Oaks, wild figs, Spanish cedars, and other tropical species rose to 150 feet. Branches were laced with lianas and adorned with air plants. Trunks were crisscrossed with vines. Treacherous canyons sliced their way between the folds of the 11,600-foot volcano. We could hear water roaring in their depths, but no human could climb down those precipitous sides. Because of the porous volcanic soils not a spring, creek, pond, or swamp stood anywhere between 5,000 and 11,600 feet on that mighty mountain. How provident of the farm owner to provide us with the one essential life necessity—water.

The whole situation was ironic, I mused while hiking. If a horizontal tunnel about 15 miles long could have been dug right

Volcán Atitlán looms above the cloud forest where quetzals nested. This tea farm was our jumping off place with jeep.

through the mass of volcano, we would have come out just above my beloved Lake Atitlán. Yet, no contrast could have been greater (short of a desert island or Antarctica). Instead of brilliant sun and sparkling water, we were enveloped in clammy clouds and ancient forests. Every noon, a cap of cumulus clouds descended over the peak, mantling and muffling everything. Awesome rains would drench the forest almost daily except during the brief two-to-three-month dry season. This phenomenon gave the ecosystem its name, "cloud forest." The abundant moisture nourished living foliage to greater greenery and encouraged dead wood and leaves to decay rapidly. Every drop was either absorbed by the plants or by the porous igneous soil.

Armando caught my eye and winked. I smiled, blushed self-consciously, and blew him a kiss. Turning back to the trail, I wondered if he still loved me. I pondered how we'd ever manage to be alone on this assignment. There'd been no time to talk during the bustle of arrival, the four-hour drive, and immediate plunge into the cloud forest.

I was relieved when we finally stopped in a gloomy but level clearing. The Mayas began cutting away undergrowth. Within an hour, they had magically prepared a campfire, built a *champa* (thatch roofed cooking shelter), and laid up a tall stack of firewood. David, Armando, and I were busy setting up our tents and stowing away the precious field equipment and cameras. Humidity and rain would be our biggest problems. Even as we worked, everyone was constantly scanning the leafy roof to look for a flash of green and red.

The quetzal is considered by many ornithologists to be one of the most beautiful birds in the world. No larger than a dove, it flies like "an arc of green fire in the sun, an emerald meteor in the mist, a cold viridian flame in rain," I was to write in my article for *National Geographic*. It takes its name from the Aztec word, *quetzalli* (tail feather), which has come to mean "beautiful" or "precious." Mexican and Guatemalan native people have called the bird quetzal for centuries. They revere it as much as Maya jade or Aztec gold.

As long as 1,000 years ago Amerindians live-trapped quetzals, plucked out their prize plumes, and released the birds unharmed. (The four, long, tail coverts grew safely back after the next molt.) The plumes were reserved for royalty and priesthood alone. Any common person who dared to use them was punished. If he or she killed a bird, they faced the death penalty. In those days both Mayas and Aztecs worshiped a feathered serpent—called Kulkulcan by the Mayas, Quetzalcoatl by the Aztecs. It is depicted in hundreds of glyphs on stelae, stone carvings, and temple stones as a fanged rattlesnake covered with quetzal feathers.

Even today, tradition stands strong. The quetzal is Guatemala's heraldic emblem. The unit of currency bears its name. The bird also appears on the country's flag, coat of arms, stamps, paper and silver money, arts and crafts, and road signs.

The name of the second largest city is Quetzaltenango—"place of the quetzal." It was near there that the Spanish conquistador, Pedro de Alvarado, confronted in battle Tecúm Umán, the great Maya chieftain. Legend relates that Alvarado mortally wounded the Maya leader. As he lay dying, a giant quetzal fluttered down from the sky and fell dead on his chest. Thus, say the Mayas stoically, their race lost its freedom to the Spaniards. The graceful quetzal is considered a symbol of liberty even today.

The popular belief persists that the bird cannot live in captivity. I believed this, too, until I saw two perfectly healthy quetzals in the Bronx Zoo aviary. They have been there several years, but have never bred. I was about to discover why during our two-month sojourn on the volcano.

Early next day we began our quest for the quetzal. To my surprise, the March morning dawned clear and sunny, yet cool enough for a wool sweater. The cloud forest resembled an emerald-and-gold cathedral. A riotous choir of birds greeted us. Toucans tooted, wrens trilled, euphonias sang, woodpeckers drilled, guans gabbled, and redstarts whistled. But nowhere did I hear a quetzal singing.

Forearmed by my experience with the giant grebes, or *pocs*, I had obtained a tape recording of the male quetzal's territorial call from Cornell University's Laboratory of Ornithology. It was a melodious two-toned whistle. I played it over and over expectantly. Nothing answered. We paired off with the workmen to cover more ground. I chose Pablo, a slim Maya lad from the Cuchumatanes Mountains. Barefooted and keen-eyed, he could slip through the forest virtually unheard and unseen. The only giveaways were the same faded red T-shirt and silvery sombrero he wore every day of his stay with us. Altogether we made up three teams, staying in touch by walkie-talkie. About noon, Pablo and I heard a faint two-toned whistle high in the canopy. Freezing in our tracks, I scanned the treetops with binoculars. Finally I saw our quarry, perfectly camouflaged, about 90 feet above our heads. How would we ever make observations, let alone take pictures, at that distance?

For a week we rose early and trekked about the cloud forest without seeing courting quetzals or finding a nest. David was growing impatient. He checked and double-checked his strobe lights, electric cords, lenses, film, blinds, rope ladder, and climbing spurs.

"Find me a nest! Find me a nest!" he chanted every evening when we assembled for our simple meal of tortillas, black beans, tough beefsteak grilled on the fire, and Guatemalan coffee. "We've only got a couple of months. The money won't last forever," he worried.

Armando and I nodded sympathetically.

"The rains are coming. I'll lose good light. Our work will be much harder then," David went on doggedly. "I must have a nest to work with. That's the only place I can be sure of photographing birds close up. When the parents come to incubate and feed the young, I'll get my best shots."

The morning Pablo and I found our first quetzal nest it happened so quietly that I was almost stupefied. Pablo simply stopped and pointed to a tree about 20 feet ahead. He turned and gave me a piercing look from dark eyes fringed by coarse black lashes. He didn't speak, just motioned over my shoulder at some bunches of bromeliads growing around a dead tree stump. In the dim church-like light, I could see nothing unusual. A gentle breeze swung the leaf blades. Two of them seemed more fragile, greener, limper. Pablo smiled. Feathery plumes hanging out of a nest hole! A live quetzal!

The male was snuggled down inside the nest cavity with only his two longest tail coverts curving up and out of the entrance. No wonder the quetzal's scientific name, *Pharomachrus*, was chosen: it means "long mantle" in Greek. This aptly describes the yard-long plumage which adorns only males.

Now our work began in earnest. David commanded everyone to exercise the utmost caution so as not to frighten away the birds. During their early stages of courting and nest building, they can easily be spooked. Only after they are incubating their eggs and watching chicks does a truly strong tie exist between parents and their nest sites. Then they'll tolerate much more disturbance and movement. The nest hole we had found was situated about 28 feet off the ground on the upper side of a dead tree. In order to get close-ups, David had to be no farther than 30 feet from the hole and level with it. He decided to erect a 25-foot tower and place his blind, cameras, tripods, and lights atop it. Our local farm workmen were invaluable now. They could shinny up trees and carry heavy loads which left the rest of us staggering. No laborer was taller than my five feet, four inches or weighed much more than I do. Yet each had incredible strength and endurance.

To camouflage our tower, aluminum ladders, wires, and batteries, David asked Armando to spray paint everything green. The mosquitoes were biting Armando furiously one morning. Snatching up a nearby can of insect repellent and applying several bursts around his head, he found to his chagrin that the label read, "emerald green." Thus he earned the nickname "Señor green ears."

After days of work, the tower and photo equipment were ready. David began his daily routine of creeping up the tower with two boys, easing into his blind, settling in for an eight-to-ten-hour day. He then sent the boys back. Birds can't count. As long as they see a few people come and go, they will not suspect that one has stayed behind. I was gaining tremendous respect for the superb know-how, patience, and alertness of this wildlife photographer. All we knew of David throughout the day was a thin trickle of smoke from his cigarettes emerging at the top of his blind. Occasionally he whispered staccato messages over his radio set. David had already calculated that during this incubation period, the birds would present themselves to his cameras only 100 seconds in every ten-hour day! Later, after the chicks hatched and began demanding food from their parents, David's chances for getting pictures would greatly increase.

Normally the female bird incubates her eggs all night and is relieved by the male early each morning. She flies off to feed and preen. Then she returns for a midday stint. He comes back again during the afternoon to brood and allow her another break until dusk. It was during this brief nest-exchange ceremony that David had to snap his pictures. The bird taking over would usually make two or three false attempts to enter the nest without going in. I called this display "bowing in." The incoming bird was announced only by a light thump as it alighted on the nest tree or by the faintest swish of wings.

Armando named the quetzal couple "*Los Caballeros*" (the elegant gentlemen) because they were so dashingly handsome. The male was shimmering green on his head, back, and wing coverts, with black wing primaries and secondaries. His little crest reminded me of a Roman gladiator's. It stood straight up above two chocolate-brown eyes and bright yellow beak. The male's curling shoulder cape was of gilded green feathers. He clung to the tree with yoked toes—two forward and two back. Neither bills nor feet are strong enough to dig anything except the softest, most rotten wood. Four elongate plumes hung below his tail. This was his shining train to impress females. Yet the male's most glamorous attribute, to my way of thinking, was the carmine-red breast and belly and the darker red undertail coverts. The female by contrast was a "plain Jane." She lacked the crest, cape and train of the male. Her breast was mostly gray with only a touch of red near her black-and-white-barred short tail.

Quetzal painting showing male and female on nest tree.   *Painting by W. J. Goebel*

While David perched in his blind, Pablo and I roamed over hundreds of acres of rugged cloud forest. Daily we searched for new nest trees, identified fauna and flora, and observed quetzal feeding and courting behavior. The birds seldom, if ever, came to the ground. They obtained water from rain trapped in leaves and air plants, and from dew. They ate grubs, snails, insects, and wild fruits, such as avocados and figs, often snatched in flight. We found nine more nest sites in dead stubs of trees. Three of the pairs appeared to be incubating eggs or brooding young. None, however, was as convenient and low as our Caballeros.

It was fortunate we had those backup birds. One morning David astonished us by tersely stating on his walkie-talkie that the Caballeros had abandoned their nest! Quickly Armando set up ladders and examined the nest tree. Empty! I combed the ground for signs. We found only two breast feathers from the mother.

"An owl did it," Armando guessed. "Remember one hooted last night."

"Yesterday an ornate hawk-eagle swooped by," said David gloomily.

"I've seen a few gray squirrels and a kinkajou," I offered. "It could be any one of those predators."

"What do we do now?" asked the ever-buoyant Armando.

"Try another nesting pair," answered David. "What have you got for me, Anne?"

Laboriously we moved all the equipment and tower to a mossy snag, 50 feet tall, standing lone and wobbly in a little canyon. On the far side, we found a flat area just big enough to take the tower. To cross over with our gear, we had to straddle and slide along a huge fallen tree trunk. It took another week of cautious labor to set up everything, including a perching tree. This was a *Cecropia* about 50 feet high, which required ten men to drag it near the nest tree and "plant" it. David's hope was that the birds would stop on one of its branches enroute to their nest hole. That way he could get better pictures by focusing on this perching tree.

Within five minutes after the fake tree was set up, a gorgeous male alighted on its lowest branch and gave a low nasal version of the territorial call. I immediately named him "The Organ Grinder" because his voice was so harsh and ragged compared to other quetzals. He treated us to some rare displays over the next few days. Once at dawn I glimpsed his giddy flight display. He spiraled up into the sky, singing exuberantly, "wak-a-wak-a-wak-a-wak!" He hovered a moment high above the cloud forest canopy. Then he dived back down into the trees where his bewitched and, he hoped, excited female was waiting. No wonder the quetzal couple in the Bronx Zoo wouldn't breed, I reflected. He can't show off with his acrobatics high in the sky. And she can't get aroused without watching him perform.

Another morning I saw him fly up to the nest hole with only one long tail plume. He seemed as healthy as ever. At once Pablo and I scrambled down into the canyon and began searching for the lost plume. We found it shortly. I climbed back out of the ravine with the feather waving saucily from my sombrero. Armando broke into laughter and immediately took out his tape measure.

"Forty-eight inches long!" he whistled. "Look at the colors change just like light on a soap bubble." He waved the feather gently in the sunlight. It caught every shade in the spectrum from yellow-green lime to turquoise to ultramarine, with occasional casts of gold and copper.

Since tail plumes are purely for sexual attraction, The Organ Grinder was probably not hampered or unbalanced by his loss. He only looked cockeyed. Apparently, plumes often come loose from the wear and tear of nest building, entering and leaving the small four-inch nest hole, and the chores of incubation and feeding young. The Organ Grinder, The Caballeros, and other quetzal pairs we watched proved that the birds do not make two doors to their nests. Popular belief says that they do so to protect their flowing trains.

I was so enchanted with the feather that I packed it up and mailed it to Dr. L. Durrell, professor emeritus at Colorado State University. He worked with electron microscopes. "Tell me what makes its many colors," I wrote, knowing he loved this sort of challenge. My colleague studied the feather at 10,000-times magnification and wrote back cryptically, "The quetzal isn't green, it's brown!"

His report explained: "Attempts to extract a pigment from the green feather failed. But a chemical test for melanin (brown color) is positive. The feather barbules are composed of granules in orderly rows spaced at approximately 5,400 angstroms apart. (One angstrom is one ten-billionth of a meter.) As the wavelength of green light is in this range, the physical phenomenon of interference makes light striking the barbules break down and reflect back green."

This phenomenon was first noted in 1960 by an ornithologist studying hummingbird feathers. It has been found to be quite common in bird feathers. All in all, I decided, the plumage of the quetzal was superbly suited for camouflage under rainy conditions in cloud forests. Then the feathers show little iridescence and blend in remarkably well with wet, shiny, green vegetation. In fact, without the sharp eyes of Pablo, I would have missed seeing birds countless times. Very often they'll sit for hours quite motionless, high in the canopy. Occasionally they'll look from side to side in a slow, suspicious manner. Also, they seldom show their red breasts if they feel uneasy.

Over these weeks I had grown quite fond of Pablo. His will-ingness to work, his broad grin over perfect white teeth, his shy-ness, were all endearing qualities. We rarely spoke, yet we seemed to be on the same wavelength. When he didn't show up one morning at 5:30 A.M., I grew concerned. After work, I asked Armando to drive me down to the finca to find him. I had imag-ined the boyish Pablo to be about 18 years old and living with his parents. To my surprise, the lad had a wife, two babies, and was at least 25. I found him lying atop a reed mat on a cement floor in the big *galería* (large open dormitory), where the coffee pickers and their families usually lived. He was deathly pale. In poorest Spanish, his wife explained he had cut his foot with a machete chopping firewood the night before. He had almost bled to death. The nearest clinic was a bumpy hour's trip down the mountain, and there was no one to drive him. So he was lying in blood-soaked rags, waiting for nature to heal him. I was ready to admon-ish the administrator of the farm, who had a jeep, and to drive him to medical help myself. However, David and Armando impressed on me that we were in a delicate position as guests of the farm owner.

"You can't interfere without jeopardizing our work," they cau-tioned me.

Inwardly I fumed, but I dared not say anything. However, I began taking Pablo meat, vitamin pills, and fresh bandages in order to speed his recovery. Each time I visited, I winced inwardly at the lack of privacy these poor people endured. Only thin plas-tic sheets, hung from strings and ropes, divided each family from one another and from the central row of wood cooking fires. Where the group's toilet facilities were, I never found out. Women routinely were seen sitting outside the building in strong sunlight picking lice from clothing and blankets. Sometimes from a child's head.

I soon had new troubles to think about. The rains had started and with them heavy thunderstorms. One night, as we were eat-ing, an earthquake set the forest jiggling and swaying. We pon-dered pessimistically what these elemental forces might do to that delicate, rotted nest stub. Yet each dawn as we approached appre-hensively, there would be The Organ Grinder, safe in his snag, the long, lone plume waving gently in the breeze. What's more we now saw that he and his wife were changing places more often and bringing morsels of food into the nest hole. Clearly their chicks had hatched. We were lured into a false sense of security.

One noon, that nest tree, slowly, silently, majestically, toppled over. No rain, no wind, no quake. It just fell. Rainwater had soaked into the rotten wood. It was a great weight to add to the tall stub. We had already suffered through three afternoons when four inches fell in a few hours. It was like living inside an all-green shower stall.

David almost choked on his sandwich. Armando and I were rooted to the ground. Then we sprang into action. We careened down the canyon, pawed through the debris, and found first one chick and then the other. Both were alive but the larger baby had a cut across its backbone, the smaller, a hemorrhage beginning on its head. Armando cradled them in his strong hands, breathing warmth over the baby chicks. From the forest, I heard the plaintive chatter of the female—"waac-a-waac-a-waac." Luckily both adults had been out feeding when the tree fell.

We hurried to the jeep, drove down to the *finca* (farm), and set up a nest box in the kitchen of the farmhouse. We asked little boys to go out and catch bugs, worms, fruits. I hard-boiled eggs and mashed avocado with the yolks. No one was exactly sure what to feed the chicks. We decided that a varied diet would provide most of the nutrients, protein and vitamins they required. I assumed the job of feeding the baby birds with a forceps, thus earning the name, *"Mama Quetzal"* (Mother of Quetzals). No mother ever had uglier offspring, however. The chicks had grotesquely bulging bellies, heavy legs, gaping wide beaks, and tightly shut eyes. Their bodies were half-naked. Pinkish, almost transparent skin alternated with rows of fuzzy black and brown feathers. It seemed impossible that such miserable-looking creatures could ever grow up to be resplendent trogons. Every two or three hours, the pair would set up a persistent, peevish buzzing noise when they got hungry. I was preoccupied all day long. Only at night did they quiet down and sleep hunched over like miniature vultures.

After three days both chicks failed and died. I felt dismal, having become attached to the noisy little beggars. We had lost a priceless opportunity to record and photograph quetzal growth literally in our laps.

This disaster necessitated serious decisions. None of our other quetzal pairs in the cloud forest was at a stage of breeding from which we could expect new chicks to photograph. We could not afford to wait through the 28-day incubation period and/or the four-to-six-week period of raising chicks. Only then would they be outside the nest and visible to cameras. It was already May. Our expedition's time and money were about gone. We decided, therefore, to break camp and travel up to the Cuchumatanes Mountains where we had heard quetzals were plentiful. With luck, we might find a pair in just the right place and at just the right time to obtain more pictures. Barring this chance, David felt we only had a 50-50 chance of having *National Geographic* publish our article and photographs.

2

A QUETZAL RESERVE

─────────

The road to the Cuchumatanes Mountains took us above 9,000 feet into a totally new world. We drove through fragrant forests of white pines, oaks, liquidambars, and firs. Their branches were weighted down with masses of air plants, golden-green mosses, fragile creamy orchids, and the spidery gray tangles of old-man's beard. Quetzals can range as high as 10,000 feet. We were nearing the locale reported to us as having birds.

As we bumped over a crest, Armando suddenly jammed on the brakes. Ahead we could see a smear of smoke and orange flames raging on the hillside. Even worse, from this vantage point we noticed nine other forest fires blazing across the landscape.

We stopped beside two soot-stained Mayas who carried axes and machetes. Smoke drifted through the jeep. Trees were crashing and sending up billions of sparks. Small birds were shrieking. We all piled out. I confronted one woodcutter with outrage.

"Why are you cutting and burning this forest?" I demanded.

"To plant our corn and beans," he answered simply. "So we can eat."

"But why not leave some trees standing to renew the forest and give you firewood? Why not protect the birds and animals?"

"It is the custom this way."

What more could I say? It was the universal answer of hungry, illiterate humans. Nothing in my Cornell classes had prepared me for this. Not only had our hopes of more quetzal pictures been dashed, but thousands of acres of wildland and hundreds of species of animals were being wiped out as we stared. Only a few old blackened stumps would stand witness among new green cornstalks. A few years from now, erosion from the heavy rains and soil compaction from the strong sun would render this land unfit for crops

or trees, man or beast. By that time, the Mayas would have moved
their fields to fresh areas of forest and repeated the process of slash-
and-burn agriculture.

This ancient method of farming is still practiced throughout
tropical America, Africa, and Asia. As long as the human population stays small, the clearings will remain small. Then trees and soil
can someday regenerate themselves. But where human numbers are
increasing, as they are in most of the world, there is relentless pressure to clear larger tracts of farm and range land. It is driving people up steep mountain slopes and into swamps and deserts where
they have no business living. There, ecological impacts are usually
disastrous.

Moreover, flames from slash-and-burn agriculture often escape
and become huge wildfires. These burn until weather or topogra-
phy put them out. Most developing countries have no fire-fighting
services, such as fire towers, observers, patrol planes, or smoke
jumpers. Seeing this one scene in the Cuchumatanes abruptly
made me realize the scope and severity of this traditional type of
agriculture when multiplied around the world.

David took the loss hard. He had no other place to go now for
his pictures. In an effort to cheer him up and save our expedition,
we spent two days combing the mountains for other nesting birds.
What we found only saddened us more. A young Maya in San
Mateo Ixtatán village eagerly offered us a dried quetzal skin for
$2.00! Proudly, he showed off the blow gun and clay pellets with
which he hunted the birds. I asked him how he could possibly hit
such a small creature with this weapon. He shrugged off his heavy
black wool jacket, raised the long tube, and unerringly hit a yellow
pine cone 50 feet away. I wondered if he had any inkling that
Guatemalan law, which has protected the national bird since 1875,
prohibits killing, trapping, exporting birds dead or alive, or molest-
ing their nests. Probably not. He told us he sold quetzals to whatever truck driver, traveler, or animal collector happened into this
remote area. Apparently hunting quetzals was common both here
and across the high border into Mexico.

After the quetzal was discovered by a European naturalist
named Mocinno in the early 19th century, the first dried specimens
were shipped to Europe. A craze to obtain quetzals began.
Thousands of birds were killed, apparently by the same method as
the young Maya had used, and their skins and feathers sent across
the Atlantic. Today the British Natural History Museum has

dozens of quetzals. Indeed, I saw them when I did some research there. Drawer after drawer of brilliant green tail feathers and carmine red breasts and withered little feet. Obviously, the persecution of this cloud forest jewel has gone on for centuries.

Retracing our way to Volcán Atitlán, we saw large tracts of virgin cloud forest being cut for firewood, charcoal, shingles, and lumber. More acres were being planted with coffee, quinine, tea, vetiver, and flowers and other cash crops. In most cases, the forest was clear-cut—that is, all the trees in an old growth stand were leveled. This allowed erosion to start and imposed a long-range threat to the entire watershed, water supply, and water quality for people and wildlife living below it.

One Sunday afternoon, we saw three men looking for wild honey. One bragged about having cut 35 trees in one year, most of them 100 feet tall with diameter at breast height (dbh) of four to eight feet!

"How do you know you'll find honey in a tree after chopping it down?" I asked.

"We see bees flying in and out of a hole," he replied casually. "So we go ahead and cut it down. Takes about five hours. Sometimes there is no honey, but usually there's a quart or two. We earn 35 to 75 cents a quart for honey in the market."

Armando broke in with, "That's a lot of work for very few centavos."

The man shrugged and nodded in agreement. "It buys a little *aguardiente* (crude liquor) and some *Mejoral* (a brand of aspirin)."

"Those big trees do a lot of damage to the forest when they fall down, don't they?" I pressed the woodcutter.

"I don't know. What difference does it make? There are hundreds of trees."

"It makes a huge difference if there happens to be a quetzal nesting in them," I muttered.

It was clear to us now that habitat destruction was the chief direct threat to the birds. The second serious limiting factor was the fragility and scarcity of nest trees.

Back at the *finca*, we soberly collected our equipment, paid the workmen, and said good-bye to the owner. He was deeply disturbed by the bad luck which had plagued us and by our stories of mountain forest eradication in Guatemala.

"Come back again if you need to," he offered warmly. "This property will stay as it is. I'll always protect our cloud forest. We love our quetzals. We may even make a kind of bird sanctuary up here."

The last person to see us off was Pablo. He ran alongside the jeep, gesturing. Glad to see that he had apparently recovered from his accident, I smiled broadly and threw him a good-bye kiss. His mouth opened, but no words came out.

"That boy is going to miss you," remarked David.

"That boy's in love," corrected Armando with a dark look backward in the driving mirror.

———

David and I returned to the United States and salvaged our story. It appeared in *National Geographic* in January 1969. I also wrote two scientific papers, "Biology and Conservation of the Quetzal," and "Behavior and Feather Structure of the Quetzal." With these publications in hand, I started to think how I might use them. Could they serve as leverage to obtain grants and establish a quetzal reserve? As far as I knew, not one protected area existed anywhere from southern Mexico to western Panama—the birds' full range of 1,000 miles. Yet, as we'd painfully seen, the species was becoming rare and endangered.

If it had been possible to make a grebe reserve at Lake Atitlán, as I'd done in 1966 to 1968, why not one for quetzals in the cloud forests of Volcán Atitlán? As good luck would have it, Armando came to visit me at Christmastide in Ithaca. With his usual optimism, he encouraged me to try. I wrote several exploratory letters and was gratified by the responses. The plantation owner in Guatemala was all in favor and ready to donate 1,000 acres for a sanctuary. Money was promised by World Wildlife Fund, USA, and the Cleveland County Bird Club in Norman, Oklahoma. My main stumbling block was to get leave from the university.

Upon completion of my thesis and degree, I had accepted a teaching position at Cornell. In one day I leaped from graduate student to assistant professor. My finances after four years of graduate school and foreign field work were so limited that I *had* to take a job. Luckily, there was enough time over spring vacation, 1969, to return to Volcán Atitlán. Armando and I met with the same courteous landowner, and we created our plans. He graciously offered us a small guesthouse and the same five Maya laborers as before. These generous arrangements made a world of difference in saving time and energy camping and cooking in the cloud forest. Also, it offered some precious privacy. The boys were pleased to see Armando and me again. Pablo stared at me, but said nothing. I had long forgotten his odd farewell behavior of the year before. But Armando hadn't. I noticed a subtle change in the way he spoke to Pablo.

Our first task was to make a census of quetzals and recheck all the nest trees where we had worked before. It was an ideal time, for courting season was underway. Every morning the silvery two-toned whistles of males echoed from the treetops. This helped me estimate the size of quetzal territories. During the reproductive season, each pair defends a territory of 1,000-foot radius around its nest tree. This tree varies in height from 12 feet to almost 150 feet. A home range is roughly 15 to 25 acres per pair. All told, there were about 22 quetzals, and maybe ten nest sites, on the proposed refuge.

Next we had to mark the boundaries. With machetes, the Maya laborers and I lightly blazed two three-foot swaths across the 5,000- and 8,000-feet elevations over rugged terrain. It was laborious and exhausting work. Both the eastern and western boundaries were naturally delineated by very deep, impenetrable canyons running up the volcano. I painted and lettered two large signs reading QUETZAL SANCTUARY. The workmen erected these at the southern corners.

Meanwhile, Armando was overseeing another phase of the project: making artificial nest boxes. I had decided that one management technique which might help the quetzal population was to provide safe homes on live trees. If wood ducks, martins, and bluebirds can use artificial nests, why not quetzals? These boxes were roughly the size of a wood duck house. Each one had a layer of sawdust in the bottom, a rubber (inner tube) roof cap, and a little ladder inside so the chicks could climb out when ready to fledge. Pablo was indispensable at this point. He could climb like a monkey. He installed almost all of the 16 nest boxes about 20 feet high on living trees. We were careful to place the boxes where there were no nearby branches, vines, or lianas to provide access for predators. We wrapped tin flashing around the trunks of the nest trees so no animals could climb up either. I doubted that any quetzals would use new nest boxes this breeding season, but I hoped they might accept a few the following year. All in all, I was pleased by how smoothly and quickly work went.

One Saturday afternoon after the Maya men had finished, I

Anne adapted design of wood duck boxes to make artificial nest boxes for quetzals. Birds used them after a year.

got a hankering to camp alone in the cloud forest. The April moon was full and dry season was almost at an end. I asked Armando to drive me near the site of our old expedition camp and help me set up a tent. This done, he seemed loath to leave. He tied his dog, Jessie, a strong German shepherd, to a tree.

"Go on," I chided him gently, "nothing's going to happen. It'll be like a camping trip in the Adirondacks. I do miss them a lot."

Armando shook his head disapprovingly, but gave me a kiss and left. I settled down by the campfire to listen to the evening sounds and soak in the atmosphere. A soft mist began filtering through the forest and gradually thickened. The light turned a somber gray. Tree trunks looked black; leaves, pewter. It became a monochromatic, mysterious world. The only sounds were the campfire's crackling and the occasional large leaf dropping noisily to the jungle floor. Then Jessie began to growl: low, deep-throated, and menacing. I stared into the forest. Nothing. I grabbed my flashlight and heaped more wood on the fire. I remembered the machete lying inside my little orange mountain tent. When I crawled in to get it, I realized it felt much safer inside. I settled down in the center and tried to figure out what was upsetting the dog. A mountain lion? They were very rare on the volcano and not dangerous. Perhaps a coyote? The only other large mammals were peccaries, deer, foxes and margay cats. I doubted jaguars would still roam the volcano since it was mostly ringed by farms below. Jaguars were my favorite mammal. I knew they were also harmless. I heard a slight shuffling nearby. Jessie's growls increased. The firelight threw dancing shadows on the thin tent walls. I wondered if my silhouette was visible. Finally, I lay down flat, clutching the machete, and waited. After an hour, the dog quieted. I sensed that danger had passed. I crept out, rekindled the fire, and cooked my supper.

Later, trying to sleep, I cursed myself for insisting on this mini-outing. Because of the mist there was no moonlight to admire. No intriguing noises broke the night's deathlike hush. No owls. No wind. Then, suddenly, from far down the volcano, drums, rattles, bells, and shouts reverberated. What could it be? The sounds grew louder. Should I run and hide? Stay? Now I was *really* scared.

To my utter relief, I heard a new sound— a jeep rattling up the dirt track. It could be only one person—Armando! I raced downhill to meet him. He leaped out of the Land Rover and grabbed my shoulders. "Are you all right?" he demanded. "I had a feeling something was wrong."

Throwing myself in his arms, I told him about the strange events and asked him to listen to the clatter and banging below us.

"There was just an eclipse of the full moon," he explained soothingly. "Those superstitious Mayas believe that something is eating up the moon. It's not foggy lower down, so they can see it disappearing. They run outside and make lots of noise to 'save it.'"

Even as he spoke, a pale, watery shaft of moonlight slipped through the fog and threw a glow on my tent. The clouds were lifting and a breeze began. The forest was coming back to life.

"But the other noises you heard earlier," said Armando gruffly, "I don't like that. Jessie's got a good nose. Someone was up here."

"Maybe it was a couple of our workmen having fun," I suggested.

"I doubt it. They respect you too much," murmured Armando, fingering his revolver. As he turned to spark up the fire, I'd never seen him look so grim. He pulled a small flask from his jacket. "*Aguardiente*—white lightning," he explained. "You're nervous as a cat. Take a big swallow and relax, Anita. I'm staying here with you tonight, love."

Gratefully I obeyed. The raw liquor hit my stomach like a blow. A warm flush spread over my body. Bright blue-white moonbeams streamed reassuringly into the cloud forest. Above the sheltering canopy of trees a clear ebony sky strewn with stars stretched into space. Maybe the quetzals were sleeping that night, but Armando and I didn't as we delighted in this rare, private and beautiful night together.

The next week I devoted to the last and most enjoyable phase of setting up the reserve. I spent two days training the five workmen. Three would be paid as private game wardens to patrol the sanctuary on weekends. The other two would act as honorary ones, filling in when needed and acting as guides for visitors. Since the farm had no public access and the reserve was to be opened only to scientists, photographers, conservationists, and educators, we were not too concerned about enforcement.

Then I lectured to the farm's schoolchildren, explaining why the quetzal was very special as Guatemala's national bird. Why we were trying to save it and its cloud-forest habitat. I used David's slides, the owner's projector, and a portable generator. I hoped the children would carry this conservation message home to their parents. The little tykes sat absolutely spellbound. They had never seen colored pictures on a wall. What a marvelous teaching technique. I would love to travel about Central America with a van, a portable generator, projector and screen, giving conservation lectures in remote areas.

My final duty was to meet with adjacent landowners and help them form a non-profit conservation association for legal registration of their reserve. We hoped that the Ministry of Finance would thereby declare the land tax-exempt. The owners were taking 1,000 acres out of possible cultivation and donating the land for a protected natural area. It seemed right that they receive compensation from the government. We chose the name "Asociación Atitlán para la Protección del Quetzal" (Atitlán Association for the Protection of the Quetzal).

On our last day at the *finca*, we came down late from the volcano. I walked into my guesthouse bedroom and stopped abruptly. Someone was in my bed! In the dim light, I couldn't make out who, but it seemed like a fat person. I screamed. Armando raced up and stared into the room.

"Get back!" he ordered, pulling me into the kitchen. "Stay here!" He pulled out his revolver and grabbed a flashlight. Then

he slid sideways against the wall toward the room. I froze in horror. I saw the bright beam play across the bed. Armando took aim.
Half a minute of tense silence passed. Then his body relaxed and
the gun dropped. He motioned me to his side. Together we
approached and stood looking down at—a dummy!

Someone had stolen into my room while I was out working
and cleverly put together a caricature of me. It was authentic from
the beat-up sombrero to the pair of worn hiking boots. Only one
thing was wrong with the likeness—the dummy was pregnant!

The whole creation had to be the work of a sick mind. And it
had to be someone who knew me well, knew my clothing, knew
our schedule. It had to be one of the five Maya men we worked
with. Stunned, I mentally ran over the list. We both spoke the
name at once—"Pablo!"

Armando broke into a harsh tirade. "It was Pablo who tried to
sneak up to your tent the night of the eclipse. It is Pablo who
made this dummy because he's heartsick for you."

I hated to agree, but the evidence pointed that way. The entire
situation made me feel sad for the Maya lad. "I'll speak to him in
the morning," I began. "The poor fellow..."

"No, you won't!" stormed Armando, shoving the revolver back
in his belt. "Anita, I'll handle it!" And with that he ran out into
the night. I never knew what happened.

We left early next morning. Armando scarcely talked. On the
trip from Volcán Atitlán back to Lake Atitlán, I did a lot of thinking. In two days I had to return to the university and it would be
months before I could see Armando. He wouldn't enjoy coming
to the states again. If we were to live together, it would have to be
in Guatemala at the lake where Armando had his roots and a
position of good standing. He needed to be where schooling and
Ph.D.s were unimportant compared to his sharp native intelligence and mechanical skills. Was that enough for me?

I had yearned to be married to Armando for over three years.
We had dreamed of each other across 2,000 miles. But it was an
either-or situation. Little or no compromise.

A decision was forming deep inside me, as dramatic as driving
from the dim cloud forest to the sparkling blue lake, as symbolic
as growing from graduate school to my first professional job. I
knew I must be independent. This time I didn't cry when I flew
back to the university.

UPDATE

- David's and my article for NATIONAL GEOGRAPHIC magazine appeared in January 1969, entitled "The Quetzal, Fabulous Bird of Maya Land." I also wrote special quetzal pieces for DAS TIER magazine in Frankfort, Germany, called "The Resplendent Quetzal," and for LIVING BIRD of the Laboratory of Ornithology at Cornell. I donated some of my quetzal tapes to the Library of Bird Sounds there, as well.

- A couple of years after installing the artificial nest boxes, the farm owner wrote that two of the boxes were in use by nesting quetzal pairs. This generous and helpful man died in the late 1970s of a fatal disease.

- The quetzal reserve, large portions of surrounding cloud forest above the tea plantation and other large farms, and the rocky volcano top have recently been combined as a Biodiversity Reserve under supervision of the private University of the Valley in Guatemala City. Research projects in ecology, botany, quetzals, and much more are planned.

- During the civil war in Guatemala, guerillas were reported camping in and around the quetzal refuge and higher up on the volcano slopes. It is not known if they planted mines there.

- Armando died of a heart attack at Lake Atitlán in the early 1980s. I only saw him once from the time I left him after establishing the quetzal reserve. (Perhaps a lifetime of smoking and drinking orange juice with two raw egg yolks every morning contributed.)

3

ANEGADA

That year found me teaching at Cornell. This was my first real professional job. It was heartwarming that Cornell University, where I'd been both an undergraduate and a graduate student, had hired me. It felt great to be teaching in the field of natural resources and earning a good salary.

Nevertheless, it was an intoxicating day when a colleague wrote from the Caribbean Research Institute of the College of the Virgin Islands, asking me to participate in an ecological survey of the most remote island in the American and British West Indies. Anegada! The very name, lyrical and wild, conjured up visions of white sand beaches, coconut palms, tranquil blue seas, coral reefs, and sun as penetrating as an acetylene torch. I knew Anegada lay equally positioned between the Greater and Lesser Antilles, yet it bears no resemblance at all to its mountainous sister Virgin Islands or to Puerto Rico. It actually looks more like flat Anguilla and Barbuda, about 75 miles away.

The Institute was trying to assemble a team of scientists to visit Anegada and gather basic biological information. Field data was needed for analysis before a sprawling development corporation from England could move ahead with plans to build a large retirement community and tourist resort. It had already leased 6,000 of the island's 9,592 acres. The Institute was very keen to do a baseline study prior to major construction and discover what natural resources needed management and protection. It hoped to use isolated Anegada as an ecological reference and benchmark in relation to highly developed Caribbean islands. The island's value as an indicator of ecological change caused by modern development would be unquestionable. A quick review of the literature at the university library indicated that only five or six scientists had ever worked there. None had attempted to specifically enumerate or describe the major habitat types of this island or list all its birds and mammals. Its main claim to zoological fame was the presence of a huge, rare, endemic lizard—the Anegada ground (or rock) iguana, *Cyclura pinguis*—about five feet long. At once I was captivated by the chance to collect new scientific information and be a "mini-pioneer" in the protection of this remote island.

I wrote back and agreed to come during Cornell's month-long Christmas vacation. My trip was financed by a grant from the Division of Research at Cornell University. All equipment and logistics of travel would be taken care of by the Caribbean Research Institute. I could now see the benefits of having a Ph.D. Already grant money was far easier to obtain and people had more confidence in my ability. Strange how one piece of paper could make such a difference in doing conservation work . . .

When I stepped off the plane in St. Thomas on a January morning, the blazing sun nearly blinded my winter-weak eyes. I blinked like an owl and reached for sunglasses. The tangy sea breeze began clearing my sinuses. How good it felt to be back in the tropics. None of the other team members had arrived. Each had listed different dates of availability. Instead of tackling Anegada in a concerted effort, we would be doing piecemeal studies over the next several months. The team consisted of two marine biologists, a botanist, a herpetologist, a marine archaeologist, myself as wildlife ecologist, and possibly a park planner. The pieces of this ecological picture would be a long time coming together.

Nevertheless, I was here and ready to go. The hours were ticking relentlessly toward my reluctant return to the classroom.

By midafternoon a young student assistant had been located, his camping gear assembled, and our supplies piled on the dock. The captain of the college research boat, however, was not eager to start out on this four-hour run late in the day. The reefs north and east of Anegada are treacherous and extensive. Over 200 wrecks are charted for Horseshoe Reef alone. Channels are poorly marked. Moreover, the seven-by-three-mile island barely presents any profile to the navigator. Most ships give the island a wide berth. Dusk was falling when the lavender smudge that was Anegada first showed on the horizon. The sea was alive with phosphorescence, sparkling and winking in our wake. The captain steered carefully toward the only channel and jetty on the island's entire shoreline. Behind it, a few hundred yards away, lay "The Settlement," Anegada's only hamlet.

When we finally docked on the leeward shore and began

unloading, thousands of mosquitoes swarmed over us. We worked faster and faster to avoid the ravenous insects. Soon a jumbled heap of scientific gear, sleeping bags, tents, backpacks, and food lay on shore. The captain hurried us off his boat. He was anxious to get back to St. Thomas before midnight.

"Be back for you next Saturday," he promised, then eased cautiously away from the rotting wharf.

Jim, my student assistant, and I were left alone on shore with the topsy-turvy mess of equipment. "Let's straighten this out," I said irritably, as the boat dwindled in size upon the moonlit sea. "We've really got to find some repellent and put up our tents. We may as well camp right here tonight."

Now the sandflies from nearby mangroves discovered us. Maddening! Within half an hour we had managed to organize things and get a small smudge burning with driftwood and dry seaweed to drive the bugs away. Jim started to crawl into his tent, then backed out, groaning, "Oh, no, there's no netting! It's rotted out." In a hurry, he had grabbed the wrong tent for this kind of job.

"Well, you can sleep in mine," I offered, glad now that I had insisted on bringing my own field gear. (This was only one of many times when I've had to share my shelter with needy colleagues.) "How about a cup of cocoa?" I said comfortingly to the young, distraught and tired helper. "Then we'll sleep better."

"What would I do without you?" Jim murmured. "Okay. Where's the water?" he asked, unearthing a pan.

Then it hit me. Water! The one most important thing we needed was water. No one had thought to ship a goodly supply for our week's work, so accustomed were we to turning on a tap. Yet, without at least two gallons apiece per day, we could not survive field conditions on this semi-desert island. I remembered reading that Anegada has no fresh surface water at all. Inhabitants get their meager supply from sinkholes and depressions in the limestone where a few fresh-water seeps and rainwater collect. We didn't want to drink from those, and we didn't know where they were yet.

The coincidence of having worked on Volcán Atitlán up at 6,000 feet with no available surface water, and now at six feet above sea level equally lacking in water, did not escape me.

"We'll have to go to The Settlement first thing in the morning," I decided. "There are supposed to be three hundred blacks living there. Maybe we can *buy* some water. Otherwise . . ." I let my words drift off. This was *not* the right way to begin a field expedition. We were here with nothing to drink, over 100 pounds of equipment to move, and one topographic map. After the onslaught of insects we were experiencing, it was imperative that we move across to the windward shore and camp on a beach. The sea breeze would blow bugs away and cool us in the heat of the day. We could make a base there as well as anywhere, as long as we had drinking water. For the survey, I'd planned to do trapping and netting of small mammals and birds at the five major ecosystems on the island: beach scrub and dunes, freshwater sinks and seeps, salt-water lagoons, dense bush of the interior, and The Settlement.

For now, we slacked our thirst with two cans of peaches in syrup.

Shortly after dawn, we walked into the town. We followed a well-worn path and were soon on "Main Street." This one-track limestone lane was lined with tiny wooden shacks, weather-beaten to pewter-gray. Each one had a cistern with its pipes leading to the rusty sheet metal roof. I didn't see how people could ever collect and keep sufficient rainwater to survive all year since Anegada receives only about 30 to 40 inches annually, mostly in rainy season.

On all sides of us, old tin cans, faded cardboard boxes, plastic bottles, broken glass, discarded metal drums, and nondescript rubbish lay in profusion. Apparently, the residents of The Settlement just threw refuse on the ground and let the antiseptic sun, salt air, roving dogs, and hungry rats perform their cleansing acts. Not a tree in sight. The bald white limestone was as hard as cement. One small shop was open. Otherwise, the place was deserted.

Then I noticed a very old man rocking on a shady porch. His clothes, his beard, and his fedora were all various shades of gray, blending with the silvery boards behind him. If not for his fringe of snow-white crinkly hair and the creak of his rocker, we might have walked right by him.

"Hello, sir," I called companionably, stopping and looking at him.

The creaking stopped and a pair of beady brown eyes bored into mine.

"Hello, missus," came back a high-pitched voice. "Did you just come in by boat?"

"No, we arrived last evening," I replied in a loud voice, not sure how well this gaunt gnome could hear. "We came in from St. Thomas. We're here for a week to study the animals."

"That so?" he asked politely. "Well, come right up here and tell

me about it, missus."

I gave Jim a look of relief and we walked up to the old black man and shook hands.

"Mr. Wallace Vanderpool, your servant," he said deferentially, almost bowing.

I found myself wondering if he was a descendant of slaves and where he came from. This elderly man lacked the proud carriage and vitality of Latins I had worked with. He seemed fragile, humble and stooped. Only his eyes hinted at an

Mr. Wallace Vanderpool relaxing in his Anegada home.

underlying spunkiness.

Sitting on the railing of the porch, Jim and I told Mr. Vanderpool our names and what we planned to do. He rocked rhythmically and seemed quite interested. Then he jumped nimbly to his feet. "I'll just get you both some lemonade, missus," he exclaimed. "You must be right thirsty."

Jim and I thanked him. I had a secret horror, however, of greenish liquid full of rust specks, algae, tiny lizards, and amoebas. To our surprise, the three chipped jelly glasses he carried out looked clear and lemony. Their contents tasted even better. He must keep his cistern strained and scrubbed, I decided. Thanking him for the treat, I asked Mr. Vanderpool if we might find a place to buy water during our stay. On many Caribbean islands, it's as expensive as soda pop or gasoline.

"Why, right here," he said pertly. "You just come and get all you want, missus. No one's charging you for no water."

"But you won't have enough to last you till rainy season if you share it," I protested. "Of course I'm paying."

"Well, Missus Anne," he explained, "I have a big cool cistern half full, a well in the yard, and a couple of sinkholes in my crop field. I use the sinkholes to water my pets and plants, the well for cooking and washing, and the cistern to drink. Now, how's an old man like me going to use up all that water? I don't work out in the hot sun much any more."

Nevertheless, we agreed on a small fee for the water. Mr. Vanderpool said he would provide the jugs. Jim volunteered to walk in from our camp to pick them up at dusk.

"Would anyone have a jeep?" I asked dubiously. "We have a lot of gear to get up to the north side of Windlass Bight."

"Of course, we do. Andrew, my next-door neighbor, can take you over—and bring the water," he added cannily. "Since the development company came over here, most of the men have given up lobster and conch fishing and have gone to work building roads. They make a lot more money. A few have even brought jeeps and cars over here." He shook his head sadly. "I hate to see and hear the change. Used to be all we heard was the wind and waves and birds, day in, day out. We ate lots of good food from the sea, too," he added. "Now, it's candy and crackers and sody pop and canned spaghetti. Car engines and boat motors." He spat distastefully over the railing. "I miss those fresh groupers and conch chowders, missus, and now and again a crawdaddy."

I perked up my ears. An introduction—be it largemouth bass, a weed, or a construction company—could change a whole society's health, diet, and way of life. I wondered if a protein deficiency might be showing up here.

"Are the people still healthy?" I asked. "Are their teeth good?"

"Oh, I don't know, Miss Anne," he answered plaintively. "I know *I* don't have the get up and go I used to, but then I don't go to sea no more. Our boats are all moldering by the dock. You must have seen 'em, Jim. The sea is good for a man. It makes him strong. So does its food—them shellfish." He grinned impishly. Then added, "There's been a lot of changes here."

Clearly, Mr. Vanderpool didn't have any medical information of interest. Besides, the company had been here less than a year. Perhaps it was too early for physical changes to show up in the

Fishing sloops rotting near shore after develpment company hired local men to build roads for tourist resort.

islanders' blood, teeth, body fat and bones.

"How far is it to Windlass Bight?" I asked, gently bringing him back to the present. "We'd like to camp over there."

"'Bout a league," answered Mr. Vanderpool.

"How far is that?"

"Well, I'm not sure," replied the wrinkled fisherman. "Maybe five or ten miles. We don't use miles here. Leagues is left over from the English pirate days."

"Jim, what do you say we take our lunch and walk over there? Time how long it takes. Andrew can bring our gear when he gets home from work, if Mr. Vanderpool would be good enough to arrange it. That way we can start exploring the island and save some time."

Jim looked at me dumbstruck. I knew precisely what he was thinking. To leave a pile of valuable equipment unattended in St. Thomas or St. Croix would be foolhardy. It would be gone in ten minutes. But I had an intuitive feeling that this man was deeply honest, and the island was still untouched by racial strife and human deceit.

"It's all right," I said softly to Jim. "I know Mr. Vanderpool will watch out for us."

We reached the great white beach of Windless Bight at noon and took shelter under an overturned rowboat near the dunes. My thermometer read 92 °F, and the sand was blazing hot. Beyond the beach a sheltered shallow lagoon of purest Caribbean blue ran out almost half a mile to a great toothlike reef. It separated the island from the Puerto Rican trench. On the horizon, the water was an angry blue. Here the five-mile depths of the trench suddenly came up against Anegada. It was a tremendous change in relief—28,000 feet of depth to about eight feet. The sea balked at this sudden restraint after its free fetch of over 4,000 miles from Europe. It threw itself ceaselessly against the long coral strands.

We rested through the midday heat, bathing, sunning, and sleeping. By four o'clock the heat dropped, so Jim and I headed to the three southwestern salt lagoons shown on the map. I was eager to scout the area and run our first trap line. The sun was setting when we broke through a fringe of mangroves and gazed out on a brick-red body of water. Three Bahama ducks were preening nearby and a great blue heron stood statuesquely in the shadows. Two mangrove cuckoos called sweetly from the underbrush. Then the sharp rattle of a belted kingfisher surprised us as he flashed by. Seconds later, a small black bird streaked over the salt lagoon close to the surface with a neat "*zit-t-t-t-t*" sound.

"What was that?" wondered Jim aloud.

I rapidly ran through Bond's *Birds of the West Indies* in my mind. I could come up with nothing that small, that black, and that fast. Then it struck me—a bat! "There must be bats on this island, Jim. But where in the world would they roost? There are no caves here."

"Unless they fly down into the sinkholes?" he countered.

"Oh, my word, can you imagine that! We'll have to find out if they do. But first of all we have to identify them. Let's put up the mist nets here," I said excitedly.

It was an odd but strangely lovely scene—the dark-green band of mangroves edging the peaceful lagoon which had turned almost scarlet at sunset. At least a hundred agile little black bombers crisscrossed the water with their *zit, zit, zit* sound. They were probably feasting on mosquitoes. The cuckoos sang their twilight song. A small flock of egrets flew overhead silhouetted against the saffron sky. From time to time a hint of cool breeze ruffled the still water and carried in the muffled roar of the reefs. A soothing spot.

Then in the distance we heard the noise of a jeep missing on at least one cylinder. We hurried back to Windlass Bight and found

Andrew waiting for us. Our camp gear was neatly piled above the high tide mark, and assorted jugs and bottles, totaling ten gallons of water, stood in a row. Andrew was an affable, tall, enormously powerful black, who had worked his way up to foreman on the construction crew.

"I be here at dis time every day all week, missus," he promised. "And don' you worry none 'bout de water. I'll bring ten gallons. It be clean." Then he left before it got dark, since he had no headlights on his jeep.

Jim and I set up a cozy camp. Everything was intact. Jim attached a plastic tarp to the back of his tent to keep out any vagrant mosquitoes, while the front was left open to the wind which blew in continuously and was the best repellent possible. My tent opened right out towards the lagoon. We cooked a hot supper that night, with cups of tea to quench our thirst. Then we fell into our sleeping bags. Far out across the moonlit lagoon the Atlantic thundered on Anegada's great reef, lulling us deeper and deeper into slumber. I felt privileged and humble, knowing not one human being stood between me and the shores of Spain.

The results of our week's field work were surprising. We learned that the only native mammal on Anegada is the little fruit-eating bat (*Artibeus jamaicensis*). The bats did indeed roost by day in sinkholes. In fact, Jim climbed down into one with a young local boy to verify this. Undoubtedly, other indigenous mammals once inhabited Anegada, such as *agoutis*, (a rabbit-sized rodent), wild guinea pigs, certain insectivores, and rice rats. However, over the centuries, they were either wiped out by exotic introductions which arrived by sea or ship or were trapped out for food. Interviewing Mr. Vanderpool later, I heard that Anegada had been visited by Carib Indians, buccaneers, Spanish sailors, a few colonists, slavers, and traders. Accompanying these sporadic visitors had been black rats, house mice, house cats, and some domestic livestock. All of these became feral—that is, they roam about in a wild state. The feral creatures—cattle, sheep, goats, donkeys, cats—have vied with native wildlife and eventually taken over. Lacking natural predators, they increased until their grazing, browsing, and preying decimated the native fauna and flora of the entire island. Then they, in turn, became pitifully scrawny.

Colonists and sailors harmed the little island, too. The land was cleared and burned off for farming. The trees were cut for firewood, charcoal, lumber, and ships' timbers. Such treatment soon reduced vegetation to a few scraggly trees, thorny shrubs, weedy plants, and cacti eking out an existence upon the eroded limestone. The only places where residents can farm on Anegada today are in pockets and depressions of limestone where some nutritive soil still lies.

Jim and I encountered mature trees only in the area behind Windlass Bight and Loblolly Bay. This dry forest stood 25 feet high and contained West Indian birch, strangler fig, lignum vitae, and mahogany. The "bush," as it is called, is the chief habitat of the huge Anegada ground iguana. Other Caribbean islands— Hispaniola, Grand Cayman, Cuba, Exuma, Andros and Turks islands—have or have had their own species of iguanas. None as large or as threatened, however, as the Anegada one.

Our exploration of the bush enabled me to create and sketch out boundaries around a proposed fenced preserve for these endemic lizards. Rule One: *Save the habitat in order to save the species.* In the face of a proposed international airport, golf courses, industrial sites, retirement homes, tourist hotels, a generating plant, and a sod farm, I wondered if my recommendation would be accepted.

The other sanctuary I proposed was a large waterbird refuge at Red and Flamingo Ponds. Although we saw no flamingos during the survey, Mr. Vanderpool recounted how the great ruby-pink birds used to be seen here by the hundreds. Sometimes, he said, they even nested. Gradually, however, they decreased as a result of poaching and egg stealing by the natives. He had seen no flamingos since 1968. "Fillymingo," he explained, "is considered a great delicacy in these islands."

"Do you eat their eggs sunny side up or scrambled?" I quipped, thinking he was joking.

"Oh, fried," he replied seriously. "Fried fillymingo eggs is mighty tasty, Missus Anne."

This information helped explain the vast decline from hundreds of thousands to roughly 20,000 flamingos in 1971 in the Caribbean area. Today the birds nest successfully only on Inagua (Bahamas), Bonaire (Netherland Antilles), and the Yucatan peninsula (Mexico). In these three places, flamingo reserves have been established and low-flying aircraft are prohibited from passing over the areas in order not to frighten and stampede nesting adults and young. They must keep an altitude of 2,000 feet.

At the end of the week, Jim and I said good-bye to our good

friends, Mr. Vanderpool and Andrew, promising to see them again in three months. I planned to return to Anegada in April for more birding and mist-netting. Hopefully I'd see some exciting new migrants in spring.

4

WINDLASS BIGHT DREAM

M y second visit started off like clockwork, except that again no other team member was available and I had no assistant. This didn't worry me. I felt quite at home on the island. Windlass Bight would be my base again while I resampled the five ecosystems. As long as water could be delivered, I'd manage alone. Andrew gave me a bear hug of welcome and helped me set up camp on the beach. Yet at evening time, he seemed reluctant to leave me five miles from the nearest person. I assured him that my log cabin in the United States lay the same distance from my closest neighbor in winter. He seemed dumbstruck.

How was he to know that most of my young life I had dreamed of living alone in a cabin in the woods or on a trop-ical island. The cabin had become a reality in the Adirondacks. But relatively uninhabited small islands are hard to find and even harder to buy. Nevertheless, my dream was coming true on this assignment, if only for five idyllic days.

Andrew left plenty of water by my tent and drove away shaking his head worriedly in the gathering darkness. I unpacked my gear, ate supper, and fell asleep listening to the muffled boom of the Atlantic.

The days slipped by as smoothly as the clear lapis lazuli waters of the lagoon which ebbed in and flowed out with the tides. Each morning I awoke in the cool dawn, took a quick dip in the sea, and even shivered as I dried myself before a little campfire. I birded till nine, then checked the mist nets and released any trapped birds. By eleven the heat was mounting, so I returned to the beach and upturned rowboat. I sat underneath the boat, cooled by the breeze, and wrote down my field notes. This spring visit was really paying off. I had already observed 12 species not seen in January. Three birds were outstanding finds—a piping plover never before record-ed in the entire Virgin Island group at any time of year; a marbled

For five idyllic days Anne camped alone at Windlass Bight facing the Atlantic. It was her base for ecological work.

godwit which had been seen only occasionally in winter in the West Indies; and a cattle egret, a recent immigrant from Africa. Another interesting discovery was a metal band that Mr. Vanderpool had obtained from a duck hunter during the winter of 1970. He gave it to me, puzzled by my excitement. I explained that many waterfowl have bands put on their legs in the USA to trace their migration routes and distances traveled.

Later, I checked it out with the Migratory Bird Population Station in Laurel, Maryland. It had been placed on an adult drake blue-winged teal in Maine—2,000 miles away!

Late afternoon found me setting off again to check out some new corner of the island. Andrew delivered my water at dusk and stayed to chat by the campfire until he could barely see his way back to The Settlement. After supper, I'd sit awhile on the powdered sugar beach or skinny-dip in the tepid lagoon. Floating on my back, watching the moon rise, my body gleaming and silvery as a fish, I truly felt like a marine animal. Far off to the north, the ocean thundered restlessly. I thought of all the white-toothed silvery shapes hunting along the reef in front of me by night; just as the black, furry bats were sonaring in on bugs at the salt lagoon behind me. Here in the peaceful shallows no danger lurked. I rolled over like a seal and paddled back toward the tent and my campfire. Later, snug in my sleeping bag, I listened to a lone mockingbird singing his heart out to the moon. Spring's mating urge was upon him—and millions of migrants winging north across the Caribbean. Some might even end up in my Adirondack forest. For the first time, I felt a pang of homesickness for my cabin. But that homecoming had to wait till May.

By the end of that serene week, I had counted 55 species of birds—28 of them first records for Anegada Island.

Later, I would write a scientific paper on "Birds and Mammals of Anegada, British Virgin Islands," for the *Caribbean Journal of Science*, 1973.

Then, on the last evening, a jarring element inserted itself into this dreamlike life. Andrew arrived early with his jeep and announced that "de plant doctuh" had arrived. He was camped by the shell mounds near the east end of Anegada. He'd been there three days, but no one had seen hide nor hair of him. Andrew, out looking for his strayed cow, had happened upon the botanist.

"Mon, dat doctuh, he got de fancy food and tent and everyting," exclaimed Andrew, "but de site no be good. No, missus. No one go down dere much. De bugs be bad."

"I should go visit him now and see what he's doing," I said. "Otherwise the boat will come tomorrow to fetch me and it'll be too late. We might be able to share some information."

"Well, you gonna break de camp here anyway. Let's go dere now," Andrew offered. He made short work of loads with his gargantuan arms.

An hour later we were in the jeep bouncing over pocked limestone, with the land growing poorer and less vegetated as we headed southeast. I noted stripes of International Orange on the rocky ground. Ahead, a huge heap of weathered conch shells rose like a monolith. Beside it, close to a salt pond, stood an elegant green stand-up tent with its fly stretched out like an awning. Around it were a folding table, chairs, an ice chest, a huge lantern, plant presses, and boxes of canned goods. No one was there. Peeking into the tent, I could see several half-empty tins on the floor. Small land crabs had apparently smelled the food and eaten their way up through the canvas floor to feast. They now scuttled back into their holes like sneaky thieves. Andrew waited uncertainly. It was growing dark and he longed to traverse the winding track home while he could still see. Yet he was most concerned that "de plant doctuh" had not come back, and that I still had to set up my camp.

"It not good to be out in de bush so late," he warned.

I searched about for a note, map, some clue as to where the botanist might have gone. Nothing. Then we both heard the sound of clumsy footsteps stumbling toward us. A thin, disheveled, middle-aged man appeared, limping badly. Andrew and I rushed over to help him. Instead of a greeting or thanks, we received a glower.

"Who are you?" he demanded suspiciously, looking from one to the other of us, then around his tent. I introduced Andrew and myself, explaining I had just arrived to discuss our joint research for the Institute before I left Anegada next day.

"Can't do it," was his abrupt reply as he hobbled toward his chair and threw down a heavy knapsack. "Got to press and identify these specimens. I'm finding dozens of species never recorded here before."

"Are *you* painting those orange lines on the limestone?" I asked curiously.

"Yes," was his curt reply.

"Why?"

"Gridlines," he answered, throwing a machete carelessly on the ground. It rang cruelly as the stone nicked the blade. Then the botanist sat down and slowly began to ease off his brand-new boots.

"You have some terrible blisters," I sympathized, leaning forward.

Again he glared at me. I stepped back. Painfully he pulled off his socks and revealed two fluid-filled circles the size of silver dollars on his heels.

"What possessed you to bring new boots here for your field work?" I asked good-naturedly.

He gave me a strained look and made no answer.

"Let me boil up some water, prick those blisters, and drain them properly," I offered. "They should be bandaged, too. Is your gas stove working?"

"No, it's *not*," he spat. "Leave me alone. I'll be all right."

Andrew and I looked at each other in amazement. Such behavior was hard to fathom. I decided to try once more.

"Look," I said gently, "you'll never be able to finish your field work with feet like this. You need medical attention, some soft slippers, and a good meal. Let us help you."

"I don't have any slippers," he answered peevishly, "and I forgot the gas for the stove. I've been eating cold canned goods." Then to our astonishment, he burst into tears.

Suddenly I realized the man was close to heat exhaustion and was almost incoherent. Andrew took over. He ambled up to the botanist, lifted him bodily, and carried him carefully to the jeep. He ignored the pronounced flinch and grimace the white man made. "We gonna take you to De Settlement, mon. You be in no shape to travel de bush, Mistah Doctuh. Dey be a nurse der."

Next morning, a very dejected botanist accompanied me on the boat back to St. Thomas. He took nothing with him but the plant press, his half-filled knapsack, and a pair of Mr. Vanderpool's slippers. Whether he ever went back to Anegada I don't know.

——————

Back at my cabin in the Adirondacks, I typed up field notes and relived the calm and beautiful days at Windlass Bight in my mind while reviewing my photographs.

Reports eventually came in from other scientists as they completed their parts of the survey. To my initial recommendations I added two more. One was to set up several pristine dune-beach parks along the windward shore. We worried that the development company might bulldoze the usual three lines of barrier dunes flat. This is often done to add more shoreline property and raise the value of a modern waterfront development. The ecological backlash of this real estate maneuver would be the loss of natural stability and protection afforded by the dunes against hurricanes, high seas, and beach erosion. Pristine dune-beach parks could serve as prime water recreation areas. Anegada's beaches are practically unparalleled in the West Indies.

My second recommendation was to make an historical natural monument encompassing the old conch shell mounds and adjacent salt flats at the eastern tip of Anegada. These undoubtedly are both pre-Columbian *middens* (kitchen refuse piles left by early Arawaks) and post-Columbian shell mounds. A search through the discarded shells might yield valuable information about the early fauna and the archaeology of this unique island perched against the Atlantic. It might also show trends in decreasing size of conches, indicating overfishing.

In general, our reports advised against lavish developmental changes which would attempt to make Anegada look "civilized," greener, or more attractive by north-temperate-zone standards. Golf courses, a sod farm, nurseries filled with exotic plants (and insects), grass lawns, and flower gardens did *not* belong on this remarkably uncontaminated and waterless island. As far as we could learn, Anegada was one of the few places in the entire Caribbean which had so far escaped chemical fertilizers, pesticides, phosphates, fluorinated hydrocarbons, weed killers, electricity, and (until the last few years) even gas-driven engines. As such, it was an unusual find and a reference point for environmental "purity." Moreover, Anegada had an abundance of the two most precious ingredients for ecotourism—sun and sea. It could survive on its natural treasures as it was.

I never saw the final report from our "team," or an environmental impact statement. I don't know who read our individual reports. No one asked any of us to return to the island. However, through my grapevine of colleagues, I heard that the English development company abandoned its project in 1973. Next, that the government of the British Virgin Islands might encourage tourist development. Five years later, I heard that this, too, had been given up. Later, plans were afoot to set up an industry to quarry sand on the island. The Anegada community successfully vetoed this on the grounds that the excavations would make the land more vulnerable to flooding and the enterprise would generate no jobs for island residents. They were not trained to run heavy mining equipment. Then there was talk of using the island for military target practice; and drilling for offshore oil. These projects also fell by the wayside.

And so today, as far as I know, Anegada is still drowsing under the Caribbean sun. Some men have returned to fishing and conching by the old-time methods, exporting some of their catch to the Virgin Islands and Puerto Rico. Flamingo Pond has officially been turned into a preservation area. Iguanas still scuttle through the bush, I hope.

I learned two important lessons from this assignment. The first was that hands-on teamwork is essential. In handling ecological surveys, there have to be coordination, good timing, cross-fertilization, and personal commitment. Second, I realized the need for careful preparation and adequate field gear. A successful expedition and ecological analysis can stand or fall on a rotted old tent or a new pair of boots.

UPDATE

- As of 1998, very little development, other than two very small hotels and one tiny campground, has occurred. Population of island is 162 people.

- The British Virgin Islands National Parks Trust (established in 1961) today runs 17 park units in B.V.I. They are overseeing conservation programs for both Anegada flamingos and iguanas. A large area of flamingo and iguana habitat, along with adjoining north shore windward beach shoreline (where I camped) has been proposed as a protected natural area by the government. Due to a century-old unresolved land title issue between the local Anegadian community and the government, there has been a delay of 25 years in establishing this park.

- Nevertheless, in 1998 the B.V.I. National Parks Trust appointed its first Senior Terrestrial Park Warden, Mr. Rondel Smith, on Anegada. He will supervise a reintroduction program of the West Indian Roseate Flamingo. The birds will come from Bermuda Aquarium Museum and Zoo, where a successful captive breeding program exists. He will also supervise a rehabilitation program for the Anegada Rock Iguana, including a headstart facility for juvenile iguanas and research on feral cats which prey on young iguana.

- At least 40 humpback whales still breed and bear their calves offshore of Anegada each year.

- Dr. Edward Towle, who first brought me to Anegada, just retired as president of Island Resources Foundation. He is still Chairman of the Board. We have been in touch all these years. His philosophy of conservation in the Caribbean is that slow, steady pressure, incremental progress, and continuing public education efforts are what it takes in most areas.

5

BARÚ and BENJAMIN

———

Quetzals—iguanas. Atitlán—Anegada. I was more and more drawn to independent field work. In June 1971, I made a crucial decision to go free-lance. Since I'd saved enough money teaching at Cornell to survive for a year, I could move to my rustic Adirondack cabin and use my home as office and base of operations. That would cut down overhead. My good guide friends, Bob and Rodney, assured me $3,000 was enough to live on for one year.

Bob advised, "If you drink a lot of whiskey like I do, you'll need about $3,500."

Rodney cautioned, "You can manage on $3,000 if you don't travel any farther than Utica. I never do."

I smiled. In those days I drank nothing alcoholic; however, I sure did plan on going a lot farther afield than Utica, N.Y.! I had made enough contacts in the last five years to bring in some paying assignments as an ecological consultant and writer-photographer. I reasoned that, with most professionals tied down to academic or institutional schedules, a person who was free and flexible might hold an edge in obtaining worthwhile short-term assignments.

At the end of the second week without a paycheck, I knew this was a big psychological turning point. No academic institution, no sugar daddy, no independent source of income was backing me up. From now on, I was strictly on my own. The realization was both exhilarating and frightening. I needed a lot of faith.

I got by for the first half-year on small writing jobs and day consultancies. Then, on a blustery day in January 1972, the first big foreign ecological assignment came. I had trudged over the frozen lake on snowshoes to pick up my mail. On returning to my toasty cabin, I sat by the crackling woodstove and opened my mailbag. Surprise! A cable from Switzerland fell out. With cold-numbed fingers I tore it open. The International Union for Conservation

of Nature and Natural Resources (IUCN) was requesting I go to
Panama for a month and conduct an ecological survey of its first
national park, Volcán Barú. Moreover, they wanted me to hire a
photographer to document the entire expedition. I let out a whoop
of exultation which echoed across the hoar-frosted hills and startled a few white-breasted nuthatches and snowshoe hares. Here
was my opportunity to earn good money, learn new techniques,
meet foreign professionals, and travel to a different country. Best of
all, I'd be contributing to Panama's newborn national park program.

The incongruity—not to mention the size—of the project did-
n't really hit me until suppertime. How was I going to get all my
tropical field gear—tent, mist nets, traps, weather instruments,
cook set, canteens, sleeping bag, cameras, film, tapes, notebooks,
and the rest—out of the cabin? How would I carry it two miles
down an ice-bound lake to my truck? Where would I find a photographer who might be ready on such short notice to spend a
month climbing an 11,400-foot peak in Panama? My jubilance was
so great, however, that I simply glossed over these logistical problems. Instead, I sang a jolly song to my dog, Pitzi.

Fortunately, friends loaned me a snowmobile. Despite blizzards
and deep drifts, I was able to drag two toboggan loads of equipment
to my truck fairly easily. I wrote to a list of free-lance photographers. Phone communication was a problem. I didn't have one, and
the closest pay phone was five miles away. I finally chose the photographer by mail. Clyde Smith was becoming well known for his
excellent pictures in *Adirondack Life* magazine. The man arrived at
my cabin on snowshoes, swiftly made out a contract for us to sign,
and headed off again into the teeth of a snowstorm. I decided that
if Clyde Smith could conduct his business this efficiently in an
Adirondack winter, he'd do okay on a Central American volcano.
And he did, although he'd never been to the tropics. The only
drawback was he spoke no Spanish.

Clyde and I flew to Panama City with about 300 pounds of gear.
We were met by government officials from the Ministry of
Agriculture and two of our new Panamanian teammates: Dario
Tovar, chief of Panama's budding National Parks Service, and
Javier Ortega, a young forester who was to be our driver.

Mr. Tovar explained that the survey had been requested by the
former Minister of Agriculture, Carlos Landau. This farsighted
gentlemen was convinced that a national park would bring in eco-

tourism dollars. It would also preserve the most unusual mountain flora and fauna of western Panama. It would protect the volcano's watershed against erosion, flooding, silting, and decreased water quality downstream. His belief was affirmed by a United Nations Food and Agriculture Organization (FAO) study. It pointed out that Panama could profitably develop six national parks. Barú could be its number one attraction, with quetzals as a main feature.

The next day the four of us traveled along the Pan American Highway to Davíd, Panama's second largest city, near the Pacific Ocean. Until now I had not been aware that the Panamanian isthmus curves in an east-west direction. Somehow I imagined it ran north and south and was all tropical. However, its cool western highlands are the market basket for the entire country. Temperate zone food and flower crops thrive here—cauliflower, potatoes, green beans, and carnations. I found it hard to believe, too, that frost frequently dusts the top of Panama's continental divide.

Off across a wide stretch of cattle pasture, we got our first glimpse of Volcán Barú. It certainly didn't look like the highest

Volcán Barú from a distance at 5,000 feet. Main crater on the right. Volcán's height is 11,400 feet.

point in the country (11,410) feet. More like a large, lazy hill with a few irregular lumps on its sides—rather as if a cook had carelessly frosted a cake with a blunt knife. Little did we realize, looking up from sea level, how grandiose its geological formations were.

We began our first week of reconnaissance around the *eastern* base of Barú, climbing as high as 7,500 feet. We worked out of the pretty little resort town of Boquete. Each day we visited the key areas proposed for park development and possible visitors' interpretive centers. One such site lay beside Río Bajo Chiquero. A river literally sprang out of the volcano side, cascaded down a wall of sheer rock in a lacy water veil, turned into a tumbling, gurgling stream, and hurried away toward the Pacific. I tried a dip in the freshet and found it crystal-clear, toe tingling, and almost too cold for comfort. As I dried myself, the liquid warbling of American dippers (water ouzels) floated over the streambed. It made me think of Colorado's Rocky Mountains, where I'd done my winter study of mule deer for a master's degree at Colorado State University.

Another beautiful spot lay 1,000 feet above the stream valley in a magnificent primary forest of magnolias and oaks. Some trees stood 100 feet tall and had trunks four feet in diameter. As we stepped to a lookout point at the forest edge, Panama's famous *bajareque* (misty sprinkle) was gracing Boquete. Shafts of late afternoon light played hide-and-seek with the bajareque as we watched, forming single rainbows, double rainbows, triple rainbows. The mist turned pink and lavender. This phenomenon occurs when light rain is skimmed off the tops of heavy cloud banks held against the Atlantic slopes and is blown over the continental divide by strong trade winds. Gently it falls out miles away on the Pacific slopes and valleys from seemingly cloudless skies.

Each day some new dignitary came to visit us in Boquete. I was delighted by the officials' interest and the logistical support we were being given. As far as I was concerned, though, the most valuable person we met in Boquete was Benjamin Cuevas Montezuma of the Guaymí tribe. He was the government's only guardian for this huge proposed park. I took one look at the sturdy Guaymí who was to guide us up the volcano and was impressed. His muscular shoulders were to prove invaluable for carrying our scientific equipment, food, and precious water jugs up to the summit. His keen eyes and nose were incredible at finding hidden animal trails, signs, and scents. Most of all, his strong stoical nature was to help us endure the hardships that lay ahead.

Early the next week, we began phase two of our survey with explorations on the *western* slopes of Barú. The vegetation and landscape were much drier, starker, and sparser than around Boquete. A great lava discharge from Barú's fiery past had strewn rocks and rubble over much of the ground. Looking up, we saw an intimidating sight. The volcano's summit loomed, looking more craggy and steep than it had from any other angle thus far. Gazing at the mountaintop, I whispered nervously to Clyde, "I doubt we'll ever make it to the top with all our gear. What do you think?"

The raw-boned, rangy photographer squinted his blue eyes and reconnoitered from long-distance the best route. He was an excellent mountain climber and specialized in mountain photography. He shot me a comforting look and said simply, "We'll make it."

I sensed we were both eager to begin the climb and get to know that lofty peak. But before we could tackle the summit, we had to finish this week of field reconnaissance on the lower western slopes. An exciting aspect of our team cooperation was working closely with the Panamanian technicians. Javier identified tropical trees and showed me new species. Dario explained the country's natural resources program in detail. I reciprocated by teaching them how to make soil measurements, take weather readings, trap

Field team at work: Dario Tovar, chief, National Parks; Javier Ortega, right, forester; and Anne, ecologist.

and net wildlife, and identify birds. Clyde struggled to learn Spanish and took lots of pictures. At that time (1972) this type of team approach and photographic documentation was most innovative. Panama was one of the first Central American countries to consider parks and work cooperatively with outside experts.

The regional forester came to lead us up a rough jeep road to the
7,500-foot contour where the park's proposed boundary lay. We
planned to set up camp there and make a new study site. As we leveled off into a small valley, the sight made us cringe. Dario cursed.
There, backed right up to the park's border and probably intruding
upon it, was brand-new pastureland. Not a tree had been spared.
Downed timber lay scattered every which way, waiting to go up in
flames or down in rot. Cows were already grazing on new patches
of grass. When we stopped to get out of the jeep, we heard the
steady chop-chop-chop on nearby hillsides and the crashes of
falling trees. It was the Cuchumatanes Mountains in Guatemala all
over again. Disgruntled, we held a quick discussion. Stay? Turn
back? Search for another study site?

Suddenly I heard the "*waac-a-waac-a-waac*" alarm note of a
female quetzal. Amazed, I quickly hiked partway up a hill clothed
with untouched cloud forest. I played my old quetzal recording
from Volcán Atitlán. Immediately, a male bird responded with his
territorial whistle. An hour of observation convinced me that we
had stumbled onto a large group of the gorgeous trogons. These,
however, had the shorter tails of the southern subspecies. The
longest plumes measured 24 inches. I hurried down and persuaded
my team members to stay. We made our field headquarters at the
edge of the pasture after all.

Soon I estimated a population of about twenty quetzals. All
were engaged in early courtship. Almost every morning I saw
bunches of three to eight birds chasing one another, calling seduc-
tively, and flirting. Once three females and five males performed a
provocative "ring around the rosy." The "gents" flew 'round and
'round a small sapling with their long green tail plumes fluttering
behind, while the "ladies" chattered boisterously from its branches.
One cool, misty evening, a lone shimmering green quetzal alighted
only five feet above my bright orange tent and calmly surveyed me
as I oiled my boots. Evidently the birds here had never been bothered by people or land clearing. Actually, the new openings in the
forest enabled me to obtain far better observations of the birds than
I had in Volcán Atitlán's dense cloud forest. Clyde was able to
obtain pictures of the shy trogons without all the elaborate equipment David Allen had used. He needed no tower, no blind, no
strobe lights. The species was at the southernmost point of its range
here. Unlike the birds I had studied in Guatemala—the northern
subspecies (*Pharomachrus mocinno mocinno*)—this was the southern

subspecies (*P. m. costaricensis*), smaller and less brilliant.

According to Dr. Alexander Wetmore's *The Birds of the Republic of Panama*, 1972, quetzals were quite abundant on the slopes of Barú between 1856 and 1902 at elevations of 7,000 to 9,000 feet. Since then, their distribution has been greatly reduced due to increased human activity. Even though these birds are not subject to as many pressures as in Guatemala, they are disappearing fast because of clearing of cloud forests and collecting for zoos and aviaries. I learned that quetzals were being sold by a German firm in San José, Costa Rica, for roughly $250 a pair. The air shipper guaranteed to deliver the birds alive. We found quetzals only in remaining swaths of virgin cloud forest on the eastern and western sides of Barú. The Pacific slope was under intensive cultivation with livestock and grazing as high as 8,000 feet.

It was dry season in Panama—not too hot, not too cool—so our work was pleasant. Javier and I took several environmental measurements: air and soil temperatures, soil samples, small mammal census, humidity, wind velocity. Javier made a forest profile. Benjamin showed me the ancient, deep trails of tapirs and the rootings of peccaries. Clyde went exploring. To our concern, however, the wind blew stronger every day. One night, as it was buffeting our camp at 40 miles an hour, Clyde discovered a small forest fire. Sparks had blown down from one of the woodchoppers' campfires into a mass of dry fallen treetops. Flames were already racing up the ravine toward our campsite. Clyde alerted everyone. We charged in with shovels, machetes, sticks, and a few pitiful pails of water scooped from a tiny creek. If we didn't put out the fire at once, it would destroy our campsite and equipment and probably penetrate the cloud forest. We slept uneasily after that, tossing as fitfully as the trees in that gale.

I was awakened at dawn by the sound of a small tree cracking. It fell on the tent where Dario and Javier were sleeping. Fortunately it missed both of them. My own little pup tent blew over during breakfast. Benjamin squinted up at Barú's cloud-streaming peak and said quietly, "The wind is very strong up there. We cannot climb tomorrow as planned. It could be 100 miles per hour. We'd be blown right off."

Dario looked disappointed. He had hoped to scale the summit with us, have a look around, then return to his office in the capital. Clyde and I were frustrated, yet we agreed it would be foolhardy to force this third and most important phase of the survey.

Instead, we packed up our tents and drove to Davíd to see Dario off. It was a good chance to renew our supplies and have clothes laundered. Benjamin helped me push a cart around an air-conditioned supermarket, choosing lightweight foods for our stay on the summit. Suddenly he said shyly, "I know how much you love the quetzals. Sometime I would like to take you into the Guaymí reservation where I was born. I want to introduce you to the chief. He has a special hat filled with quetzal feathers. He wears it once a year for a corn harvest celebration."

I stared at Benjamin in surprise. A Guaymí chief! Quetzal plumes! Ceremonial headdress! Hearing this inside a super-tech food market, I marveled at how varied the world is away from academia. How very unscientific. Cultures colliding with cultures. I felt curious and re-energized.

"Is it far from Davíd?" I asked.

"Only an hour by car or bus, then eight hours by horse. I know a place to rent horses, too. We could get there in one day," he replied.

Just then I saw the headlines on a newspaper by the checkout counter: WINDS HIT 65 MPH AT DAVÍD AIRPORT. It was a "*norte*" (norther) just like those at Lake Atitlán. This one was apparently stronger and lasting longer than most. I knew from experience in Guatemala that we'd have to wait another two to three days until it blew itself out. We actually had an enforced "vacation" ahead of us. The thought struck Benjamin and me simultaneously. "Why not go now?" I cried, eager to witness a native custom involving quetzals and to photograph and describe it.

We finished shopping in a hurry and went to find Clyde and Javier. Over a fragrant lunch of *arroz con pollo* (chicken and rice) and cold Panamanian beer, we made plans. Everyone was enthusiastic except Javier. He had never ridden a horse. This mini-expedition would be money well spent if it expanded our knowledge of the area and the customs of native people around the national park.

Next morning found us speeding along the Pan American Highway by jeep to our "jumping off" place. Benjamin directed Javier through a ramshackle hamlet to a poor farm. Four cadaverous horses stood with their heads hanging. After a short bargaining session, we swung into the saddles, equipment tied fore and aft, and urged the gaunt creatures to walk. Our way wound through dry and dusty range land, third-growth tropical woodland, across a shallow river, and up into scrubby-looking hills. The land seemed badly overused. The cattle were as thin as our mounts. In midafternoon, Clyde's horse simply lay down and refused to get up. Six hours of carrying his 200-pound frame plus camping gear was more than she could manage. We unbuckled the saddle and packs and left her behind to rest. Clyde walked. By four o'clock we began passing stilt huts that looked like Seminole *chickees* in the Florida Everglades. Just before sunset, we reached a large hut where a friend of Benjamin's lived.

"We'll camp here," he told us, "and go on early in the morning. The chief lives about half an hour from here in a large group of huts. But we must water the horses now, let them rest, and wash ourselves."

While Clyde and Javier set up the tents, Benjamin and I led the horses to the watering place. I followed him confidently through a cool green forest and up a small gully to a spring hole. The pool was no bigger than a wash basin, cupped with mossy stones, and clear as champagne. It was the only water source within two miles. I watched this dependable, diffident man fill our canteens and pots and coax the horses to drink. Then he took off his shirt and sluiced water over his head, face, armpits and torso. His brown taut skin glistened like waxed mahogany in the last ruby rays of the sun. Clean, he shrugged on his shirt and led the horses quietly back. I stayed behind to rinse off my own sweaty body. I realized again how very fortunate we were to have such a guide.

That night I stayed awake a long time, staring out my tent flap toward the Pacific. Tomorrow I would meet a real Guaymí chieftain and see a secret ritual. This sure surpassed teaching Introductory Wildlife Conservation to 500 students and sitting through interminable committee meetings! Far off along the coast, a few tiny ship lights winked. They seemed to signal "You're right. You're right."

My evening imaginings of the Indian ceremony seemed pallid compared to the day's actual event. Benjamin had us up at dawn, getting ready for the visit. He again washed his muscular torso and donned a brand-new light green *guayabera* (shirt). Then he stroked fragrant pomade onto his glistening black hair. Clearly this was a big moment in his life. I teased him lightly. "Why, Benjamin, you look as if you're going to a wedding."

He flashed a rare smile and said, "It is the first time gringos have come to my home."

Until that moment I'd not realized how little known and untouched this tribe is in the modern world. It's one of three Amerindian groups—the San Blás, Chocos, and Guaymí—and occupies the westernmost highlands of Panama. The total population was between 30,000 and 40,000. Few Guaymís speak Spanish, and fewer still want to be integrated into Spanish Panamanian society.

We reached the cluster of huts around eight o'clock and found a few families sitting on raised wooden floors. They looked out at us with large, luminous, black eyes. Two young women dressed in long colorful patchwork gowns were pounding wheat in a huge log mortar with heavy pestles. The rhythmic beat resounded through the clearing. Old men were weaving thin strips of palm fronds to be used in making Panama hats. Elderly women were fashioning beautiful beaded necklaces called *chaquiras*. As we arrived, all stopped what they were doing and stared at my blond pigtails, Clyde's blue eyes and cameras, and Benjamin.

A wizened short man came forward and introduced himself with great dignity. He was the chief indeed, but hardly what I expected. He wore a very old, mildewed tuxedo jacket in our honor. His son-in-law, next to be introduced, sported a pink metal construction hard hat and Western-style shirt and pants. Obviously the men had dressed up in their finest. Clyde and I glanced at each other and suppressed our giggles. To have even smiled would have been the rudest of behaviors. We nodded respectfully and shook hands. The wife of the chief now extended her tiny clawlike hand and grinned a toothless greeting. After these formal introductions, no one knew what to do next.

Clyde saved the day. He offered a small flask of rum to the chief. Ceremoniously, the elder uncapped it, took a swig, and passed it to his wife. She downed a healthy gulp and passed it back. Three times they shared the potent liquor. Then they offered it to the hard-hatted son-in-law. Other Guaymís began edging closer. Their mood was quickly mellowing.

Benjamin whispered something to the chief. He went into his hut and came out with a long, hollowed-out bamboo pole. Gently easing a plug from each end, he began pulling out one, two, three— twenty quetzal plumes! With greatest care, he stuffed them into the band of an old sombrero covered with sequins. Finally a headdress of shimmering, two-foot-long emerald feathers stood above the gaudy crown and trembled in the breeze. Reverently the chief placed the spectacle on his head.

Now he spoke to his wife and son-in-law who scurried into the huts. The son-in-law came back with charcoal, an ancient red lipstick, and some white claylike material. Deftly the old man applied a geometrical pattern to his face. Then, wonder of wonders, he started painting mine. Benjamin stepped to my side and said softly, "You may feel honored, Anna. My people decorate their faces only for special occasions. You are a special guest. The chief is putting on a design which fits you alone—the jaguar design. His

The Guaymí chieftain paints Anne's face with a special honored jaguar design.

wife would be pleased if you would wear a Guaymí dress when you dance with them."

Dance! Who said anything about dancing? I'd come to see a quetzal ceremony. The only dancing I knew were rousing Adirondack square dances. Suddenly it looked as if I had to be part of it. Javier was grinning in approval while Clyde looked speechless. For once he even forgot to take pictures. The son-in-law started playing a flute, while another man began blowing into a conch shell. A small drum was added to these instruments.

Now Benjamin brought a long, polished pole and handed it graciously to the chief. "Although this is not the right day to celebrate," he explained to us, "he will show you a bit of the *balsería*. It's an old, old game we play every spring to celebrate the corn harvest. Only the strongest, most agile men play. They must avoid being tripped up by the balsa stick and must stay on their feet for hours, even if they've been drinking *chibcha* (a fermented corn liquor). The champions of the balsería usually become chiefs or respected elders," he said. "Now watch!"

The Guaymí chief and Benjamin play the balsería game with a stout stick, each trying to trip his opponent. Winner stays erect.

The old man swung the pole at Benjamin's muscular legs. He leaped nimbly out of the way, then pranced about like a prize-fighter waiting for the next thrust. The chief feinted and swung again, almost but not quite catching him off guard. I could see that Benjamin probably would have become a leader had he stayed on the reservation. He had the strength, endurance, and even temperament of a chieftain. Not to mention the last name of Montezuma!

After a while, the tempo of the music increased. Young girls, women, and men formed a conga line. With much good-humored laughter, they urged me into the line. I quickly caught the beat and mastered the steps. The old chief dropped the polished pole and went to the head of the line. He pulled us along in a shuffling, weaving dance, his quetzal headdress waving woozily. A more ludicrous sight would be hard to imagine. Here I was at ten o'clock in the morning, supposedly conducting a serious ecological survey, in a tight, bright granny gown, my face painted, dancing with abandon in a remote corner of Panama.

———

Benjamin was noticeably morose on our way down from the reservation. Reining my horse close to his, I gave him a questioning glance. "Qué pasa?"

Turning to me, he said simply, "My wife died near here." A tear glittered in one corner of his eye.

"Was it long ago?" I asked shocked.

"About four years. She was bitten by a snake while gathering wild fruits."

"Was there no way to save her?" I gasped, my heart going out to this bereaved man.

"No. It was much too far to the clinic, and we had no horses," he replied stoically. "She died quickly."

We lapsed into silence, letting our tired mounts pick their way through the scrubby woods. Then Benjamin spoke abruptly. "I left the reservation after that and went to work picking coffee around Boquete, as many of my people do. The best beans are grown on the slopes of Barú. Instead of coming back here after the harvest, I stayed out. It was too lonesome even with my own people. I began to work for the Department of Natural Resources cutting trails up the volcano and guiding officials. Then there was talk of a park and I was made a guardian. This is the first time I've been home since I left."

"Wouldn't you rather live on the reservation now?" I inquired. "It seems like such a pleasant life."

"No," he said gloomily. "There are too many dangers facing us here."

"What do you mean?" I asked.

"In the eastern part of our reservation, Panamanian mining engineers have discovered the largest copper deposits in the world. They are building a huge plant and digging a mine on our land. My people tell me that the government will build a school for the Guaymí children and teach them Spanish. They will show the men how to operate heavy machinery." He shifted in the saddle and went on. "The government wants to mix us up with Panamanians and make us disappear. No one is proud of the Guaymís. Soon we will lose our customs, our clothing, our language, our beliefs.

"Also, between here and the volcano, they are building a large reservoir and hydroelectric plant. Again they will use the Guaymís as cheap labor. Gradually my people will drift away from their homeland and their traditions."

"But surely other Guaymís feel as you do," I protested. "They won't let that happen."

"Yes, some do," agreed Benjamin, "especially the ones who worship Mama Chi."

"Who?"

"Mama Chi. It's a new religion that started about fifteen years ago. A young Guaymí woman had a vision by a spring of water. She was told to start a new cult. Worshipers of Mama Chi do not drink chibcha, will not take part in the balsería, and try to keep the old ways. Many Guaymís here on the reservation have joined this religion."

I was amazed. The more I traveled abroad, the more I learned of the occult, the magical side of life. Just imagine starting a new religion. The straight, hard lines of science mattered little here. People did not think or function as I had been trained to do. It was a humbling experience.

A new thought began formulating in my mind. Turning in my saddle toward Benjamin, I blurted out, "It sounds like the Guaymís in Panama are just as threatened as the quetzals!"

He nodded. I'd never considered that human beings—be they Guaymís, Eskimos, Bushmen, or Amazonian Amerindians—could fall into the category of rare and endangered species. Yet their homelands were being threatened by technology and industry just as wildlife habitats were. The same kind of repercussions were resulting from bringing in heavy machinery as from introducing exotic species. Was cutting cloud forest for tea and timber any different from making a copper mine on an Indian reservation? Was bulldozing primary dunes on a small island for new real estate development any different from setting up schools for children never before exposed to a foreign culture and language?

Benjamin and I were both silent and morose as we continued down the mountain to our jeep.

6

A STARRY NIGHT

———

Back at Barú we found that the north wind had died and the days were calm, clear and warm. We decided it was time to climb to the summit and camp there for as long as we needed to survey the area. Benjamin led the way with a heavy canvas knapsack full of foodstuffs. Javier plodded along glumly under a cumbersome pack frame with a plant press tied to it. Clyde darted here and there taking pictures, seemingly oblivious to his 60-pound Kelty pack. I brought up the rear, trying to take notes, identify new birds, handle cameras and binoculars, and cope with my 35-pound pack.

Lunchtime found us at Portrero Muleto, a curious craterlike depression on the eastern slopes at an altitude of 9,500 feet. We clambered down. Steep andesite walls rose on three sides, while ahead we could see toward the summit through a V-shaped cleft. My legs ached and my back was soaked with sweat as I sank down on the dry, cracked mud and pumice floor of the false crater. Sun-bleached bones of tapirs were scattered among the tussocks of grass. I munched a sandwich and drained my canteen. Looking over at Clyde, I thought of asking him for a few extra swallows, then noticed that his canteen was also empty. Benjamin had insisted that each of us carry a two-gallon plastic jug to be filled on Barú's upper slopes. But where? We hadn't passed a stream, spring, or seep anywhere since the 7,500-foot contour. I thought longingly of the clear, cold Río Bajo Chiquero and its countless little waterfalls. All Volcán Barú's water was springing out of the porous volcanic soil far below us, just as it had at Volcán Atitlán. How would we survive strenuous work at these altitudes without that precious liquid?

Now Benjamin's knowledge of the area came into play. He led us up a narrow ravine and into a small bamboo glade. A pool no larger than a dishpan lay filled with cool seepage water. Evidence was ample that wildlife came here to drink and bathe from miles around. Dainty tracks of brocket deer embroidered the pool edges. Bird prints of every size crisscrossed the damp earth. Wet mud had been packed down into a wallow for wild peccaries. As we approached, we heard the splashing of a black robin in the "dishpan." With infinite care, Benjamin filled our four jugs and every canteen. I immediately dropped halazone tablets into each container. This bamboo glade was the last watering place we were to find.

The added weight of our jugs (a pint's a pound, the world around) plus the ever-higher elevations made the final part of that climb a torture. Even after we stopped in an elfin woodland draped with delicate green mosses and gilded by the setting sun, I could not find the energy to appreciate it. My groaning muscles were about to signal a halt when Benjamin thoughtfully dropped back to offer encouragement. The 11,410-foot peak was in sight, he said. Already he'd found a level camping spot 300 feet below the summit and half a mile away. Supper would be ready by the time I got there. Then he sprinted ahead.

I broke through timberline, tottered up a tundralike slope, and stopped still in my tracks. A full moon was lifting through a blanket of gray clouds far beneath me. In the opposite direction, where the sun had set, luminous shafts of rose and gray were shooting up. Benjamin was crouched over a campfire, boiling rice. Clyde had one tent set up and was erecting another. Only Javier, crumpled beside his plant press, looked as exhausted as I.

At dawn, after a good night's sleep, I scraped the frost off my backpack, donned an Icelandic sweater, and gratefully gulped down a cup of hot Panamanian coffee. Now I was ready to tackle that last stretch to Barú's peak. We negotiated a knife-sharp ridge where the mountain fell away on both sides for a thousand feet. Then we climbed hand-over-hand up the rocky summit. From our vantage point, we could see both the dark blue Pacific and the gray-green Caribbean. What a superb lesson in geology and geography. The Talamanca Range melded into even higher peaks in Costa Rica to our west and fell in lowering humps eastward toward the Panama Canal, 275 miles away. North, we could count at least eight mountains more than 10,000 feet high along the continental divide. (Barú actually stands a little south of this central spine.) Beyond it, toward the Caribbean, the hills were broken, rugged, and heavily forested. This was an area of extremely heavy rainfall. In fact, clouds were thickening above the coastal plain as we watched. Neither roads nor towns existed in that direction, save for foot trails and the seaside village of Bocas del Toro. This provided free access for wildlife to migrate in dry season between Barú and other mountains down to wet lowland rain forest. This wide, vast, wild corridor was extremely important for the animals' survival. The other three slopes of Barú had already been encroached upon by human development. Fortunately, the park's proposed plans protected this forested avenue.

From Panama's highest point, we could also look directly south into Barú's crater complex. "It looks like a huge doughnut," I exclaimed to Clyde. We could see the deep break in the rim from which scalding lava had poured long ago, devastating the western slopes. In some pre-Pleistocene era, geologists say, the volcano grandly blew its ejecta over a 700-square-mile area. Since there are no definite records of eruptions in historic times, we didn't worry about any great blow-ups during our expedition.

The crater complex looked so fascinating that we immediately decided to explore it. The weather was ideal—clear, 70°F, and calm. We threw lunch into one pack, climbing ropes and first aid kit into another, and scrambled over to the bottom of the giant doughnut. Scaling its sides looked hazardous. Giant blocks of lava, scorified as moon rock, lay jumbled one upon another. I could teeter some of them by gently pushing with one hand. Among them, deep holes sank into darkness. Clyde stared into one of these. Suddenly he announced that he was going to rope down inside. Benjamin, eyes aglow, volunteered to join him. At once, I denounced the idea as crazy and profitless. "If either of you gets hurt," I protested, "it could prove fatal. We're at least eight hours' fast walk straight down the volcano and another hour and a half by jeep to the hospital in Davíd. One whole backbreaking day just to reach good medical help."

But Clyde and Benjamin stubbornly insisted. "Who knows what we'll find in there?" said Clyde excitedly.

"I've been to the top of Barú more times than anyone in Panama," exclaimed Benjamin, "yet I've never had a chance to go down inside it."

How could I stop them?

Producing two 50-foot coils of stout line, Clyde tied one end to a pinnacle of rock and eased himself into the bowels of Barú. Benjamin followed close behind. Soon I heard a bellow, "We're down 35 feet. There are some weird-looking plants growing down here!"

Benjamin roping down rock upthrust in main crater of Volcán Barú, Panama.

Credit: Clyde Smith

"*Plants!*" Javier jumped off a boulder and pressed his face into the hole.

"What do you see?" I asked eagerly.

"Nothing but Clyde's flashlight," replied Javier.

Minutes later, Clyde and Benjamin squeezed back out with some choice specimens. The plants were roughly the size of African violets and covered with short tan hairs. Javier promptly popped them into a plastic bag and sealed it tight. They might be a new species or first records for the volcano. (It turned out to be a fern, *Elaphoglossam*, an uncommon plant found at high elevations.)

Then we continued up over the crater rim and looked down. The scene was as bleak, lifeless, and blasted as any I'd ever witnessed. Barú's eruption must have been incredibly powerful. Four small craters lay within the main doughnut-shaped mass. We clambered down and scrambled from crater to crater, trying not to scratch ourselves on those cruel rocks. Surprisingly, a pair of large-footed finches appeared from nowhere and hopped after us curiously. A few frail plants struggled from cracks and ledges, kept moist by passing clouds.

The sun paled for a moment and a chill crept into the air. Wisps of clouds trailed through the crater complex. A few minutes later a patch of fog enshrouded us. High noon. Gray scud filled the doughnut hole. I became completely disoriented. There was no sun, no wind, no shadows.

Things I'd only read about in ecology books were happening right before my eyes on Barú.

That day the phenomena of horizontal precipitation and microclimates became sharply evident. Strong mountain convection (orographic) currents were forcing up warm, humid Pacific air and condensing it above our heads into clouds. I recalled the same cloud cap appearing over Volcán Atitlán each noon. A considerable quantity of water was being caught, condensed, and collected by plant leaves, branches, and epiphytic vegetation from these fogs, mists, and clouds which drift by more or less *horizontally* in the tropics at high elevations. Such moisture, in the form of tiny droplets, was supporting a miniature community of mosses, ferns, orchids, subalpine flowers, and shrubby plants.

I rested briefly under one leafy shrub whose canopy contours exactly matched the colorful carpet of mosses and lichens underneath on which I was sitting. Outside these contours, the ground was as bare and stark as a desert. We also found a dwarf tree clinging to the southwest crater wall where most clouds rolled in. Its branches were covered with hundreds of small magenta orchids like bright balls on a Christmas tree—the only cheerful sight in that drab world. Life on the edge...

This miracle of horizontal precipitation, interception, and condensation has been studied by Dr. L. R. Holdridge, renowned tropical ecologist. Working in Panama's Talamanca Range, he found that sideways-blown water, derived from condensation in cloud forests, makes a great difference in the total yearly runoff down-slope. High altitude moisture can add as much as 20 inches annually. This becomes very important to the humans and animals that live far *below* the mountain tops and depend on running water for survival. It is also critical to the regulation of stream flow, erosion control, irrigation projects, potential hydroelectric plants, and large-scale ranching operations downslope.

Any tampering with the delicate water regime at high elevations would only lead to troubles below. If vegetative cover were cut or burned *above*, decreased stream flows in dry season, more rapid runoff in wet times, excessive leaching of the fragile, unstable soils, silting of streams, landslides, and losses of fish and wildlife would result *below*.

Toward late afternoon, the clouds lifted. We climbed back out of the crater and headed for camp. To the west, towering thunderheads glowed peach and ivory atop the purple skyline of Costa Rica. Here and there along the rough ridge, a dead bush stood starkly silhouetted against silver clouds boiling up over the Pacific. It was the most dramatic sky I'd ever seen.

Back at our tents, Javier busied himself with pressing and labeling plant specimens. Clyde was numbering his film rolls and captioning them. Benjamin was cooking supper over a smoky fire. I sat apart, staring over the coast where the waning moon would soon appear. I was lost in thought about the experiences of that day. It seemed more important than ever to secure this mighty volcano as a national park.

I shifted uneasily. My mind was jumping all over the place. There was a pressing need for more food and fiber to feed and clothe Panama's ever-burgeoning population. Yet, decreased quality of life for humans and wildlife alike would result when agriculture, ranching, and lumbering were practiced in the wrong places—like on Barú.

Panama's Department of Natural Resources (RENARE) had reported that recent removal of cloud forest on Barú's midslopes had resulted in a bad flood along the Río Caldera in November 1969. It had washed out homes in Boquete, plus croplands, bridges, and trees. The channel had been widened several hundred feet in places. In the Río Chiriquí Viejo, another stream springing from the mountainside, average annual water temperature had risen by 5°F over the past 30 years. At one period, the water silted so badly that introduced rainbow trout disappeared. RENARE had estimated that 90 percent of the original native forest below 6,000 feet was gone from Barú.

I caught Benjamin's steady gaze upon me. "Qué pasa?" he asked quietly. "Are you tired, Anna? Are you hungry? Supper is almost ready. We have rice, beans, cheese, and coffee," he said, as if to cheer me.

"No, Benjamin, it's not that. I'm just worried about the water," I said abstractedly, unprepared to explain the full ecological function to him at that moment.

"The water!" he exclaimed. His face fell. "I was afraid to tell you about that. We are almost out of water."

Perplexed for a moment, I realized that he meant our drinking water. Even though none of us had bathed, laundered, or even brushed our teeth in the last 24 hours, we were using it up at an alarming rate just for cooking and quenching thirst. Only one gallon of the initial eight remained.

"Javier and I must go down to Portrero Muleto early tomorrow and bring up more," Benjamin announced seriously.

This meant that we would accomplish only half the work I had planned at the summit. However, we could not survive without this vital life-support item. So the next day (and once again after that) the two men had to climb down about 4,000 feet, then backpack four full jugs to the top of Barú.

Lack of summit water also caused an absence of mammal life here. I had seen only droppings of forest rabbits and rootings of coati mundis. The larger mammals—puma, tapir, jaguar, peccary, ocelot, deer—moved down to the wetter Caribbean slopes during dry season. Yet, to my surprise, small birds were plentiful. They apparently existed on dew, condensation, and wild fruits, as did quetzals. My favorites were the volcano hummingbirds, flame-throated warblers, and yellow-thighed finches which flitted brightly through the elfin woodlands. At dusk, if we were quiet, we could hear black-billed nightingale thrushes singing eloquently.

In my proposed park planning report, I decided to recommend several strategically placed water catchment basins for wildlife. These would provide water for both animals and people at the summit and also serve for fire fighting. In addition, I would strongly urge the provision of well-built garbage pits and rustic outhouses. Signs of *Homo sapiens* lay all over the summit, despite the difficult ascent. Beverage cans, broken rum bottles, plastic debris and toilet paper littered the trails. There were blackened elfin woodlands as evidence of campfires gone wild. Dozens and dozens of names and dates had been painted on rocks. Nevertheless, periodic cleanups and removal of garbage could be done by volunteer Boy and Girl Scouts. (Scouting was very popular in Panama.) Privy holes could be covered with dirt, new holes dug, and outhouses moved by park rangers. The Panama Audubon Society and ANCON (*Associación Nacional para la Conservación de la Naturaleza*) might also volunteer to help the park.

Benjamin told me that roughly 800 to 1,000 people had climbed Barú in 1970-1971. Given that number of people *before* it was formally declared a national park, I wondered what the use—and abuse—would be like *after* it opened officially. The current population of Panama was about 1,500,000, excluding the Guaymís, other tribal Indians, and Canal Zone residents. This number is expected to zoom to 3 million or 4 million by the year 2000. Panama is probably the most prosperous country in Central America, has the highest per capita income and gross national productivity. It is a key nation in the banking world. Yet it contains the smallest number of people working in agriculture and ranching, and has one of the highest urban populations (45%). It was 56% in 1998. All these statistics portend more active participation in outdoor recreation in Panama. I figured that Volcán Barú would become a prime target for local residents and foreign visitors.

What facilities would be built here? I worried. Would paved roads and plush accommodations like those in the Everglades and Grand Teton National Parks be created? Or a golf course beside the sparkling Río Bajo Chiquero? A cog railway or a car route right to the top of Barú? A revolving restaurant at the summit? Not everyone agrees that a national park's chief function is to conserve wildlands, wildlife, and natural beauty. The possibilities made me cringe.

Meanwhile, we still had more work to do. After taking weather data and soil samples, running a trapline, and censusing birds, as we'd done at our eastern and western 7,500-foot study sites, Javier and I collected subalpine and elfin woodland plants. The plant press soon was bulging—seventy-two specimens! When Javier groaned at the thought of carrying this heavy weight down the mountain, I reminded him that these were probably the first plants ever collected atop Volcán Barú. They would make a fine addition to the University of Panama's herbarium.

On the fifth evening, Benjamin sadly announced that our food was nearly gone. All we had for supper was oatmeal and rice, with half a cup of cocoa apiece. For breakfast next day, we ate just oatmeal. We *had* to leave. No need to push our luck. Another norte might begin, or an accident befall us if we were in weakened condition. Nonetheless, we had camped longer on top of Barú (to our knowledge) than any other group—ever.

After our scanty supper, Benjamin said he felt like climbing to the summit. It was an exceptionally clear night. Would Clyde or I care to join him? Javier was already snoring. Clyde chose to work again on his films. I rallied. When would I ever be on Volcán Barú again? The waning moon had not yet risen, so we walked by starlight. Distant halos of light hung over the hidden towns of Boquete, La Concepción, and Davíd. Benjamin pushed ahead on his steel-springed legs. At last mine gave out, and I sat down exhausted. "Go on without me," I urged. "Do you have a flashlight?"

"Si, Anna."

"Be careful, Benjamin."

Minutes passed. The only sounds were the low hoot of an owl and the occasional clatter of a stone falling from under Benjamin's boots. Staring at the cascade of twinkling stars swathing the sky, I pondered on how soon the volcano would be declared a national park. There were 1,200-odd other parks in the world. Could Barú become a model for other countries where cloud forest and mountain sanctuaries were urgently needed. Barú had all the right park prerequisites: extensive area, outstanding natural resources, the beginnings of an effective system of protection, and ecotourism.

My friend, Dr. Norman Myers, a wildlife ecologist, has often called conservation "the art of the possible."

Just then a light blazed from the summit—Benjamin's torch! He blinked three times at me. I answered back with three flashes. My spirit soared up beside him through that starry night. He was standing on the very apex of Panama. He was the king of Panama. He was the highest man in the world for all he knew of Mount Everest, the World Trade Center, and space ships. That night, that mountain, and that countryside belonged to Benjamin, a simple, uneducated Guaymí, a dedicated though lowly government employee. It belonged to him more fully and more deeply than it could ever belong to those of us with our diplomas, cameras, and plant presses.

Perhaps, I thought, conservation *is* possible in Panama.

———

Next day we made the descent down dizzying slopes and dangerous scree safely. We arrived in Davíd—11,410 feet to sea level in eight hours—famished and with splitting headaches. After four aspirins each and a short nap (which gave our bodies time to adjust to the barometric pressure), we were ready to dive into an enormous Chinese dinner. Gorging ourselves, we discussed plans for the next two days. We had to pack, repair equipment, and sort out our specimens. Then we needed a day in Panama City to visit government offices, make our final report, and express our thanks.

To my surprise, Benjamin asked for his pay and the next day off. He said he had a sick uncle in the Davíd hospital. He had seen him before climbing the volcano. He now wanted to check up on his relative. I readily agreed, but asked that he be back in time to see us off. I was much too fond and appreciative of our Guaymí guide to leave without saying good-bye. We waited two extra hours for Benjamin. Clyde and Javier fidgeted to drive off, but I refused.

Benjamin finally showed up. His face seemed strangely altered. Could he have been drinking? Or just sleeping after the weeks of hard work?

A moment later I was deeply ashamed of my suspicions. When Benjamin hugged me good-bye he whispered in my ear, "Anna, my uncle is better. He is going back to the reservation. And I met a girl, a Guaymí girl, under a tree outside the hospital. Her husband abandoned her, and she has a little baby."

"Oh, Benjamin," I sighed. "I'm glad for your uncle, but how sad for the girl. What will become of her and the baby? Are there shelters for women here?" Then it dawned on me. "Oh! How wonderful! Oh! Did you feel affection for each other?"

He nodded. "Yes. Right away. It happens like that with us Guaymís." He looked at me sideways and smiled. I saw happiness in his wide black eyes for the first time since I'd met this taciturn, sturdy companion. Then he broke away from us and waved farewell.

I left Panama next night believing that Volcán Barú and its cloud forests would be saved. And believing that not only conservation, but many other things, are possible in this world. Perhaps it's because I still see Benjamin standing under the stars on Barú's summit.

UPDATE

- Volcán Barú National Park is still the same size—35,000 acres; however, it now is contiguous with two new transfrontier parks in Panama and Costa Rica. These are both named La Amistad, or Friendship, National Parks. All three are part of a World Heritage Site declared by UNESCO about ten years ago. It totals 567,845 hectares, or 1,402,577 acres, which is the single largest natural forest unit in Central America today. The Site has enormous conservation value in terms of biodiversity. It contains 180 endemic plant species and is one of the last refuges for jaguars, ocelots, and tapirs.

- Volcán Barú National Park did not remain intact, unfortunately. Some new logging roads reach above 6,000 feet in the park's highlands where oaks are being cut and private farms established. These roads have caused erosion of the volcanic soils.

- Telecommunications towers have been built on top of the volcano (highest point in Panama), resulting in serious erosion, visual pollution, and lots of garbage on top and in the craters.

- Benjamin is currently working as a ranger in the Panama frontier park, La Amistad.

- ANCON (National Association for Nature Conservation) has become the leading NGO (non-government organization) in Panama and works closely with the National Park Service. It has done surveys, drawn up species lists, studied proposed park boundaries, and educates the public in conservation. A committed, spunky group.

- The population of Panama (1998) reached 2,735,943 in a country of some 32,000 square miles. The protected areas system includes 14 national parks, covering 3,399,117 acres.

- Two new threats to the World Heritage Site on Panama's side are a recent highway, which opened up the untouched rain forest east of Barú from Chiriquí to Bocas del Toro; and the Chiriquí-Bocas del Toro oil pipeline, which caused construction of an adjacent highway. Since 1988, settlement, logging, cattle grazing, fires, illegal hunting, and erosion have increased. Overall integral management of Barú's watershed is crucially needed.

7

CONSERVATION MADE EASY?

---

y next big consulting job came by mailboat directly to my log cabin dock on a hot, sunny July day in 1973. Pitzi, my German shepherd from Guatemala, had pranced down to meet the mailman and bring back my mailbag in his mouth. I rewarded the fawn-colored male with a cookie, then opened the bag. Inside was a cable. It read: CAN YOU JOIN SURVEY TEAM AS WILDLIFE ECOLOGIST FOR PROPOSED NATIONAL PARK DOMINICAN REPUBLIC AUGUST 1ST? REPLY AT ONCE.

August 1 was only three days away. Immediately I boated out to a pay phone and dialed my colleague, Dr. Edward Towle, director of Island Resources Foundation. He was in the Virgin Islands assembling the survey team. His voice cut clearly across 2,000 miles between the Adirondacks and the Caribbean. He explained that this project would be jointly sponsored by the Dominican Republic government and by part of a huge multinational corporation, Gulf+Western Industries, Inc. The team would be large—composed of Dominican sociologists, anthropologists, archaeologists, botanists and American park planners, marine biologists, and me as wildlife ecologist. Dr. Towle described the proposed park as flat limestone country, consisting of an almost uninhabited island and wild peninsula in the southwestern corner of the Republic. He assured me that we would have the best of accommodations and transportation in the field. Gulf+Western was generously supplying all logistical support.

Until then, I had never heard of this company. Now I learned that it owns vast acreages of sugarcane and ranchland in the Dominican Republic. Paramount Pictures is one of its subsidiaries. It stands among the top corporations in the USA.

"Well," I mused, after hanging up and leaving the broiling phone booth, "this should be interesting. It will be a new approach to do conservation work for a giant corporation. I wonder how effective we'll be?"

I began frantically packing and skimming through my library on Caribbean fauna. All my field gear had to be carried in one backpack, a huge duffel, and two camera bags. Pitzi was taken to the kennel. Mail was stopped. Somehow I managed to be on a plane to Santo Domingo in time. I arrived by van at La Romana, a coastal company town near the proposed park, just in time for an evening briefing. A dozen scientists clustered in a smoke-filled room, poring over maps and making travel plans for the next day. Since the park area had no roads, no towns, no airstrip, and no docking facilities, other than a small Navy station on the island, getting into it was a major problem.

We split into three parties. The archaeologist, an historian, and two sociologists would drive way around to Boca de Yuma, a tiny fishing village. This was the closest approach by road to the proposed park border. From there they would walk south into the park and begin looking for caves where ancient Indian petroglyphs (rock carvings) and paintings were said to exist. They would also check to see whether any scattered squatters might be eking out an existence along the coast. The marine biologists and a park planner would cruise over to *Isla Saona* (the Island of Saona) in a sport-fishing boat and make their initial reconnaissance of beaches, reefs, bays, and islets. The third group, which included a geographer, botanist, a park interpreter, and me, would survey the entire 103,474-acre tract by helicopter. Our task would be to observe by air the various ecosystems within the park and note the condition of its forest cover. Helicopter! Guatemala and Panama were never like this. I could see that we were part of a tightly coordinated, efficiently run, well-planned undertaking. It should yield fast and accurate results.

"Remember," cautioned our team leader, "this is not an in-depth, complete survey. This time it's a 'broad brush' treatment. We just want to know what's out there. Right now no one knows what birds, mammals, beach resources, types of trees, archaeological remains, and so on are in the park area. Later, we can concentrate on details. We have only five days to work, so find out all you can."

With those heady words ringing in my ears, I went to my hotel room and began laying out clothes and equipment for the early morning flight. It would be my first helicopter ride. I could hardly wait.

A company car whisked us to the La Romana airport right on time. A shiny Bell Ranger sat trimly on the heliopad. A mechanic was finishing up the preflight check and another was topping off the gas tanks. The pilot, a stocky, blond Texan with Vietnam experience, lounged expectantly in a small waiting room.

"Ready?" he asked, rising.

We followed him out to the chopper. I climbed inside first and took a seat beside the right side front window. The others squeezed in to the back seats. The Ranger carried five people, including the pilot, and the rear passenger compartment was complete with radio-phone, bar, and leather padding. Breathless, I listened to the rotors starting to hum, to turn, to whirl. An infernal racket and quivering shook the chopper. I held my breath. Suddenly, without the slightest jerk or shudder, the helicopter eased into the air, tilted forward and down, yet rose swiftly. I watched the airstrip diminish beneath us and the hazy outline of the peninsula come into focus ahead. It was covered with dry, low, dense woods. The botanist shouted in my ear, "That's probably the largest contiguous tract of subtropical, dry-to-humid, lowland forest left on any Caribbean island. Just look—no one seems to be living there at all!"

We flew down the western side of the peninsula over narrow, immaculate white beaches and aquamarine water. This leeward side looked limpid, calm, and shallow. At the base of the peninsula, about ten miles from the upper park border, we reached a huge bay, Bahía Catalanita. The water shaded to jade and yellow-green over the turtle grass flats. Around one islet, Isla María, I saw a cloud of black specks dancing. Tapping the pilot on his shoulder, I motioned him downward. He put the Ranger into a fast descent—almost too fast. Before I could warn him, we were almost on top of a huge breeding colony of man-o'-war (frigate) birds. Afraid that the rotors' downblast would terrify them, I motioned hastily to the pilot to veer off sideways. There, at a safe distance, we hovered a few feet above the mangroves and watched those elegant birds soar and wheel above their nests on slim, eight-foot wings.

The park interpreter caught my eye and yelled, "Great place for a nature boardwalk and birdlife display."

I nodded enthusiastically. Then, like a giant hummingbird, we sideslipped off across the bay and approached Isla Saona. It appeared almost flat except for an upward tilting of the northeast-

ern coastline. This culminated in an outcrop known as Punta
Balajú (Whale Point). There the Caribbean changed to the royal
blue, deep, and turbulent Mona Channel. It was a favorite route of
migrating whales. Off to the east, 40 to 50 miles away, lay Puerto
Rico.

The chopper leaned sideways and I gasped. The seatbelt bit into
my side and stomach. Our pilot was treating us to a close inspection of the old lighthouse on Saona's southeastern tip. In a blur, we
circled the rusting light on top. Then we darted off along Saona's
southern coast. Enchanting empty beaches flashed by. We detoured
around Mano Juan, a Dominican Republic Navy base, so as not to
alarm the 200 sailors there. Then we were flying over lagoons as red
as those on Anegada. I strained to see a flamingo, but nothing
moved on those vast, wind-ruffled surfaces. Again we turned hard
about and headed back up the center of the island. Like the mainland peninsula it was largely forested, with no lakes, ponds,
streams, or swamps. No fresh water—anywhere.

Now we had come full circle around Saona and were ready to
fly up the eastern, or windward, side of the peninsula. To my astonishment, a totally different scene met our eyes. There was a tiny
clearing with five huts and huge conch piles on the southeastern
tip. From there, roughly 16 miles up to the village of Boca de Yuma
at the northeastern end, the entire coastline was a series of raw,
rocky escarpments. Open ocean dashed ceaselessly against cliffs.
Grottos, natural bridges, and blowholes had been carved out by this
endless pounding. Where land had risen in geological times, sea
caves and hollows had been left pocking the cliffs. Reaching the
park's northern border, the Ranger climbed steadily up into the sky.
From 2,000-feet elevation, the pilot pointed down and yelled to us,
"Notice the fault line that runs across the peninsula here. It's more
or less the proposed park boundary. North of it you'll see the beginning of cane fields and ranches that run up into the mountains on
the north coast. The whole park, including Saona, will be about
420 square kilometers."

This would truly be a park of impressive size and quality for the
Caribbean. Four other areas in the Dominican Republic had
already been designated as national parks, but all these were pri-
marily forest reserves and not open to the public. In addition, at
this time, no national park service existed. The concept of this
park was to provide preservation of its natural resources, encourage
local use and tourism, and engage in an active program of educa-

tion, interpretation, and research of this natural area. These aims could have far-reaching environmental consequences and provide a model for any new parks in the future.

Already the Ranger was descending and the airport ahead was growing larger. Our flight time had passed like a whirlwind. I felt as if we had been airborne a few minutes, though my watch told me it had been over three hours since we took off. My ears were still ringing after I ducked beneath the revolving rotors and joined my teammates in the waiting room. "Can you imagine any better way to examine an area?" I exclaimed giddily.

"But at what expense!" replied the Dominican botanist soberly. "That Ranger runs a hundred and fifty dollars an hour to operate if it costs a penny. Our little morning exploration probably cost the company a cool five hundred, not counting the fuel."

I was astounded. I'd never really thought about what our survey work would ultimately cost. I queried the botanist, "Who is really footing the bill?"

"The Gulf+Western Dominican Foundation is providing funds to inventory and evaluate the park's natural resources and to develop master plans," he explained. "The Foundation exists strictly to bring about the best and most imaginative use of Gulf+Western philanthropic funds in all types of human development. This national park isn't the corporation's only interest, but perhaps it's the most important for our island's four million inhabitants."

Later that day, I happened to stroll past several huge sugar warehouses. Each was the size of my former high school and each was packed to the roof with fragrant raw sugar. I stood for a moment trying to translate that enormous aromatic tonnage into dollars. Next I attempted to trace the path from here to U.S. supermarkets where sugar sat in prim bags on shelves. I knew that a pound of sugar sold for 10 to 15 cents down here in the Caribbean; in New York State, for 40 to 50 cents at that time. Quite a markup. My consulting fee was $100 U.S. dollars per day, plus airfare and housing at the company hotel. Clearly conservation efforts cost a lot more handled this way than the way I'd done it on a shoestring in Guatemala. I finally gave up trying to calculate what it meant. What really mattered was that Gulf+Western corporation wanted to help make a national park for the Dominican Republic and was willing and able to be its sponsor.

The next three days zipped by. The sportfishing boat took us for a closer look at the man-o'-war-bird colony and to dive on a couple of reefs. I bird watched at one end of Saona Island, getting a total of 65 bird species. The rest of the fauna was typical of an oceanic island—small mammals like mice and rats, a few reptiles, and insects which had reached Hispaniola on natural rafts. Large mammals could not have arrived by any means save importation by man, as on Anegada. The habitats I saw seemed relatively untouched and not yet destroyed by feral stock. The area was too dry and fragile to withstand much exploitation by humans or domestic stock. In general this boded well for national park development.

The population of the Dominican Republic was increasing at three percent per year. It was far wiser to preserve this unique peninsula and island as a park now, than let it fall into second-rate cultivation and pastureland by squatters later. As a national park, it could meet the recreational needs of people and still keep its ecosystems intact.

Our last day at La Romana, we were called in to meet the head of the Gulf+Western Dominican operation. He would assist the team leader and key people in making decisions about the park and also serve as liaison between the government and corporation. We were late returning from the sea, so I ran to his office without so much as putting on my sneakers. I made a cursory examination of the room—no desk, no papers, no briefcase, no smiling secretary in a corner. Rather, it held an assemblage of stunning Cuban mahogany and leather furniture; photographs of tennis and polo players, racehorses, and prize bulls; bridles, bits, stirrups; and burlap sugar sacks tastefully tacked to the walls. What sort of office was this for a corporation head?

Then the door opened, and a compact, lithe, heavily mustached man clad in impeccable khaki pants and a white polo shirt slipped in. I was suddenly embarrassed by my cut-off jeans, bare feet, hunting knife at my belt, and pigtails. I looked like a ragamuffin. To compensate, I murmured a greeting in Spanish and then offered the most formal "thank you" I could muster for Gulf+Western's help and hospitality. Apparently, I was the only one of the Americans who spoke that language, though most of the Dominicans knew English. I received a firm handshake and warm glance from the C.E.O.

He spent the next hour and a half with us, listening to the results of our survey, looking at maps, asking a keen question now and then, and nodding at our plans for future research. He said little and took no notes. Yet his dark eyes probed us intently. I gradually realized that a photographic mind was recording every word and detail. No phone rang, no secretary interrupted us. We might have been having an animated afternoon social get-together rather than a planning session that involved millions of dollars and a hundred thousand acres of undeveloped land. Then, abruptly, our host stood up, shook hands with each of us, and excused himself. A moment later, his receptionist bustled in to usher us out.

"My boss has never spent so much time with anyone except the highest executives of the company," she fussed. "He must be *very* interested in this park and in your survey work." As the others filed out, she detained me with a courteous hand on my arm. "The C.E.O. was so pleased you spoke Spanish," she said warmly. "He hopes that you can come back to continue your research and especially to be here for the official declaration of the park, if possible. You would be able to explain the master plan to his Dominican colleagues and the government officials."

Once again, my Spanish had served me well. "Of course," I told her with a broad smile, "I'd be honored."

As a matter of fact, wild horses could not have kept me away. It wasn't every day that a wildlife ecologist got in on the ground floor of exploring new territory and helping to create a new national park. Conservation had never seemed easier.

8

DOMINICAN ESPRESSO

Back at my Adirondack cabin, I spent a week catching up on mail, phoning people, and paying bills each morning. Afternoons I tidied up my woodlands. The winding trails were raked smooth. My fir forest was combed over for fallen branches. The outbuilding roofs were swept clean of needles. Then each evening I built a blazing bonfire and cooked my supper over all that debris.

Hummingbird feeders were filled and hung back outside. I took my morning dips with loons, happy they received me back and returned my low tremulos. Once I had reconnected with my resident wildlife, land, and cabin, I felt centered. Now it was time to begin one of the most pleasurable and fascinating aspects of my ecological work.

After every distant consulting job, I spend an equal number of days preparing a report. It is liberally illustrated with photographs taken in the field. Luckily I have a large library of field guides, ecology books and natural history texts.

It's easy to research information needed just by pulling books off shelves and sitting down to read on my sundeck. As I write up field notes and caption photos, I relive every moment of every trip. Purple finches warble, waves lap on shore, a raven croaks, spruces sigh in the breeze. What a superlative office! I pictured the other members of our park team working in staid city offices with traffic noise and sirens in the background.

Within three weeks all our reports were submitted to the Gulf+Western Industries office. Counting our survey, the planning and mapping work, and illustrations, a total of 60 days had been devoted to the proposed park.

Then a year passed while our reports were assembled, translated, printed and bound in handsome master plan portfolios. Finally, they were distributed to top Dominican government officials, including President Juan Belaguer. In September 1975 he officially declared the area _Parque Nacional del Este_ (National Park of the East).

Soon afterward, I was invited to the Dominican Republic to participate in the first big planning session. Key people from the government, Gulf+Western Industries, and the Museum of Dominican Man were participating. Flustered I stood up to address these august persons: the corporation head for Dominican operations, a high-level general and admiral of the Dominican Army and Navy, a young chief of the brand-new park service, and the Museum's director. Carefully, in Spanish, I described the general ecology, natural resources, and main attractions of the park. Next I outlined our plans for future study and tourist development. Bound copies of the master plan and pictures were passed around the table.

When it was over, the C.E.O. shook my hand warmly and thanked me. "I'd like you to do an in-depth survey of the park soon, help lay out the road, pinpoint visitors' centers, and anything else needed. We'll provide whatever you want—helicopters, assistants, boats," he said, matter-of-factly. I was speechless. It was like being asked to play God. I managed to nod agreement. He gave my hand another firm squeeze and added, "Everyone is enthusiastic about the park. We can expect good cooperation from all these interested organizations." Then he was gone.

I reserved three weeks in which to make the survey and returned after Easter in 1976. My plan was to cover roughly the same route we had flown over. I'd start at the northeastern corner of the park below Boca de Yuma and walk the entire perimeter of the peninsula. I'd end at Bayahibe, a beautiful beach used by the company's hotels, just above the northwestern corner—a distance of 35 to 40 miles. Much of this coast was not accessible by motorboat because of the rough seas, high escarpments or shallow mud flats. Then I would cruise over to Isla Saona and walk its southern shoreline from Punta Catuán to Punta Caña and the old lighthouse at the easternmost point—roughly another 15 miles. While backpacking, I planned to observe birds, particularly the spring migrants, and run a small mammal trap line each evening. Extensive notes and photographs would be needed of the different ecosystems. During the last few days I'd work with Gulf+Western engineers on laying out a roadway into the park.

I had asked for two Dominican assistants. One would carry an extra pack with snap traps, live traps, bait and water; the other, an extra tent, bedding, food, and water. I would be loaded down as usual with cameras, binoculars, notebooks, field guides, my own tent and sleeping bag. But I wasn't exactly prepared for the type of assistants waiting. Luis was 75 years old and could neither read nor write. He had spent his entire life on Isla Saona. The second, Ramón, was about 55, tall, and weighed less than me. His cadaverous frame and hacking cough were not promising for the rugged trip ahead.

Yet the old adage, "You can't tell a book by its cover," had never proved truer. Luis and Ramón turned out to be the hardiest, sweetest, most considerate field helpers I've ever had or probably ever will again. Luis easily toted his 50-pound pack all day, helped set traps, made the campfire each evening, and imparted fascinating bits of natural history. He apparently could survive on about three cups of water a day. His years on Isla Saona as a hunter and fisherman had created a stalwart woodsman. As for Ramón, he managed the food pack, cooked all our meals, told us sea stories, and maintained a jolly mood. Not for nothing had he been a popular mate on numerous fishing boats around the Dominican Republic. Within the first 24 hours the two black men and I had become fast friends.

One major goal of our field trip was to find, if possible, a very rare and endangered insectivore, the Hispaniola solenodon. This small, secretive, slow, nocturnal mammal is found only in Haiti and the Dominican Republic. It has been almost exterminated due to land development, deforestation, hunting by dogs, predation by feral cats and mongoose, and capture for zoo specimens. The solenodon's range and numbers are completely unknown. I hoped to find a few of the long-snouted, bewhiskered, little creatures in Parque Nacional del Este. Perhaps they were surviving in the caves, sink holes, or hollow trees of its dense forestbush. Photographs showed it to be not much larger than an opossum, with the same naked tail and clawed feet. I knew that solenodons mainly eat ants, roaches, grubs, and worms, as do its relatives the shrews and tenrecs. It has also been implicated in feasting on poultry and gorging on vegetable crops. Luis was carrying several large, collapsible live traps which we would bait with delectable tidbits. Hopefully we'd actually see and photograph one of these unusual creatures.

The main problem we faced and could not conquer was water. I knew that the heat would be brutal at midday. We would each require several quarts daily just to maintain our well-being. A

Gulf+Western engineer had warned that we would find no drinking water at all on the peninsula nor on Saona. Only the little naval station had a supply brought in by boat each week. I couldn't afford to send Luis out every day or two to replenish our water as Benjamin had done on Volcán Barú. When we were near the bottom of the limestone peninsula it would mean a 25-mile walk round trip. Furthermore, no boats could land on that craggy, wave-lashed eastern coast.

Our only hope was the Ranger. I found the Texan pilot and presented our problem.

"Yeaaah," he drawled affably. "I could drop off ten gallons of water every other day in between my other duties. Generally I'm flying over the cane fields most days, dropping off machinery parts for broken tractors and giving visiting firemen the royal tour." He yawned widely. "Put some X marks on this chart for me. Take a can of bright orange spray paint along to mark the places you want the water left. I'll see you get five two-gallon plastic jugs every other day."

"Oh, that's super!" I smiled. "We can probably get by on less, but one of the jugs might leak or break. If you drop them off late afternoon we'll be using a lot of water at supper, washing up, filling our canteens and so on. That way we'll have less to carry the next two days."

"Well, I can't promise for sure when I'll get them to you," he hedged, "but I won't let you die of thirst, okay? Say, be sure to mark an area about 20 by 20 feet with the spray paint so I can see where you are. Now tell me, do you want to be dropped off and picked up, too?"

I nodded. "Please take us to Boca de Yuma early tomorrow. Then come and get us near the man-o'-war birds rookery next Saturday. I jotted down the date and X'd the map. "Do you remember the spot from our first trip?"

He said yes. I chuckled. Probably after ferrying soldiers and supplies around Vietnam, this would just be a milk—I mean, a water—run. I estimated we would walk five to eight miles a day, which meant he'd have to make three drop-offs during the week. Surely no water had ever been so expensive or as difficult to provide.

Next morning a wide-eyed Luis and Ramón accompanied me to the airport and shakily entered the helicopter. My initial excitement was nothing compared to theirs. These men, who had never been higher off the ground or the sea than a treetop or a flying bridge, must have been close to heart attacks. On our swift flight over to Boca de Yuma, I was more intrigued in watching their faces than in scanning the landscape below. As soon as we landed, the pilot unstrapped our three backpacks and unloaded three jugs of water.

"See you in a couple of days," he said, waving nonchalantly. Then the chopper rose noisily over our heads and clattered away. Luis and Ramón were so rattled and the silence seemed so enormous that we sat down under a small tree and ate lunch just to get back to normal. Then we helped one another into our packs, picked up the jugs, and began walking south.

Less than half a mile inside the proposed park border we reached the first interesting area. A 30-foot gray-and-white cliff dropped down to the choppy sea. Atop it grew a little woodland. Its canopy had been sheared off as neatly as if by a pair of giant garden shears—an example of pruning by the salty sea wind. A short while later we emerged on a rough, flat, bare coastal shelf of blackened limestone. We followed the merest hint of a trail. Ahead a spout of foaming water abruptly shot up out of the rock.

"Old Carlos's blowhole," announced Luis, grinning from ear to ear. "I've heard of it for years, but I never walked this part of the peninsula before."

The geyser spurted up every few minutes, then fell back into a large grotto in the limestone. Beneath us I could feel the rock shudder and hear a dull booming. Although the hole was a good 200 feet from the ocean, an underground passage evidently allowed breakers to push inland and blow out into the open. Old Carlos of the Dominican Republic was as regular as Old Faithful in Yellowstone Park.

After I photographed the huge blowhole, we trudged on along the exposed coast. Sun and wind beat into our faces. The Mona Channel, restless and blue-gray, heaved to our left. A perpendicular, 120-foot escarpment rose in tortured patterns to the right. There might be a splendid view from the top, but I could see no way to climb up there. I made a note to recommend a circular iron staircase be built against the cliff to a lookout on top.

I heard a sudden intake of breath and turned abruptly. The two men were quite a distance behind me, adjusting their packs. "Must have been the wind," I thought and walked on. Again, that strange sound. I stopped in my tracks and looked around. No animals. I glanced overhead. No birds. Nothing but scrubby sea plants, sand, and black rock. Then the sucking noise came once more. Easing out of my pack, I began a minute inspection of the ground. Luis and Ramón caught up and helped. To our amazement, we found a hole, no bigger than a pencil, going straight down into the rocky pavement. Periodically a long sigh escaped from it. Then I realized the whole of this coastal shelf was undercut and under enormous pressure from wave action. Somehow, air was being forced in and out of that tiny blowhole as the sea rose and subsided. Someday, given time for wind and wave action, it might enlarge and become Old Carlos the Second. I made a small orange X mark with the spray paint. We must be able to find this incredible phenomenon later on and use it as a public interpretive display.

We continued down the coast all day, marveling at the sea grottos, sea caves, and blowholes we found. The only signs of human habitation were faint tracks, bits of dried donkey dung, and the shorn trunks of thatch palms. Apparently people came here to harvest the huge fanlike leaves for roofing their huts. The poor trees didn't have a chance. Once their leafy heads were topped, the wind and sun discouraged them from living. One rule in the park, I decided, would be no harvesting of thatch palms. The scenery would be much more natural, photogenic, and diverse with clusters of palms standing green and tall.

I was beginning to realize that our first trip in the Ranger over the park had been like an impressionist painting. As the team leader had said, "a broad-brush treatment." Now we were doing the fine pointillistic work, going step by step over the area. The two extremes were absolutely necessary to any thorough ecological coverage.

That evening we made camp on a circle of sand surrounded by cruel limestone outcrops and near a dry wood. We had the ocean breeze to discourage insects and a source of firewood at hand. A thin skein of clouds slid over the sky, turning the sea to gunmetal gray and cooling the air. After the 90-degree heat of midday and our seven-mile hike, I was ready for a bath. The only place was the sea. How could I manage? To climb down that steep, spray-wet cliff would be foolhardy. No bay or beach broke this entire coastline.

Ramón solved the problem. Handing me a plastic pail and a length of light nylon line, he suggested I dip up water from the cliff top and take a sponge bath. "That's what we do aboard the fishing boats," he explained.

Luis and Ramón at first campsite on windward coast, Dominican Republic. Water jug delivered by helicopter on right.

Putting a few rocks between me and the men, I found a little indentation at the edge of the high escarpment and flung down the pail. When it seemed to have filled, I gave a yank to haul it up. But a big wave caught the pail on its outgo and tugged back at me. For a second I teetered on the brink. If I had fallen, I probably would have been dashed upon the rocks. Even if I managed to swim out, how long would it take my helpers to discover my plight? How could they pull me up the cliff? Had they brought a long, heavy rope? Shaking, I grasped a corner of rock and braced myself. Moments later, I pulled up the pailful of water. The cool salt water on my naked body felt wonderfully refreshing, but the close call sobered me.

When I returned to the campfire, both men were staring nervously toward the sea. Ramón jumped up and grabbed my arm. "Anna, are you all right? What a fright you gave us! We couldn't see you, yet we didn't want to disturb you bathing. If you'd fallen in and drowned, Luis and I would probably have been convicted of murder."

His dark face looked terrified. I realized that he spoke the truth. No one would believe two simple native workmen if a high-paid foreign female consultant in their company suddenly disappeared at a remote place like this.

To ease his mind, I laughed and said lightly, "Oh, I'm sorry, Ramón. I was just enjoying my bath and waiting for the wind to dry me off." From then on, I vowed to be extra careful and not get our little team into trouble. Somehow, the incident brought us closer together.

At daybreak I was awakened from a sound sleep by Ramón softly calling, "*Anna, Anna, es el tiempo a despertarte*" ("It's time to wake up").

I sat up in my sleeping bag and groped for the tent zipper. Ramón deftly opened the mosquito netting and handed me a tiny cup of rich steaming Dominican espresso heavily laced with sugar. What a treat! I gave him a sleepy smile and eagerly sipped the fragrant drink. Already Luis had started a fire and rolled up the other tent. Leaving Ramón to fix breakfast and break camp, Luis and I headed back into the woods to check our trapline. Most traps had been baited the evening before with a mix of peanut butter, raisins, and oatmeal. Evidently the land crabs and ants had discovered this delicacy early and cleaned it up. The bait levers of every trap were bare and most had been sprung. We caught only a couple of Norway rats and house mice in our snap traps (just like on Anegada) and a gray-and-white feral house cat in one of the live traps. I opened the door and allowed it to streak for cover. Then Luis recovered the other traps and untied the red flagging we used to mark each site.

After a hearty breakfast, we began our day's trek south. The coastal shelf widened and became sandier, while the escarpment angled back away from the sea and lowered. About ten o'clock we came upon a rude hut built of every conceivable kind of flotsam and jetsam imaginable—weathered planks, flattened tin cans, plastic sheeting, lengths of frayed line, rusty oil drums. The little yard was swept clean and bare. A few small fruit trees and beehives clustered behind the house. We approached and called out a greeting. A gaunt, very black old lady in a ragged patchwork dress peeked out. She looked us over. Then, with a toothless grin, threw her warped plywood door open wide and beckoned us in. She lived in a poverty so complete that there was nothing inside but a crude bench and table on a dirt floor, a wicker basket of eggs, and a battered old calendar on the wall. Yet this delightful crone insisted on making us coffee. She poured a dollop of precious water in a pot without a handle, blew on the embers of a tiny wood fire, and set three chipped cups on the table. All these utensils were gifts of the sea. Then she dropped a handful of ground Dominican coffee in a stained square of cheesecloth and brewed us each a cup. It seemed a novel way to make espresso. She sweetened each cup with thick honey, then sat back to watch us drink. The coffee was delicious. Our compliments soon had her beaming and bobbing her head self-consciously. She insisted on showing us the beehives, which earned her enough money to survive here alone as a squatter. She had absolutely no idea a park was in the offing, or what that might do to her way of life.

I was genuinely sad to leave the gracious old lady. She seemed as calm and pleasant as a grandmother in Kansas. Yet how tedious her life must be. It consisted of sweeping the yard, feeding her chickens, listening to the sea and tending her beehives. She had no husband, no children, no car, no horse, no burro, no dogs, no cats, no radio, no TV, no books, no magazines, no washing machine, no refrigerator, no sewing machine, no entertainment. Did she hope each day for some passerby to break the monotony?

Perhaps not. I recalled the many long periods of time I've spent at my cabin without any visitors or wish for company. Day flowed into day, filled with intellectual, athletic and contemplative activities. Each hour was filled with happiness at being in a place I loved so much. I prayed the tiny black woman also knew that peace.

I whispered to Ramón to leave her some sugar, coffee, and extra water, for we had more than enough. Then I asked her about the solenodon and showed her a picture of one. She nodded at once and said, "Oh, yes, the little *oso* (bear) comes to steal a chicken every so often. I swept one out of the chicken coop with a broom two nights ago!"

What a statement! If it were true, it meant that solenodons were present in the park. This would make the area even more valuable. They might possibly be unafraid of people. Nevertheless, I still had to prove their presence by actually live trapping and/or photographing one.

Throughout the day, we passed other squatters' huts. From what I could observe, they survived on seafood, honey, and coffee. They found items in the flotsam and jetsam, and when beachcombing. That vital commodity, water, had to be carried in from Boca de Yuma. To earn a few dollars for medicines and clothes, they harvested palm fronds, kept beehives, or made charcoal. Each person we spoke with was as hospitable, open, and sincere as the old lady.

Might there be truth, I wondered, in Thoreau's sage comment: "A man is inversely happy in proportion to the things he possesses." One disturbing activity was the charcoal making. Squatters were girdling and cutting live trees or picking up dead ones to burn in huge circles called *canucos*. Although we had not noticed these from the air, here on the ground it was easy to see that they were eating into the forest like mange spreading across a dog's skin. The piles of wood burned for hours, eventually turning into chunks of charcoal. This was bagged in burlap sacks holding 100 pounds each and packed out by burro to Boca de Yuma. There it sold for three U.S. dollars a bag. This terrible destruction of the peninsula's meager woodlands for such pitiful remuneration was a tragedy in the making.

On this expedition, I realized that conservation *has* to be the concern of a wealthy society, even though it helps all humans, rich or poor. I decided that the first thing the government should do, through its Park Service and Museum of Man, was to sponsor and pay for moving these poor squatters out into new homes and finding them jobs which would offer a better quality of life. Some could work for the park, but there might not be enough positions to go around. This was where the Dominican sociologists would come in handy, to ease the transition and integrate these people smoothly into a different life style.

At Punta Titín, we marveled again at the sea's artistry. A natural bridge stood alone, arched and symmetrical. I asked Ramón to take a picture of me standing atop it. Another blowhole here brought a spume of water up 30 feet from the ocean's surface through the limestone shelf to foam out into a natural "bathtub." The water was warm and frothy, and I longed to strip and immerse myself.

That afternoon it was time for our first water drop-off. Luis and I found a level stretch of limestone atop Punta Titín and sprayed a giant square in orange paint. Then we sat down on the windswept promontory to wait. An hour went by before I saw the Bell Ranger as a distant speck to the south. It hawked and hovered like some giant dragonfly, searching for us. Gradually it worked its way up the coastline. Now we could hear its clattering. Suddenly the pilot spotted us. The Ranger veered straight toward our point. Minutes later, the tall Texan was handing us five fresh-water jugs and glancing around nervously at his makeshift landing site.

"Everything okay?" he asked, ducking as a gust of salt spray wet his face and shirt.

"We're fine," I replied." This is a spectacular coastline. I love it."

"Great. Then see you day after tomorrow," he said, relieved. He slammed the door and roared away, leaving us with the problem of carrying all this water, plus our backpacks, off the rocky point and south. Miraculously, it was solved a short time later. A palm frond cutter and his mule passed us, heading to the cluster of huts at the

Anne and Luis load a patient little mule with water jugs for trip down the rocky coast of the proposed national park.

peninsula's end. For two dollars we hired the mule to carry all the jugs *and* Ramón, who was tiring, to the tiny hamlet of El Algibe. If we set up our base camp there, we could work our way back up the coast or west along the base of the peninsula without having to lug these heavy loads around. That night found us camped a quarter of a mile away from five wattle-and-thatched huts at El Algibe. We were kept busy fending off hungry pigs, curious children, and land crabs, until we could finish supper and hide our food. Then we paid a visit to the five families who lived there and explained our mission. In their soft drawling Spanish, they welcomed us and described what they knew about the wildlife and the sea's resources. These nomadic fisherpeople were the friendliest humans I had ever met. They brought us fresh conch, cut and marinated in

Mounds of conch shells reveal that sizes diminished from very large at bottom to much smaller at top due to overharvesting.

key lime juice. Later, they presented me with a beautiful shell.

The saddest sight in that clean little village perched by the shimmering shallows of Bahía Catalanita was the huge piles of conch shells. Conch is a time-honored and valuable source of protein all through the Caribbean. It also provides shell tools and digging instruments. I searched through the piles and measured the discarded conch shells, newest and oldest. I found that the shell lengths had diminished over the decades from roughly 12 to 18 inches down to five to ten inches. The fishermen themselves confirmed the decrease. Conchs were getting harder to find and smaller in size.

"Why?" I asked.

They shrugged. "Too many people fishing for them. Even the hotels in La Romana want conchs now for fritters and *seviche* (raw seafood marinated in lime juice). There aren't enough conchs to go around."

It was the same story of overpopulation and overuse of natural resources that I heard everywhere.

We could hardly wait for the Ranger to fly in on its appointed day with our water. It would give these good folks something to talk about for the next ten years. Sure enough, the pilot put on a nerve-tingling air show by swooping right over the huts, then descending slowly and majestically into our midst. Chickens squawked, babies screamed, small boys jumped behind their mothers' legs. Even the aggressive pigs turned tail and fled. Grinning mischievously, the Texan let everyone look in the helicopter after he'd unloaded our jugs. Then he was gone in a swirl of sand, after promising to deliver more water two days hence at the other corner of the peninsula.

Next morning we set off across the base of the park, skirting belts of mangrove and shallow lagoons, keeping just inside the forest. The bay looked like ideal manatee habitat. Luis assured me that once these gentle mammals (sometimes called sea cows) had frequented the waters. They had been wiped out by hunting. Weighing close to 1,500 pounds, sluggish and slow in movement, manatees are easy prey to hunters in motorboats or dugout canoes. The cigar-shaped creatures have no defenses except their front flippers and their flattened, strong tails. The bristles about their thick lips are for browsing on aquatic vegetation. "I hunted them for years," Luis confided, "especially during rainy season. Manatees have wonderful meat and the oil is good for lamps and cooking. They like to come around Saona and drink from underwater 'boils' in the shallows."

"You mean they drink at freshwater springs *under* ocean water?" I asked, perplexed, knowing that the air-breathing mammals drink only fresh water.

"Yes, the fresh water bubbles up from the sea floor, oh, 20, 30, 40 feet from shore in some places on the shallow leeward side. If you're thirsty, you can dive right down and have a good drink," explained Luis. "I'll take you and show you how, Anna. I've survived many a time this way."

He showed me how to swim down and hold an empty bottle upside down to fill it at a boil. Once again I marveled at that wonderful native intelligence that we so-called educated people have lost.

Now that we had left the windward coast, the heat was much more oppressive. No breeze stirred the trees. Humidity was high. Tree cutters had not penetrated this far into the interior to make canucos or skid out valuable mahogany. This portion of the park was restfully green. Later, however, we ventured out into the broiling afternoon sun to photograph the salt marsh and salt flats. It hit our heads like a hammer blow. We walked laboriously through a stand of uncut thatch palms, taking care not to cut our pants or bare arms on the knife-sharp sawgrass beneath. Heat waves wriggled on the horizon. I felt dizzy for a moment and looked down. Near the ground curved a delicate spray of lavender orchids, as fancy as any I'd ever worn to a high-school prom.

"Look, Luis!" I called.

"*Los angelitos*" (the little angels), exclaimed the old hunter, gently cupping one in his gnarled hand.

As I bent down to take pictures of these lovely orchids, I noticed several spent shotgun shells on the ground. Aghast, I called again, "Luis. Someone's been shooting here."

"Oh, yes," he nodded. "A little farther out on the flats you'll see thousands of shotgun shells."

My eyes widened. "*Thousands!*" Why?"

"This is where *las palomas* (white-crowned pigeons) come to nest every spring. They fly in by the thousands upon thousands to the western end of Saona and to the tip of this peninsula. No one knows where they come from. The trees are so full of pigeons that people can shake a dozen down from any branch. The poor people used to feed the poults to their pigs. Now only the rich people come to shoot them. I'll show you."

Far out on the salt flats shimmering with heat devils, we came upon several shooting stands constructed of shaky mangrove sticks, with thatched roofs of palm fronds. The ground around them was literally covered with shotgun shells—red, blue, green, yellow. It was almost like finding a multicolored carpet out on a desert. I flinched inwardly to think how many thousands of birds had died from these barrages. I took several photos and gathered up shells as evidence. Later I learned from the National Park Service director that this is considered the largest breeding colony of white-crowned pigeons in the world. A Dominican law protects birds from hunters, but no enforcement exists. Government officials and wealthy individuals were said to be sneaking in for shoots at the beginning of each nesting season. Clearly, one of the most pressing jobs of the new park would be patrol and enforcement work. The general and the admiral on the park's board could help with that. Until the National Park Service could train and deploy park rangers, Dominican Army and Navy personnel might be ordered to protect the natural resources of Parque Nacional del Este.

Finally, on Saturday afternoon, we arrived at the man-o'-war birds. I waited quietly for the Ranger to pick us up, exhausted but enormously content. It had been a wonderful, enlightening week.

"You take a rest for three days, Ramón," I urged the gaunt, tired man. "And please don't go back to Saona yet, Luis," I cajoled. "Just as soon as I finish helping the company engineers lay out a roadway along here, we'll be ready to go to your island to explore and trap. I'd like you both with me. We may have an ornithologist along to study the flamingo lagoons to see if a population can be built up. He'll need your help. Also, I want to climb up that old lighthouse to see the view. Oh, and I surely would like more of your delicious espresso, Ramón."

Both men's eyes lit up, weary as they were. They nodded in agreement. We barely had time to take a catnap under the thatch palms before the Ranger descended like some prehistoric bird. Then, aches and pains forgotten, Luis and Ramón jumped up and ran like kids to the open door for their *second* helicopter ride.

9

PLAYING GOD

For three days, a Gulf+Western engineer and I walked the western edge of the park, from Bayahibe south to the man-o'-war birds. We spray painted a tentative route and marked the most important biological and geological points of interest. If there can be artistry in engineering, then we had an arty road.

Where large trees such as strangler figs or West Indian birches deserved saving, we split the road in two and protected them between lanes. Where an attractive vista overlooked the placid Caribbean, we curved the road toward it. Yet not so near as to show from the sea nor to create an ugly open parking lot behind. Where limestone sinks filled with fragile ferns and air plants lay like inverted greenhouses, we bent the road away. Then we laid out a winding walking trail for plant lovers. It really was a little like playing God.

We pinpointed the best sites for small visitors' centers, bathing beaches, rustic campsites, and a small outdoor amphitheater. We also discussed building a boardwalk and blind part way out into the salt flats to view the man-o'-war birds. Everything was to be built of native woods, stones, and fibers. My interest and pride in the park was growing by leaps and bounds. Visions constantly flashed in my head of how it would look when finished with Dominican and American tourists enjoying it.

The American park planner and park interpreter were hard at work at their drawing boards. They offered us lengthy philosophical pronouncements about roads.

"They can be the beginning of the end," stated the planner gloomily. "I've seen it happen in South America. Unless you have a strong enforcement staff, rigid rules, and tight park boundaries, a road can be an open invitation to squatters and exploiters. They move into hitherto inaccessible natural areas. I hope that won't happen here at Parque Nacional del Este."

"Roads can be the 'cancer of the tropics,'" agreed the interpreter.

"Oh, come on," I argued optimistically. "This road is going to be so beautiful and the park so well run that nothing bad will happen. Besides, I think the peninsula's coastline will be better off with the road than without it. If things just drift on as they are now, there'll be more charcoal canucos, more conch fishermen, more pigeon hunters sneaking in to rip off the resources. A road can stop all that by allowing adequate police protection. Also the park's interior will be left wild."

So it went. Every evening we sat at the hotel, pondering the good or evil of national parks. It really boiled down to planned sustainable development for natural resources vs. rampant exploitation. Paradoxically, by prohibiting short-term abuse of an unprotected environment by a few people, with a national park you could provide long-term recreation and education for masses of people.

Soon it was time to go back into the field. The ornithologist, Phil, had arrived. I walked down to the marina to find Ramón and tell him about our plans. I found him looking rested and clean-shaven. We embraced each other happily.

"And Luis? Where's Luis?" I asked eagerly.

"He'll be here right away, Anna. He's been dying to get back to Saona and show you his precious island."

Luis jumped onto the dock, stalwart and sensible as ever. He gave me a big grin. "When do we start?" he asked without preamble.

"Tomorrow. By boat. The bird man is here with tons of stuff. Nets, strainers, chemicals, bottles. Can you both be ready to leave at seven in the morning?"

"Yes," they chorused.

At ten the next morning we were rolling in the gentle swell of Laguna Flamenco—so named for the former flocks of flamingos which had frequented the lagoon. The company's sportfishing boat had been put at our disposal for the week's work. The captain, Luis, Ramón, and I helped load the ornithologist's gear into the dinghy, a Boston whaler. Then we all motored ashore, pushed through a stand of mangroves, and stood at last by a huge sheet of rust-colored water.

"I'll have to spend most of the day here," announced Phil, good-naturedly, "wading in this goop and taking samples of water and mud. Then I'll strain and collect the animals—brine flies, tiny shrimp, small fishes, and crustaceans. Flamingos eat those miniature items. I probably won't be able to identify everything in the field. I'll preserve some samples and check them out at home under the microscope. That way we can get an idea of how productive these lagoons are and if they can support flamingos all or part of the year. I know that flamingoes used to be here. But what made them stop coming? Humans? Poor habitat? Hunters?"

He tugged on a pair of waist-high waders, donned an old hat, grabbed his canteen and dip net, and sloshed competently into the lagoon. Ramón had been assigned to help him that day. But all he had were an old pair of sneakers, cut-off pants, no water and no hat. Grimacing, he tightened the laces and started to follow the ornithologist. I handed him two cans of Coke.

"Be sure to put something on your head, Ramón," I cautioned him fondly. "These salt lagoons can reach a 110 degrees under the midday sun. I'd hate to have you get a sunstroke."

He looked back at me gratefully and tied an old handkerchief around his head like a turban. Luis and I watched the two men wade out through the reeking mud into that hypersaline water. We were already perspiring, just standing there. I was secretly glad not to be involved in this research.

Our job was to walk the shore from Laguna Flamenco to Mano Juan, the Navy base. I would gauge the possibility of a backpacking nature trail along the coast, with some primitive campsites and bathing areas. Later we would pay a visit to the naval officer in charge of the station and make sure he understood our mission. I didn't want the Dominican Navy to throw us off the island as spies or insurgents.

At five o'clock that evening, Ramón and Phil picked us up at Mano Juan in the Boston whaler, and we returned to the big boat. After the day's heat and thirst, it was an indescribable treat to relax in the salon on padded seats, sip ice-cold Cokes and beers, and cool off under—of all things—an air conditioner! The captain served us supper. Then we all turned in and slept like babies as the boat rocked gently at anchor. Once again I smiled to myself—Anegada had never been like this.

For four more days we surveyed Isla Saona. As dawn lit the sky with flaming banners of scarlet and cerise, I'd rise from my bunk before the men awoke. Then slip into a bathing suit and dive into the sea. As I swam and floated off the bow, they had a chance to get up, dress, urinate off the stern, and wash up without embarrassment. Climbing back on board, I was presented with my cup of steaming sweet Dominican espresso by Ramón. We'd greet one another good morning, eat breakfast, and begin the new day.

The ornithologist was finding that flamingo food was scarce in the lagoons at end of dry season. These great bodies of water evaporated and shrank. Birds would go hungry if they stayed on the island. During rainy seasons, however, Saona would be a fine stopping off place for flamingos.

"They could easily fly here from Grand Inagua in the Bahamas," explained Phil, pointing north. "There are about 10,000 birds nesting there. A 375-mile flight is nothing for them. The important point is that no one disturb them *here*. I have a suspicion that the sailors at the base may do occasional target practice on those big pink birds. That kind of activity would certainly discourage them from coming to Saona."

"We don't know for sure if they do shoot," I said, "but we can try to control it. An admiral of the Dominican Navy is on the national park board. We can ask him to put out a directive requesting Navy personnel at Mano Juan be prohibited from shooting at birdlife." (Once again I was playing God. How easy it was—when you had the right connections!)

On the third day we had hiked our way up to *Canto de la Playa* (Song of the Beach). The sand was so white it made me squint, so fine it squeaked under my bare feet, so pristine I felt like Eve. A thin stand of coconut palms rustled alluringly in the breeze. I could already imagine the pleasure tourists could have stretched out here: winter-white skin slowly turning golden brown. Or Dominican children, romping in the mild surf, while they learned about marine biology. As long as Canto de la Playa was accessible only by boat and not developed beyond a few thatched huts, it could keep its rustic simplicity and still be a joy to travelers.

On the fourth day we progressed all the way to the lighthouse at the southeastern tip of Saona. Phil walked inland with Luis to check the last lagoon at this end of the island. Ramón, the boat captain, and I decided to climb the ancient lighthouse. Inside, a steel-rung ladder stretched upward into the shadowy tower. The structure must have been at least 80 feet tall and had been abandoned years ago. I hesitated. No one knew how rusted the iron bolts and bars might be. If one pulled loose or broke in two, it meant a straight fall down the shaft to a concrete floor. I was about to say it seemed too dangerous when the captain grabbed a rung and swung himself up to the first level with all the bravado of a rooster. Ramón started slowly up next, more from peer pressure, I guessed, than from any personal sense of adventure. Out of shame I followed. If the men could do it, so could I. At least, both of them were heavier than I was. If the captain made it to the top, the rest of us could. But, if he fell, he'd probably crash us down with him. It was one of the scariest climbs of my life. My hands felt cold as ice and grabbed the iron supports convulsively.

The view from the top parapet, however, was worth it. As far as we could see, not a single human—only sand and sea and forest, wind and sun and space. To our east the Mona Channel churned deeply blue. To the west the idyllic curves of white sand edged turquoise blue shallows. Below us on the beach, I noticed gleaming white bones and decided to investigate as soon as we were down. But descending was far worse than ascending. The rungs were quite far apart. One had to rely heavily on the iron hand grips while groping with one's bare foot for a rung below. At times, my entire weight hung from one hand. I began to tremble. Ramón sensed my fear. Soothingly he talked me down, taking one bare foot at a time and positioning it above his head. When at last we stood safely outside in the blazing sun, I broke into a sweat.

The lanky Latin captain threw me an admiring glance. He turned to Ramón and, assuming I couldn't understand him, muttered, "She's got balls!"

The white objects on the beach turned out to be turtle shells and bones bleached by the sun. Later Luis told me that local fishermen prowl these beaches during late spring nesting periods. They flip over the giant green and leatherback female turtles as they are laying eggs and leave them helpless and thirsty. They kill them later at leisure, retrieve the eggs, and sell the shells unpolished for $25 U.S. apiece. Turtles have been exploited for centuries as an exotic food, and for leather goods, cosmetics, jewelry, and decorations. Little wonder there is such a dramatic decline of sea turtles around the world.

Three of the largest species—greens, Pacific olive ridleys, and loggerheads—were now designated as either endangered or threatened under the United States Endangered Species Act. In the Caribbean, greens, Atlantic ridleys and hawksbills had hit alarmingly low numbers. Along the coasts of Florida and Georgia, the thousands of greens which used to nest there have plunged to a few dozen. Yet a thriving black market for sea turtles exists. In the late 1970s, a poacher might be paid over $200 U.S. for a very large specimen.

For this reason, Dr. Archie Carr of the University of Florida started the Caribbean Conservation Association with the express purpose of saving marine turtles. Thanks in part to his influence, Costa Rica had already declared Tortuguero Beach on the Caribbean side and Nancite Beach on the Pacific coast as national parks. Mexico had made at least one turtle nesting sanctuary on the Gulf of Mexico. The Dominican Republic, too, could help protect sea turtles once Parque Nacional del Este was functioning and poaching firmly outlawed.

We were just starting to eat lunch when the company helicopter paid us an unexpected visit. It settled down near the lighthouse, and a man wearing a suit, white shirt, tie, and city shoes, and carrying a leather briefcase, climbed out awkwardly. The pilot guided him under the rotors, then turned to hand me a note. He looked with amusement at Ramón and me, our salty clothes and hair, sneakers full of mud, and burned dark as cork by the sun.

"Looks like you-all are having yourselves a good time," he jested. "This here is Mr. Brown, another park planner. An independent consultant. The park board thought he ought to spend a day with you and see what Saona has to offer. Oh, I'm supposed to wait for an answer to that note."

I shook hands with Mr. Brown, then turned to scan the slip of paper. It was in the C.E.O.'s bold, fast scrawl. "Can you please show me highlights of park tomorrow 10:00 A.M. by helicopter. Continuing on to New York City at midday."

My heart thumped. The big boss actually wanted to inspect Parque Nacional del Este. I had only two hours to compress 100,000 acres, 3 weeks of survey work, and 55 miles of walking into a meaningful interpretive package. I reached for my notebook.

"Gladly," I wrote back. "Meet you at lighthouse 10:00 A.M." Then I told the pilot, "I'll have a route planned out by morning and go over it with you then. Okay?"

"Roger," drawled the Texan. He gestured apologetically at the newcomer and said, with a slight smile, "I'll pick up Brown tomorrow. He ought to see the main highlights, also."

The rest of the day I kept busy trying to guide our visitor around Saona. First I offered to climb up the lighthouse with him so he could get a bird's-eye view of the countryside. He pointed to his shiny shoes defensively. "I'm afraid they'd slip."

"Well, you can do it barefoot. It's much safer that way," I suggested.

"Barefoot? I never go barefoot."

"Oh. Well, I believe the lighthouse can be fixed up to make an excellent educational display. Besides the splendid vista from the top, it could offer interpretation on oceanography, the island's history, shipwrecks, and need for marine turtle conservation."

He nodded and took a few notes.

We cruised back to Canto de la Playa in the sportfishing boat and anchored in hip-deep water. Since the tide had gone out, and Luis and Phil had taken the dinghy, we had to slip over the side and wade in. Our guest held back. "I wouldn't want to ruin my pants," he explained.

At that the captain jumped overboard and reached up his strong arms. "Grab me piggy-back," he offered in Spanish, "and I'll carry you in."

"What did he say?" Mr. Brown asked.

"You don't speak Spanish?" I queried politely.

"No. No, I don't."

"Well, the captain's offering to carry you ashore."

Gingerly, the park planner eased over the side and straddled the captain's broad back. He insisted on bringing his briefcase and held it over his head like an umbrella. We sat down under a palm as I began to explain my ideas for utilizing the beach in a non-invasive, rustic fashion. Meanwhile, Ramón went off with his machete to cut some ripe coconuts. Mr. Brown fidgeted uncomfortably on the sand. Already his starched shirt was soaked with perspiration and his face was beginning to sunburn. When Ramón handed him a coconut, husked and pierced for drinking, he declined. "You can get dysentery from that," he warned me in a whisper.

"Really?" I murmured. "We've all been drinking coconut milk for a week. I should have the worst case in the Caribbean, but I don't. By the way, Mr. Brown, do you have a hat? Your nose is getting quite red."

"No. I didn't bring one."

I handed him my smoky, sweat-stained bandanna. He refused it.

"Would you like to walk along the coast and see our proposed hiking and nature trail?" I asked. "I could point out some of the native vegetation to you."

"I'd better not," he said. "I'm not used to this climate, you know. I might have a heat stroke."

"Where did you say you're from?" I asked.

"Washington. Washington, D.C."

"What's the objective of your trip?" I asked, a trifle annoyed. "What would you like to do?"

"Oh, just go back to the boat and take a few more notes. I'll have to write a report as soon as I'm back."

About what? I wondered to myself.

When it was time to pick up Luis and Phil, the captain moved the big boat down the coast to meet the Boston whaler. They clambered aboard stinking of muck from the salt lagoon. Mr. Brown shrank. I was only too happy to let the ornithologist take over in the air conditioned cabin and describe his flamingo work. I climbed up to the flying bridge and sat alone for awhile, trying to quell my irritation over the incompetent consultant. Imagine an American park planner coming to a tropical Latin country without proper clothing, no Spanish, little stamina, and a big attitude. I could imagine the high fee for his in-and-out consultancy. Surely he would write a fancy report that would contribute little to the over-all project. Then my displeasure evaporated as evening came on and the sea darkened. Towering cumulus clouds turned strawberry red and slowly collapsed. A cool sea breeze blew over the bridge. I began planning the short helicopter tour for next day.

Starting at this lovely beach, we toured the park's highlights by helicopter.

It went like clockwork. Allowing for an hour of airtime, we would have an hour to make three ground stops and a quick overall aerial reconnaissance. We circled the lighthouse, then landed for a moment at Canto de la Playa, where the sandpipers did a ballet before us. We swung over the flamingo lagoons and dipped down to see the man-o'-war colony. Landing at El Algibe, the fisher folk smothered me with hugs and produced a beautiful conch shell for the C.E.O.. The Bell Ranger stopped and cut its engines within yards of my secret blowhole. I walked nonchalantly to the small orange X mark and motioned for silence. Puzzled, the big boss followed me. (Mr. Brown stayed in the chopper and threw up.) Then the sea's great breath was sucked in and let out of that tiny orifice. Now, the big boss was on his hands and knees, entranced, ignoring scratches on his polished boots, stains on his white pants. The division head for that mighty multinational corporation stuck his finger in the tiny blowhole like a child playing with a toy. Then out, then in.

"How pleasant it sounds." He smiled quietly. "Ah, Anna, I could stay here all day. No company problems out here. So peaceful." Then looking around, eyes aglow, he said, "Anna, it's going to be a fine park!"

I came back to the Dominican Republic a few months later to spend a week doing liaison and planning work with the corporation, park board, museum, and new National Park Service. The roads and buildings were slated to begin that winter. G+W offered me a retainership to consult on a monthly basis for the next year or two. I was ecstatic.

Back in New York, I had settled into my cabin and was busy cutting my fall and winter firewood. One day I drove to the city for a new saw chain and a supermarket to shop. I hadn't bought sugar for months, the price had been so high. Sometimes it reached one U.S. dollar a pound. Now, to my surprise, it had dropped back by almost half. I thought of those gigantic warehouses filled with raw sugar at La Romana. How much was a pound worth there now?

A few days later, I received a memo asking me to call Washington, D.C. Unbelieving, I heard one of my teammates from the survey explain that the crash in sugar prices had seriously affected the Dominican operations of Gulf+Western. Parque Nacional del Este was to be delayed indefinitely. The C.E.O. had been transferred. Everything was in a state of flux.

"But, but, but..." I sputtered. "How can the park just end like this? We did so much. We did everything right. Good teamwork, air and ground coverage, a super master plan, photographs, the road well routed, biological research, careful recommendations, future plans. Gulf+Western was great and had *good* intentions."

"I know, I know," sighed my colleague unhappily. "That's big business for you. The stockholders are what really matter, not natural resource consultants. Got to give them their money's worth. You can never be too sure of anything when corporation money is involved."

"Maybe," I said slowly, as the idea grew, "the only way to make conservation really work is by the grass roots approach."

After hanging up, I sat a long time thinking. Until now, it had seemed that the ideal formula to accomplish conservation work in record time was through a large corporation. They had the money, the philanthropic bent, the clout, and the high-level contacts to effect speedy change. There was no government red tape to wade through. A researcher suffered no poverty-stricken days, no lack of equipment, no crippling equipment breakdowns or lengthy repairs. The corporation merely had to decide on a conservation project, snap its fingers, hire staff, provide transportation, and the work was off and running.

Yet now I had some reason to doubt. I couldn't help comparing my Dominican Republic experience with my earlier wildlife and wildland campaigns and consultancies. Each had involved a different approach, in terms of funding, personnel, and time. Each had different results. For example, the Guatemalan giant grebe campaign (see my book *Mama Poc* about this) had started as a one-woman effort with months and months of hardship, slow work, and little money. It had grown to include both grass roots and high-government support. The quetzal cloud forest reserve was more of a private group effort—interested landowners and two cooperative conservation groups. Yet it had suffered from limited funds and equipment. Anegada was handled on a part-academic, part-private industry basis. We had a quasi-team approach which never really meshed, although we obtained some useful scientific data. Volcán Barú National Park was a joint project of government and a large international conservation organization. It utilized outside expertise and local technicians. However, it had dragged along slowly, like most government programs. Initially, it did not have large funds, adequate equipment, or manpower available. Of all these projects, the Dominican national park had seemed most likely to succeed. It had coordinated teamwork, a high priority with the government, the military, a huge corporation, and lavish funding.

Which way was best? Was there a formula to success in this field? Was it normal that some should win and others lose? Perhaps all methods are feasible, or none. Perhaps conservation accomplishments depend ultimately on personal enthusiasm, cooperation, and competency—plus good timing and luck. Oh, and throw in a Bell Ranger, too.

UPDATE

- *Despite the brief reversal in setting up this park, things went ahead later. Parque Nacional del Este was created in 1975, mainly by efforts of the Dominican Republic government. It encompasses 80,800 hectares (over 185,000 acres). Development is moving slowly ahead with visitors' centers, trails, observation points, and roads. Ecotourism has helped, because the La Romana area is very popular. Many travelers go there for a variety of recreational activities.*

- *The Nature Conservancy recently published a two-volume assessment of the Park based on a serious scientific joint research effort between Dominicans and foreign consultants. In the introductory chapter, our 1973 study and report received proper recognition as an important pioneering effort, thanks to Dr. E. Towle.*

- *Other key players supporting the Park were/are the Dominican National Park Service, the World Centre for Conservation (IUCN), the World Health Organization, World Conservation Monitoring Centre, U.S. Agency for International Development. The initial two organizations behind the first study—the Caribbean Research Institute and the College of the Virgin Islands—are now the Eastern Caribbean Center and the University of the Virgin Islands.*

- *There are presently 24 protected areas in the D.R., including 11 National Parks, one bird sanctuary, and six scientific reserves. Hurricane Georges in 1998 destroyed part of Parque Nacional del Este's interior bush forest, but Nature should restore the vegetation in time.*

10

GANDHI AND GRIMWOOD

A wildlife ecologist learns from university courses and fieldwork. However, conferences and associated field trips play an equally important role in polishing one's professional skills. Conferences can be crucially important for maintaining a sense of solidarity among scientists. They also allow the exchange of up-to-date information, rekindling of enthusiasm, and strengthening concern about mounting industrialization and technology. Meetings can give ecologists an almost religious conviction that our small community must improve the global quality of life. Lastly, governments and private conservation organizations are often galvanized into action by hearing about new environmental problems at conferences.

I attended my first, and most important, international conference as a fledgling professional in 1969. The thought of flying halfway around the world to the Tenth General Assembly and Eleventh Technical Meeting of the International Union for Conservation of Nature (IUCN) in New Delhi, India, was frightening. It was also compelling. Time to "break the ice" in my own professional circle.

New Delhi hit me as a swirl of dust, majestic palaces, strange Mogul towers, silks and saris, throngs of skinny humans, smoky sunsets, car horns, cups of fragrant tea and lingering incense. The conference itself was imposing. Famous names I had long admired became associated with real faces. During registration I met an unimaginably diverse group—a white-bearded Russian zoologist, a tanned Australian forester, a tiny 80-year-old Indian ornithologist. But, one thing bothered me: male conferees kept asking whose wife I was, or what I was doing here. It was as if I couldn't possibly have a personal professional reason for attending. Even the "Dr." before my name didn't help. A few gentlemen ignored it and just talked about trivialities. This subtle form of male chauvinism was getting me down—until I saw Mrs. Indira Gandhi.

She was invited to give the inaugural speech at our opening session. We met briefly in a hallway and stared at each other for a few seconds, woman to woman. Her wheat-colored sari with threads of gold matched her eyes. They were tawny brown, totally fearless, and demanding of respect. Never before had I met a woman with such power. For years I had been tormented by the conflict between following my career drives and maintaining my tomboyish demeanor, or, bowing to more traditional concepts of feminine roles and appearance. Seeing Mrs. Gandhi, as proud, resolute, and graceful as a tigress, I suddenly gained courage. The female role model I had unconsciously sought stood before me. From then on I mingled more easily with the conferees, quelled feelings of shyness, and began acting with assurance. Mrs. Gandhi's tawny tiger eyes stayed with me.

The other person who caused a change in my life was Major Ian Grimwood, a modest, quiet, former Indian Army officer. We often met by chance at night, pacing the open-air corridors outside our rooms. Both of us were suffering from the 12-hour jet lag. Strolling back and forth, listening to Major Grimwood describe his field experiences in many lands, I gained tremendous respect for his perseverance in practical conservation work. He spoke of his adventures as Kenya's Chief Game Warden; how he had rescued three of the last surviving Arabian oryxes (horselike creatures of steppes and deserts); and ecological surveys he'd made in the Amazon jungle.

Again, without realizing it, I had found the role model for my professional career. I wanted to be an international wildlife and wildlands consultant like Major Grimwood.

On two free days set aside for field trips, my colleagues and I visited Jim Corbett National Park and Bharatpur Bird Sanctuary. India's wildlife and wildlands are fantastic where they exist untouched and protected. At Corbett, I was hoisted up the side of an elephant onto a riding chair with six other people. We plodded through head-high grasses in search of tigers. The huge, pinkish-gray ears of our mount flapped nervously each time we surprised a black buck, chital deer, or blue bull. The landscape, seen from the back of an elephant, was dramatic. Swaying savannas stretched out on one side to a clear, foaming river. In the other direction, the forested foothills of the mighty Himalayas began. Only later, after we dismounted (we never saw a tiger) and the elephant padded softly away, the park superintendent told us of plans for a dam and hydroelectric project. It would inundate about half the lowlands in Corbett National Park!

Our second field excursion to Bharatpur was even more spectacular. We headed south toward Agra (site of the Taj Mahal) and spent the night in ornate canvas tents outside the sanctuary. Everyone rose in a frigid dawn to enter the huge heronry. A stirring was already beginning in the marshes as skeins of gray-lag geese flew into a tangerine sky. Parakeets, mynas, and treepies squawked atop the acacia trees. A Palas fishing eagle made its first stoop of the day. We climbed into a balky boat with two ragged, shivering boys to pole us through the swamps. Branches were bending under hundreds of nest platforms. Painted storks, white ibis, Eurasian spoonbills, shags, egrets, darters, herons were all awake and greeting the sun. The din was unbelievable.

Two of our hosts at Bharatpur were Dr. S. Dillon Ripley, President of the International Council of Bird Preservation (ICBP), and Dr. Salím Alí, India's leading ornithologist. They took us to see sarus cranes dancing and to observe a cooperative international bird-banding program (the Asian Migratory Pathological Survey). In the last four years, it had banded, examined, and released 80,000 birds of 1,006 species.

Dr. Alí pointed out the threats to this splendid sanctuary. People were draining it for more agricultural and pastural lands, deforesting it for firewood, poaching animals, and diverting the present artificial water supply elsewhere. Furthermore, Dr. Alí noted, cattle and buffalo, which are sacred to 85 percent of India's people, were allowed to wander at will. They often infiltrated and grazed within the refuge. I was grateful that Dr. Alí was there to fight for Bharatpur—and even more appreciative when he received the J. Paul Getty Wildlife Conservation Award of $50,000 U.S. in recognition of his labors.

These field excursions almost persuaded me that India's wildlife and wildlands had a future and that her five national parks and 100 sanctuaries were fairly secure. But then came the drive back to New Delhi. Hordes of emaciated human beings edged the roadways, barely moving aside as our cars blared their way among them. It looked as if they simply didn't care whether they lived or died. Outside the city, the landscape was drab and devastated. Now and again I saw a dead or dying person lying beside the highway. Women were filling water jugs from poisonous-looking green irrigation ditches, while a short way back in the fields men squatted to relieve themselves. One ecologist told us that 500 to 1,000 years ago this land had been forested and flowing with clear creeks. But now the *wadis* (gulches) were dry and barren. A pall of smoke and dust constantly hung in the air. This land was one-third the size of the United States but with three times the number of inhabitants (700 million-plus people, increasing by 2.5 percent annually, as of 1969). Here stood 15.5 percent of the world's population on 2.4 percent of its surface. (As of this writing, in mid-1998, India's population stood at 984,004 million—or almost one billion. The country is still the same size.)

Government and private birth control programs could not begin to keep up with the population increase. We learned that 90 percent of India's wildlife had been lost in the last 25 years. A member of the Indian Planning Commission told our gathering, "The chief ministries have a difficult task to perform in their own states. Population pressures tend to promote rather than check the constant encroachment of man on forest and wildlife. It is one of the greatest pities of democracy that trees have no votes and wild animals no constituency."

By the end of those ten days in India I was sickened and discouraged. For the first time since becoming a conservationist I wondered if it was worth it. Nothing in any college class or conference had prepared me for this shock. Yet it is something that every professional working with natural resources should experience. It's certain that the "triage" system of conservation priorities, as proposed by Dr. Thomas Lovejoy, is the most realistic way to save our natural heritage. With this method, India might be written off the list of places in which ecologists should devote time, energy, and money. How could conservation succeed where living skeletons roamed the land with desperate demands for food, water, and firewood? Conservation might be better achieved in young and relatively underpopulated countries like New Zealand, Brazil, and Iceland. Triage came as the most sobering thought of my budding career.

The second international meeting, which was to have a far-reaching impact on my thinking, took place in Venezuela, the winter of 1974. The conference was convened by the IUCN under the sponsorship of the United Nations Environmental Program

(UNEP). Financial support was given by UNESCO, the Swedish International Development Authority, and the World Wildlife Fund. It was the first such conference to bring together ecologists and planners, government conservation specialists and officials dealing with agriculture, forestry, and land use. Attendees came from all over Latin America, bent on devising ecological guidelines. These would be used in developing the American humid tropics, especially rain forests. The guidelines would be published and presented to top decision makers in Latin America, urging rapid implementation before rain forests became targets for human intervention and exploitation. Ecological guidelines would aid in the proper sustainable use of rain forests and increase long-term environmental stability and economic well-being of tropical nations.

Ecologists are often placed in the position of the medical doctor who is peremptorily summoned to effect a cure when the patient is half dead. Being "M.D.s of the environment," we should be in on the diagnosis, or decision-making process, from the beginning. Ecological factors should be considered right along with political, sociological, military, and economic aspects in every project.

After we had finished the rough draft of our guidelines, the group was invited on two three-day field trips through the Venezuelan countryside. Both trips were organized for our benefit by CODESUR (Corporación del Desarrollo del Sur— Development Corporation of the South) of the Venezuelan Ministry of Public Works, and by CVG (Corporación Venezuela de la Guyana—Venezuelan Corporation of Guyana). We would be treated to a glimpse of the wet tropics where important development projects were being planned or implemented. This was my first visit to South America as a professional and my first awareness of its vast areas and environmental problems. My world was widening.

Our itinerary read like that of an Explorers' Club expedition. Our traveling vehicle was an ancient but dependable DC-3. Its Plexiglas windows were cracked and split. We could spit right through them. All 33 participants had to strap themselves in sideways on bucket seats along the length of the plane. It hadn't been revamped one iota since World War II. Then it was used to ferry out paratroopers on jumps. As the DC-3 creakily took off from La Guaira airport at dawn, some of us remarked nervously on the possibility of crashing.

"If we do," said Dr. Gerardo Budowski soothingly, "we'd probably survive in good shape. Where else do you have so many of the world's top ecologists traveling together? If we couldn't figure out how to survive, nobody else could." Then in a somewhat more gloomy tone, he added, "If we die, the world will loose its most brilliant 'doctors of the environment.'" (He was currently Director General of IUCN.)

Conversation aboard the DC-3 flowed from topic to topic, continent to continent, as easily as flipping through an illustrated geography book. Every once in a while, a flurry of exclamations broke forth. The plane took an unnerving dip sideways as all the passengers crowded on one side or the other to see some fascinating natural phenomenon below. Meanwhile the battle-scarred plane droned imperturbably onward. I was reassured by its slow speed and steadiness.

At Venezuela's newest and easternmost city, Ciudad Guyana (not far from the island of Trinidad), we marveled at the three-year-old settlement which had started from scratch and had already tripled its original population to 150,000. Once again I was witnessing the incredible human potential for reproduction and emigration.

Not far away, along the grassy coastal plain of the Caribbean, we walked through a new pine plantation of over 50,000 acres. Hundreds more trees were being planted as we watched (as of 1978, there were 100,000 acres). The Venezuelan government was pinning its hopes on this gigantic monoculture of Caribbean pine in order to have a close, cheap source of pulp and paper products. Already some of the earlier plantings were eight years old and well over 25 feet tall. They could be cut within two to four more years. Foresters were worried lest an insect plague or disease strike the vulnerable exotic species before it matured enough to harvest.

As I walked along the orderly rows of shimmering trees, I recalled a public square in Caracas. Newspapers lay scattered by the wind on streets and discarded in trash cans. The cheaper restaurants and drive-ins served everything on paper. Supermarkets offered the same variety of tissues, paper napkins, toweling, and toilet paper as in the United States. The demand for disposable products was mounting at an extraordinary pace. Could huge pine monocultures satisfy these needs? Caribbean pine has shown itself quite resistant to pests for fifty years in Africa. So far it had been doing well in Venezuela. Only time will tell.

Any single species growing alone in the tropics, however, is normally headed for trouble from epidemics and insect infestations. Mixtures of species are far healthier and more resistant to disease. That was one of the ecological guidelines we had just finished writing: **diversity breeds stability.**

Winging down to Canaima National Park, we sidetracked to view the Guri Dam—largest "black water" reservoir in the world. ("Black water" simply means clear, acidic water stained brownish or blackish by vegetation or bedrock.) As we flew over this impoundment, I saw it stretching mile upon mile between forest-clad hills. Its hydroelectric power, reaching an output of 2,650 kilowatt-hours in 1977, and a projected nine million, will provide all of Ciudad Guyana's electrical needs. This dam was especially interesting to our group because no one knows what effect the impounding of black water will have. Normally clear, or "white water," reservoirs silt up quickly. Swift-water fishes die, water stagnates and turns greenish, and becomes the breeding ground for disease-bearing insects or snails. Such reservoirs lose their usefulness quickly. This more acidic, dark-colored reservoir was a new experiment in the making. Ecologists would be watching it closely.

Next we landed in Canaima-Grand Savannah National Park. The 7.5-million-acre park is now the largest in South America and one of the six biggest on earth. It provides adequate protection of the upper Caroni watershed. Its rivers head up in the park and are vital to the Guri Dam and Ciudad Guyana. Thousands of local and foreign tourists are drawn each year to the park, thus persuading many Venezuelans that conservation can pay its way.

To see the Canaima Park's crowning spectacle, Angel Falls, we had to fly into backcountry and view it fleetingly from our DC-3. That slender stream cascades 2,800 feet from the top of a table-topped, sandstone, steep-sided mountain, known as a *tepui*. A few milky clouds drifted across our line of vision, making Angel Falls seem even more mysterious and unattainable. Then, with one wingtip frighteningly close to the canyon wall, our sturdy DC-3 banked, turned, dove, and roared away from the spectacle.

We continued south over Grand Savannah. This immense, undulating land flowed beneath us like tapestry, golden tan in color and marked with monolithic tepuis and narrow black streams. The tepuis were a topic of keen interest and speculation among us. They are authentic isolated "islands in the air," rearing upward as high as

5,000 feet. Their tops support many endemic plants, including orchids, epiphytes and dwarf forests. Most have never been explored by white people. Approximately 90 such mountains dot the Guyana highlands—one of the most grandiose and magnificent sights in the world.

Dr. Budowski was explaining that, "Grand Savannah is 'starvation country'—few fish in the streams and little wildlife on the grasslands. The acidic waters and poor soils don't support much life."

I listened transfixed. That countryside called to me. I wanted to come back and work there. The vast savannah felt free, clean, and wild. Yet without fish and wildlife, what use or pleasure was it to an ecologist?

We leaped across Venezuela to the Río Negro and the conjunction of this country with Colombia and Brazil. The meeting point is marked with one huge "sugar-loaf" mountain which we circled lazily like a giant, if ragged, vulture. This was my first sight of the Amazon basin—that enormous lowland rain forest which is the largest on earth. The green carpet rolled out to the horizon on every side, cut here and there by sinuous brown rivers, seemingly untouched.

When we landed at San Carlos de Río Negro for the night, we had the opportunity to inspect one of the "new towns" being built by CODESUR. The basic purpose was to draw out indigenous, free-roaming Amerindian tribes from the rain forest, settle them in cement-block houses, and give them a few modern amenities. These were piped-in water, outhouses, transistor radios, and rough airstrips. Sociologically and politically, it appeared a great plan to integrate the nation. But when our group of environmental doctors walked through the little hamlet, medical and ecological drawbacks became apparent.

"Those cement floors and walls will cause health problems," prophesied Dr. Budowski. "It's been noted in other new towns in the tropics that babies and toddlers who lie on cold stone floors instead of bare ground become more susceptible to respiratory and urinary infections. When they go to the bathroom, the excretions are no longer absorbed by the soil, broken down by bacteria, and eventually rendered harmless. Urine and feces puddle and pile until the mother cleans the floor."

All of us stopped to stare at the innocent-looking homes. Dr. Budowski continued, "We must remember that many indigenous people do not practice the same sanitary standards that we do in temperate climates. Besides, they probably earn less than one hundred to two hundred dollars per year. How can they possibly buy soaps, diapers, cleansers, disinfectants? Let alone brooms, mops, and vacuum cleaners?"

We strolled on through the streets. "This new life style invites flies and filth," he went on. "Forest people have been semi-nomadic for centuries. They put up simple thatched huts with dirt floors, farm and graze as long as the soil holds out, and then move on to the next patch of wilderness to repeat the process. This simple way of life is sound for both humans and the tropical rain forest—when groups are small. But when people are brought into these new towns, they are more or less trapped. They can't move the cement-block houses, yet the soil will wear out just as fast around the new town as it did around their jungle huts. Where do they go?"

We had come to an overturned tree with its root system standing perpendicular to the ground. We could easily see that the topsoil was about four inches deep above sterile white sand. The tree's roots had compensated by spreading out in a splayed, oddly-flat pattern.

"Look here. When soil is exposed like this," explained Dr. Budowski, "water and sometimes wind quickly strip it down to the underlying sand, then gnaw away at the edges, creating larger and larger sand patches. Desertification in the rain forest."

"Another thing," broke in Dr. Ray Watters, a tropical ecologist from New Zealand, "it's been found that when thatched roofs are replaced by tin ones, many natural insect predators like spiders, lizards, and bats lose a home. Then insects increase around human habitations. The human diseases borne by them may also thrive. Malaria and dengue are two bad ones."

I found this conversation strangely disturbing. Around us the jungle pressed in—wild, fecund, teeming with life. Yet here stood these squat, conventional, ugly concrete houses, rectangular lots, squares and streets, and a newly bulldozed airstrip large enough to accommodate a Hercules transport. Man had imposed a precise mathematical design and theoretical social order upon a natural, healthy, functioning environment. The government plan wasn't working exactly the way it was supposed to.

I knew that each South American nation which shares the huge Amazon basin had plans to invade this "last frontier." Just as we

"won our West," Venezuela is "conquering her South." She is trying to consolidate her native tribes and impart a nationalistic spirit through radio programs broadcast daily from Caracas. They are
picked up by lonely radio towers deep in the jungle. The new town
we were examining beside the Río Negro was only one of hundreds
of examples of twentieth-century developments infiltrating
Amazonia.

Clearly, our ecological guidelines were needed. But had we gotten them out in time? Would they be accepted and utilized? Might
the sights we were witnessing this week be forerunners of the same
ecological and human devastation I had agonized over in India?

A third and most auspicious meeting took place in San José,
Costa Rica, in December 1974. It was the First Conference on
National Parks in Central America. Representatives from every
Central American country, including Mexico, Panama, and Belize
attended. Thanks to Rockefeller Brothers Fund financing, the
need for parks in this part of the world was finally being acknowledged and considered.

It was none too soon. With the shining exceptions of Costa
Rica and Panama, attempts to establish national parks in Central
America had met with little success. A number of factors contributed to this: border squabbles, political changes, public apathy,
a general ignorance about conservation and its benefits, plus a lack
of trained managers of natural resources. Most areas declared as
parks or reserves were "parks on paper." Compared to the United
States, Canada, and Africa with their long, proud old traditions of
national parks, Central America was just a teenager.

As I sat and listened, four delegates from each Central
American country (representing natural resources, ecotourism,
culture, and planning) began to formulate plans for "pilot parks."
These prototypes would have easy access from metropolitan areas
and contain outstanding natural and/or cultural features.
Participants made lists of other natural wildlands worthy of park
status. In time, these would become "frontier" parks, wildlife
reserves, biosphere reserves, marine national parks, multiple-use
areas, and archaeological parks. The enthusiasm of the delegates
was noteworthy. This remarkable initiative was the beginning of a
Central American system of national parks. Ninety days later they
had an official request for assistance at the United Nations

Development Program in New York. In less than a year, they had written management plans for each of the pilot parks.

At the same time, again with generous support from Rockefeller Brothers Fund, a Wildlands and Watershed Unit was agreed upon. It would be housed at CATIE (*Centro Agronomío Tropical de Investigación y Enseñanza*—Tropical Agricultural Research and Training Center) in Costa Rica. This unit would assist Central American governments in establishing pilot parks and managing their natural resources.

I had no way of knowing then that my attendance here would lead to a future consulting job at CATIE. And to a deep involvement in the entire Central American park system through a *National Geographic* assignment. Such are the surprise spinoffs of conferences.

After the official meeting, I joined a few colleagues for a field trip to Monteverde Cloud Forest Biological Reserve in the Tilaran Mountains. How comfortable it felt to be back in one of my favorite ecosystems. We hiked down a muddy trail for a while. Then I told my companions to go on without me. "I'll wait here and listen for quetzals," I explained, settling down on a moss-covered log.

I leaned back and relaxed. Four o'clock. Clouds and mist were enveloping the forest in an unearthly light. High above the trade winds roared over the 4,000-foot crest of the mountains. The noise was as constant as sea surf. For six months, the winds blew thus. The other six months, rains fell and the winds were light and variable. From the top of a monstrous gnarled oak, I heard the familiar chatter of a male quetzal. A moment later, he swooped like a flash of green lightning across a clearing and up into another giant oak. As he passed, a shaft of sunlight streamed through the scudding clouds and lit up his crimson breast.

Just to see that swift streak of splendor made the whole field trip worthwhile. I silently congratulated the World Wildlife Fund, USA, and the Tropical Science Center in Costa Rica for joining funds and forces to save this remnant wilderness which eventually totalled 98,800 acres. Much of Costa Rica's high oak and cloud forests are being cut and burned for charcoal and lumber. This reserve is much bigger than my 1,000-acre quetzal sanctuary on Volcán Atitlán. It probably holds today the largest remaining population of quetzals in Costa Rica.

Now the sun shaft switched off abruptly and a thick mist muffled the forest. I could feel my clothes dampening in the high humidity. I sensed the mosses, lichens, liverworts, air plants, fungi, and trees around me also absorbing moisture. Monteverde was like one huge sponge, soaking up water and releasing it slowly throughout the year. The cloud forest made life possible downslope. Because of its small clear streams, a little Quaker colony nearby made cheeses, small farmers downslope grubbed for corn and beans, and wild animals drank and bathed. The last tangerine spokes of sunset probed up from the Pacific. They dispelled the mist again. My friends returned. We stood silently watching the gilded moss, the bronzed trunks of oaks, ripe raspberries turned cardinal red. Then we descended slowly through that golden world, hearing the trade wind grow fainter and fainter.

There have been many other conferences in many different countries. Some people have called me an ecological elitist because I travel to exotic cities and into beautiful hinterlands. Others have accused me and my colleagues of being "First World jetsetting, overeducated preservationists," using up too much airplane fuel. Still, I'm convinced that conferences are essential to being a good ecologist and concerned doctor of the environment. They help me keep my fingers on the pulse of the planet, maintain a global perspective, and stay motivated and informed.

Wherever I go and whatever I see, two things support me: Mrs. Gandhi's undaunted tigress eyes and Major Grimwood's quiet assured dedication.

11

A PANDA and SOME LIONS

One day toward the end of August 1974, I received a startling letter. Dr. Fritz Vollmar, then Director General of the World Wildlife Fund, International, in Switzerland, was writing to invite me to the Fourth International Conference in Geneva, November 2–4. I was to be awarded the 1974 Gold Medal for Conservationist of the Year. It was in recognition of my work in Central America with the grebes, quetzals, and Volcán Barú. I immediately wrote back, agreeing to come and accept this great honor.

Meanwhile, I was working at my cabin on an article about the Adirondack Park for *National Geographic*. I wanted to illustrate it with a picture that would capture the essence of an Adirondack autumn. I needed rafts of Canada Geese floating on a misty lake at sunrise—tendrils of rosy mist rising against a backdrop of high mountains cloaked in colorful leaves—a balsam or two silhouetted in the foreground as a frame. I knew of a probable place to take this picture. On October 2, when the weather cleared, I drove off with my dog, Pitzi, to camp near there. We slept in the back of the truck and woke to hear a faint musical babbling. This meant wild geese were on the lake. I drove along an old logging road and parked on an embankment at the edge of a steep shoreline.

Crisscrossing two cameras with telephoto lens over my shoulders, I eased open the cab door and very slowly stood up so as not to scare the birds. I hushed Pitzi, who was sitting on the cab seat, then reached up to the cab roof. The night had been cold. Frost whitened the grasses, bushes, and top of my truck. I felt for a hand-hold, climbed up onto the cab, and encountered a cold, slippery metal surface. Instantly I lost my balance, slid backward, spun away from the truck and down the embankment.

I must have fallen 12 or 15 feet. The breath was knocked out of me, causing several awful groans. Next I realized that something was crushed inside between my hips. I managed to roll onto one side which felt better. After about 15 minutes I was breathing more normally and thought perhaps I could crawl to the truck. But the pain was too great. All I could do was pull myself forward a few feet to within sight of the road.

The situation was alarming. I was about five miles from the nearest building, on a seldom-traveled log road, lying helpless on the ground with the temperature about 28°F. No one knew where I was.

An hour passed. Then I heard the low hum of a motor. Miraculously a game warden cruised by on patrol. There was an early bear season underway, and he was checking on hunters. He spotted the truck, then the dog, then me. When he saw me shuddering, his first impulse was to carry me into his warm car. But some instinct warned me this was wrong. I begged him not to move me. Between shivers I blurted out, "Get my sleeping bag and pack in the back of the truck."

He covered me up and laid down the pack. Gently he unlaced my boots, drew them off carefully, and told me to wiggle my toes. I did. "Well, that's a good sign," he said, leaving the boots on the ground. "I think your back is OK! I'll have to leave you here a while," were his next words, "and go find help to pick you up with a stretcher."

How I dreaded to be left alone, but it was the only way. After 45 minutes, he returned with two men and a wooden door. I crawled slowly onto the hard surface, then they slid the door into the back of my pickup. The officer had radioed out to the nearest volunteer ambulance. Shortly, I was slid into the ambulance, still on the improvised stretcher, for I would allow no one to move me. Then we headed for the hospital 80 miles away.

From the time I was found until arrival at the emergency ward, only three and a half hours passed. It was an evacuation of great speed, efficiency, competence, and kindliness.

At the hospital I was informed that my pelvis and ribs were cracked on the left side. Because I was whisked out of the woods, my truck, dog, two thousand dollars worth of camera equipment, sleeping bag, pack, and boots were left scattered all over. The men who rescued me went back to salvage things and find a home for Pitzi. Without the assistance of these wonderful people, I would have been completely lost.

Fortunately, I did not have to be in a cast but was kept flat on my back for three weeks. The doctor said I would be on crutches for two months, could try walking after eight weeks, driving after three months, and expect full recovery in about six months. Those early days were among the bleakest of my life. Serious questions about my future tormented me day and night. Would I be able to continue as an ecological consultant? Or would I be crippled for life? How could I earn my living in the interim? Mostly, how would I manage to accept my medal?

My new physician, Dr. Mike, was a good-natured and practical man. He thought it over and gave his verdict. "*If* you promise to travel to Europe in a wheelchair and don't go kicking up your heels, or doing any of the crazy things you like to do, you can fly by November first. But remember, those bones aren't knit yet. If you fall, you might be in trouble. If this accident had happened even a couple of days later, I could never let you travel."

Now that I knew it was possible to fly, I began realizing the logistics were almost too complicated to arrange. Who would drive me the 150 miles of bone-jarring roads from the Adirondacks to the airport? How would I pack? What would I wear, let alone how would I dress myself? Could I get my hair done? Who would wheel me on and off the plane and meet me in Switzerland? Truthfully, setting off across the Atlantic in this totally helpless state seemed like the scariest thing I'd ever done. But I wouldn't consider *not* going. Not for a minute.

It worked out beautifully. Thanks to loyal friends who rigged a mattress in their van, an obliging beauty shop, and the courtesy of the airlines, I found myself aboard a Swissair jet the night of November 1. To my amazement, Dr. S. Dillon Ripley, then Secretary of the Smithsonian Institution, and my benefactor of the International Council for Bird Preservation (ICBP), sat to my right on the same plane, going to the same conference. He graciously kept an eye on me throughout the trip.

In Geneva, the morning of November 2, Dr. Thomas Lovejoy of World Wildlife Fund, USA, met me, wheeled me past customs, collected my baggage, and drove me to the hotel where the conference was already in session. Deftly, my friend pushed me into the back of the auditorium to a spot where I could hear the proceedings.

At once, knowing I'd have to make an acceptance speech for the medal, I started surveying the room, calculating the shortest distance to the podium. It seemed miles away. Pride would not let me be wheeled up there. I was going to use crutches as I'd been taught by the physical therapist. There were highly waxed parquet floors. Definitely dangerous. Gorgeous little Oriental rugs scattered here and there. They would have to go or I'd risk becoming a flying carpet myself. I needed a high stool next to the mike, so as not to stand too long. And a remote control to the slide projector. I worked out my moves as carefully as a general deploying troops into a minefield. This done, I took a look at the conference members.

My heart gave a lurch. At the head table sat Prince Bernhard of The Netherlands, then President of World Wildlife Fund, International; Prince Philip of England; the Maharani of Jaipur, India; assorted Ladies, Ambassadors, Barons; a millionairess from Canada; and Dr. Ripley. The audience was sprinkled with other famous scientists and royal personages. It was the *Who's Who* of the international conservation world. How could I ever get up in front of such people in my condition? No way!

I motioned frantically to Dr. Lovejoy. "I can't go through with it," I whispered desperately. "You accept the medal for me and show the slides, Thomas."

"Nonsense," snorted my sensible friend. "You've flown all this way to get it. You can do it. You're just exhausted from the trip. Why don't we get you a room for a few hours? You can take a hot bath and sleep a little. I'll come get you shortly before four o'clock, when the presentation is scheduled. You'll feel better about it then."

"But the rugs, the floor, the podium..." I began. "It's all too tricky to navigate."

Thomas was already wheeling me firmly to the front desk of the hotel. Charming the receptionist, he arranged for me to have a room for six hours. Minutes later I was inside an enormous high-ceilinged bedroom with tall French windows. I looked out on a rose garden still in bloom, cobalt Lake Geneva, and the snowy Alps behind. A crisply uniformed maid drew a hot bubble bath in the biggest tub I'd ever seen. She fluffed up those heavenly Swiss down comforters, opened the bed, and undressed me. Half an hour later I was fast asleep.

As Thomas had predicted, I felt a bit more confident in the afternoon.

When Dr. Vollmar called my name, and I had to crutch forward like a hoptoad, I almost lost nerve. There was no running back through the audience. Shakily I balanced myself to face Prince Bernhard. I looked straight at him, noticing that he was a very good-looking man who appeared comfortably like a commoner in a brown plaid sports coat, slim-cut brown trousers, beige shirt, and soft tie. He read from a parchment scroll, smiled kindly, and handed me a small royal blue box. Trembling, I opened it. There lay a stunning, round gold medal with the World Wildlife Fund symbol, a giant panda, on one side and my name and the date on the other. The Prince shook my hand warmly and gingerly gave me an embrace. I almost fell off my crutches. Then Dr. Vollmar stepped forward with a beautiful gold Rolex watch, again with my name and the date inscribed on the back. This was an extra surprise. I was tongue-tied.

Yet the speech had to go on. Recovering my composure, I shared with the audience those months of conservation work in Central America. And then it was all over—the hand-shaking, the thank-you's, the cocktails, the accolades. Once again I was sound asleep under those cozy comforters while an early November snow-storm from the Alps dusted the roses outside my door.

Anne displaying her Gold Medal and Rolex watch awarded by World Wildlife Fund, International, in Switzerland, 1974.

Next morning, Thomas said casually at breakfast, "Why don't you come with us to London tomorrow? Remember, Mr. Getty is giving a small luncheon for the jurors of his new conservation prize and for those of us at World Wildlife Fund who administer it. You've been appointed a juror and you were invited. I'm sure he'd want you there. He's so proud of his new philanthropic interest."

I looked at him doubtfully and sighed. "It's so far and I feel so helpless traveling by wheelchair."

"You've already done more than that," he rebutted. "Albany, New York, to Geneva, Switzerland, is over four thousand miles. London's just a hop and a skip away. Besides, I'll be along to push you around," he added impishly with a boyish grin.

I grinned back. Why not? Like receiving the gold medal, it was a once-in-a-lifetime opportunity. I was curious to meet J. Paul Getty, "richest man in the world." Besides, I was too tired to fly home right away across the Atlantic. Perhaps I could rest a few days at the London home of an old friend, archeologist Colin Wyatt, whom I had met at Maya ruins in Guatemala.

"Okay, Thomas," I said, "I'll go. Just let me wire a friend to see if I could stay there a couple of days."

In London, I found myself with Dr. Ripley, Thomas, and the dashing Peruvian conservationist Felipe Benavides, then president of the Peruvian branch of the World Wildlife Fund. "Please may I drive you all to the Getty place in my car?" asked Mr. Benavides gallantly as we came to the airport door. A long, slim, gray Daimler limousine with a uniformed chauffeur was waiting. I was helped into the back seat, while Mr. Benavides sat in front, turning at once to talk to us. As we drove through downtown London, he energetically regaled us with accounts of his work in Peru.

His principal contribution had been saving the vicuña, once the prized beast of Inca royalty. Vicuña populations had fallen from an estimated two million animals ranging throughout the Andes Mountains to less than 7,000 scattered in the Peruvian highlands. The scarce, ultra-soft fur was selling for $90 or more per pound. Under Felipe's prodding, the Peruvian government had set up a 16,000-acre National Vicuña Reserve in 1967. It also signed a pact with Bolivia banning vicuña hunting for ten years. Mr. Benavides was instrumental in saving other endangered animals and certain wildlands in the Amazon basin. His black eyes snapped, his moustache bristled, and he minced no words in denouncing his countrymen who were exploiting wildlife. I was beginning to see that one did not "meet" Felipe Benavides, one "experienced" him.

Thomas turned to me and whispered, "Don't tell anyone, but Felipe will probably be the first winner of the new $50,000 J. Paul

Getty Wildlife Conservation Award."

My mouth dropped open and I listened with new respect to the elegant Peruvian. The miles slipped by. It was well past noon. My tummy was rumbling. We seemed to be driving endlessly through London. "I thought we were going to an apartment house in town," I murmured to Thomas.

"I think Getty's house is on the outskirts," Thomas replied non-committally.

Now we were on a "dual carriageway" (super highway), speeding smoothly through misty English countryside. The Daimler slowed and turned in at an imposing iron gate between high stone walls. A quaint cottage stood at one side and a cheerful woman called out through a loudspeaker, asking for identification. The chauffeur produced our invitations. We waited. Felipe fidgeted. Evidently, security was checking us out.

Then, with all the grandeur of a Hollywood production, the 20-foot ornate gate swung slowly open. A guard beckoned us in. We followed a curving road through emerald fields where sleek horses grazed, past majestic oaks which might have shaded Robin Hood himself, up over a knoll with a sweeping vista of forests, fields, and "Sutton Place."

By rights it should have been called a baronial manor house, for it was a shade too small to be called a castle. It was far too lavish and large to be anything else. We rolled up the circular driveway and parked beside other Daimlers, Rolls Royces, Bentleys, and Cadillacs—all quite different from my rusty 1967 pickup truck in the Adirondacks.

Chauffeurs surrounded our car and helped us out; butlers opened doors and took coats; maids helped me to the powder room. Then I was in the drawing room, about to meet Mr. Getty.

I saw nothing at all imposing about the man at first glance. He didn't have Mr. Benavides' flashing eyes and his charisma; nor Dr. Ripley's gracious poise and patrician face; nor Prince Bernhard's sportsman physique and charming manner. His suit was drab, his face dotted with blemishes, and his hands shook ever so slightly. The multi-millionaire stood, slightly hunched like a hawk on a perch, awaiting his company. He seemed to be looking down at us from the height of his accumulated wealth and years. Then our eyes met. His were pale blue, as keen and penetrating as a falcon's. Crutching my way closer, I shook hands. I sensed the tremendous concentration behind those hooded lids. I felt as if an electric calculating machine had just digested me.

Overtired from the trip, I asked to sit down. A butler helped me into a huge leather chair. A moment later, to my surprise, he assisted Mr. Getty to one beside mine. We looked at each other with a touch of chagrin: he for the toll of his 86 years, I for the aches of my accident.

Politely, I praised him for establishing the Getty award, largest of its kind in my profession at that time. He nodded. Then for want of anything better to say, I asked, "Would you like to see my medal?"

He nodded again. I reached for my handbag, then remembered I had left the box in Felipe's car. An ambassador was standing nearby. I called to him sweetly and asked if he'd mind running out and getting it. (It wasn't every day I found such a fancy errand boy.) He literally rushed out the door, then back to Mr. Getty's side. I opened the box and showed off the seven-ounce circle of gold gleaming on blue velvet.

"Nice," he responded coolly.

After that, I could think of nothing to say. Mr. Getty, for his part, seemed glad of the silence. And, so, together, we rested and watched the buzzing cocktail company.

It was hardly what I'd call having "a few people in for lunch." When the head butler announced the meal, over 30 dignitaries trooped to a table longer than my entire log cabin. Mr. Getty presided at one end. There were so many pieces of silverware that my mother's carefully taught etiquette failed. All I could remember her saying was, "Always start using your eating utensils from the outside in." I did so, wondering how I'd ever get through 12 pieces of silver without several faux pas. When the wine butler came to fill the first of three crystal goblets, I ordered milk. "Good for broken bones," I said apologetically. I could have sworn he winced.

Course after course arrived on what looked suspiciously like golden platters. The meal took two and a half hours. I used only seven pieces of silverware. At the serving of demitasses and brandy snifters, Mr. Getty stood up, thanked us all for coming, and invited his guests to go outside to see his pets. Then he shuffled off, imperturbable, to take a nap. The guests were diverted to the back garden for this rare treat of Getty's pride of lions after lunch.

Feeling unable to trust myself on crutches on a lion-filled lawn, I decided to obey Dr. Mike's orders. Instead I stayed inside and hobbled from room to room in the mansion. Eventually I came to a huge living room with walls covered by enormous paintings. A great fire burned in the hearth, consuming not logs but whole tree trunks. I worked my way around the room, gazing at Madonnas from the eleventh, twelfth, and thirteenth centuries. Gradually it dawned on me that I was seeing part of a fabulous art collection. I had not realized that this was one of Mr. Getty's hobbies. At the head of the room, I came face to face with a very elderly man, bent like a fiddlehead over a cane. He was in the company of a gentle young woman. His progress about the chamber was as slow as mine. She introduced us, pronouncing my name perfectly with a French accent, and then said, "Sir Julian Huxley."

The shock of white hair lifted, the kindest eyes imaginable looked into mine, and the tortured frame straightened for a moment. I sputtered, "Dr. Huxley! Oh, how *wonderful* to meet you! You don't know how I admire the work you did on the great crested grebes in 1914. It helped me so much with my research in Guatemala on the giant pied-billed grebes."

I stopped. I was sounding like a schoolgirl talking to a movie star. Yet it was true. Out of that whole day, amidst the Bentleys and butlers, the priceless paintings and golden platters, the lions and wines, this world-renowned scientist was the greatest treasure I'd found. His early ornithological work had been a tremendous inspiration. And how very opportune. Just a few months later, Sir Julian died and the world lost one of its greatest humanitarians and scientists.

The day had been too much. While the other guests were still outside, I dialed my archaeologist friend, Colin, to ask if he'd come for me.

"I've been expecting your call. *Of course* you can stay here just as long as you like," he said jubilantly. "We have so much to catch up on since Guatemala. I'll come for you right away. Where shall I pick you up?"

"At Paul Getty's estate in Surrey," I said.

My friend never missed a beat. "Righto," he said cheerily. "It's only half an hour from here. I know the place. See you." And he hung up.

Colin marched in just as the rest of the guests were filtering back, talking vivaciously. "Colin," I called from the depths of the leather chair where I'd collapsed. I struggled to get up, then stopped. The guests had fallen silent and were all staring at the

ram-rod straight, silvery-haired and mustached man. He was wearing plum-colored jeans, a flowery Western shirt, and a gorgeous
embroidered shepherd's coat from Afghanistan. In that conserva-
tive gathering, he stood out like a hollyhock in a bed of ivy. Again
manners failed me. What to do? Should I introduce him? How to
explain my friend's predilection for traveling to the earth's most
remote and bizarre places to do archeological digs, clothe himself
in native attire, and not give a tinker's damn who saw him?

The day was saved by a voluptuous millionairess who cried out,
"Oh, Colin, my dear! Why, I haven't seen you since St. Moritz
three years ago."

Much hugging and kissing ensued. Colin had never bothered to
tell me that he was a former ski-jumping champion. Then, to his
great glee, Colin was introduced to Mr. Getty, just back from his
nap. The old gentleman merely nodded sleepily and pleasantly at
this audacious newcomer.

Finally, Colin helped me tenderly out to the parking lot, ignoring butlers, maids, and chauffeurs. He opened the door of a Chevy
with 1964 Wisconsin plates. He threw my overnight bag and velvet medal box onto the back seat and helped me slide into the
front. Rows of East Indian good-luck charms hung above the wind-
shield. The seat was covered with a bright Mexican serape. He
started the engine and we sped down the driveway, leaving a cloud
of dust to sift over the startled chauffeurs.

I leaned back in my seat and let out a great sigh of relief. I was
back with my own kind of people. Only after we got to Colin's
house did I think to ask him how he got away with driving 1964
American plates in 1974 England. Then, as I crutched around the
car toward his front door, I noticed the Spanish bumper sticker. It
read: *"FE EN DIOS Y ADELANTE"* (FAITH IN GOD AND
FORWARD).

That sentiment appealed to me. It had gotten me across the
Atlantic and would get me home. It would put me back on my feet.
Before Christmas I took my first steps without crutches, and after
Easter began doing field work again. This time I was to venture out
into the enormous tropical rain forest known as Amazonia.

12

MANÚ

hen J. Paul Getty established his annual wildlife conservation award worth $50,000 U.S., he made a magnificent gesture for the world's wildlife and wildlands. The public was suddenly made aware of conservationists' long struggles to save rare and endangered species and wild places. I considered it a special honor and pleasure to be chosen one of the 11 international jurors who, under Chairman Prince Bernhard, were to select recipients of the award.

That first year hundreds of applications poured into World Wildlife Fund's office in Washington, D.C. It was the funneling and filtering point for the prize. I found it agonizing to choose among the résumés of so many dedicated human beings. The jury agreed that the first recipient should come from a Third World country, must have spent several years in conservation work, and preferably be a field person rather than an academic. Imagine my joy when Felipe Benavides of Peru won.

A gala reception and dinner were held in Washington. Many Latin American dignitaries were present. Nelson Rockefeller, then Vice-President of the United States, made a brief but brilliant appearance. After the official ceremony, Felipe and his stunning wife, María Louisa, joined Dr. Lovejoy, me, and a few others from World Wildlife Fund for a more intimate and informal celebration.

"You all *must* come and review the wildlife work in Peru—the vicuña national reserve at Pampas Galeras, Paracas Marine National Reserve, our five new national parks, and most of all Manú," said the glowing Felipe. "Why not plan a trip in May during our little dry season? Thomas, you arrange it!" he ordered expansively. "Bring George Woodwell (then Director of World Wildlife Fund, USA), a couple other jurors, and Anne. I want to use my prize money to build a wildlife research center out in the *campo* (field). You can help me decide where."

Before the evening was over, a date had been set for four of us to fly to Lima, Felipe's home. From there we would go immediately to Manú National Park—the largest park in the Amazon basin and, at that time, in all Latin America. It was an untouched, primeval huge tract of lowland rain forest.

As good luck would have it, a few weeks later I received an assignment from *Audubon* magazine to do an article on the ecological situation in the Amazon. It would take me half a year off and on to survey Amazonia (the Amazon basin), dividing it into three major segments. First, I would visit Manú in May with Felipe Benavides who had helped create it. Later in November and December, the long dry season, I would take a 2,300-mile ship cruise down the Amazon River. Finally, I would drive along sections of the new Transamazônica and Belém-Brasília highways. All told, I hoped to sample 7,000 miles of the largest remaining chunk of lowland rain forest on earth. It was an area roughly equivalent to two-thirds of the continental United States (2,400,000 square miles). There were new ecosystems, countries, and dimensions to be explored. All the odd assorted pieces—starting with my broken pelvis, the gold medal, that Venezuelan conference, and the Getty jury appointment—were falling into place in an extraordinary fashion.

One evening in May 1975 I jetted non-stop from New York City to Lima with the group. We met Felipe and two government representatives there and continued at dawn to Cuzco in the Andes. At that high, windy airport we switched to a Twin Otter. My usual nervousness about flying turned to sheer panic as we rapidly spiraled up from 11,000 feet to over 19,500 and nosed into huge snowy clouds. The pilot ordered us to start breathing oxygen and pointed out two thin plastic tubes running along the cockpit ceiling. Thomas Lovejoy sat beside me, imperturbable as an eagle. Calmly, he passed the tube to me, waited as I sucked in a few breaths, then took it back. Breaks in the clouds showed a piercing brittle-blue sky above; cruel gray mountains laced with snow, ravines, and landslides below. Our plane flew right over the great spine of the Andes, humming eastward. It seemed as dauntless as a dragonfly in the face of that frigid world outside. I broke into a cold sweat and began panting uncontrollably.

Suddenly I had a flashback to my childhood. I was five, and my parents had taken me around South America on a four-month business tour. They had often described the rugged flight from Santiago, Chile, to Buenos Aires, Argentina, in a non-pressurized, twin-propeller plane of the 1940s. "You turned green," my mother told me, "and we had to give you oxygen. Yet you kept staring out at the mountains, fascinated. We could see Aconcagua—highest peak in the Western Hemisphere. Our line of sight from the plane only came two-thirds up that mighty mountain."

———

Now here I was, straddling the Andes in a non-pressurized, twin-propellered airplane, and feeling green again. Then the altimeter began winding down—19,500 to 4,000 feet. My breathing slowed and that vision disappeared. The cabin became warm and humid. We broke through cloud cover and saw the Amazon forest spreading like a green carpet as far as our eyes could see. A few minutes later we were landing at 900 feet elevation beside a temporary oil exploration camp not far from Manú National Park. Here we would board City Service helicopters for the last leg of the trip. The influence of Mr. Benavides, plus the coordination of the Getty and City Service oil companies, and World Wildlife Fund, USA, had combined their logistical support with the Peruvian Air Force and Ministry of Agriculture so we could make the trip from New York City to Manú in a miraculous 24 hours instead of traveling with jeeps and dugout canoes for about two weeks. In my case, it made my Adirondack cabin about 36 hours from Manú!

An oil engineer and a geologist met the plane and helped us out. The pilots unloaded our backpacks, tents, and food supplies. Then we walked across the enormous airstrip toward the camp's mess hall. We passed bulldozers, generators, drilling equipment, cables, hundreds of pipes, and rows of air-conditioned trailers which served as dormitories and offices for the field staff.

"Would you like to see inside?" asked one of the men amiably. We walked around a huge Hercules transport plane unloading drilling equipment and stepped into a cool blast of air. Four bunks lined one wall, desks another, a hot shower and modern toilet facilities were available.

"I can't believe all this luxury in the midst of untouched jungle," I exclaimed.

The engineer smiled and said, "We have to have it. Searching for oil in the Amazon is one of the most grueling jobs in the world. We work three weeks, then have nine days off with free air transportation to Cuzco or Lima. Besides the professional staff of engineers, geologists, and surveyors, there are over one thousand men here, most of them Peruvian laborers who cut trails for the seismic crews. They do all the manual work necessary to keep a camp like this going. Remember, we have no roads, only the Manú River and the air for transportation."

We continued past huge sleeping sheds slung with hammocks where the workmen lived and the few private campsites where female camp followers stayed. At last we came to the mess hall. The two men welcomed us into the screened open building next to the river. They set ice-cold, glass Coca-Cola bottles on the tables. We were enjoying another one of the "miracles" of modern technology—cool, pure drinks in a land whose average annual temperature probably has not fallen below 70°F for tens of thousands of years. Nothing ever tasted so good. As we sat sipping our Cokes, looking over the muddy Manú, a hundred questions ran through our minds. I started by asking, "How much does it cost a petroleum company to open and operate an exploratory camp like this?"

"About ten million dollars," answered the engineer coolly. "There are at least 15 other private companies looking for oil in Peru alone. There are others in Ecuador, Bolivia, Columbia, and Brazil. One of the most recent discoveries of petroleum is here in the upper Amazon. It might possibly yield four billion barrels a day by 1985. We're still not sure."

"How many acres does each company have?" asked Dr. George Woodwell.

"Around two and a half million," answered the geologist matter-of-factly.

"But each one's almost the size of Manú!" Felipe stormed. "That certainly doesn't say much about our priorities. One park vs. 16 oil camps!"

"Really," agreed the American engineer. "Anyway, each company leases a tract from the Peruvian government. Under their contract they can drill four test wells at two million dollars each and set up a base camp for another two million. They keep 46 percent of anything they strike; the government receives the remaining 54 percent. A contract runs for about 35 years."

I was beginning to see why gasoline prices were rising in the

United States. I had never realized how much work and money went into just finding crude oil, much less transporting and refining it. "What about ecological damages?" I queried. "How bad are they?"

"We try to keep all pollution to a minimum," said the engineer. "There's usually not much large-scale damage to the forest itself, because the total area cut down for test wells, campsites, and the airstrip comes to only two hundred to four hundred acres out of the two and a half million. The hundreds of miles of trails cut by seismic crews grow up with jungle vegetation within four to six months. At the main camp, we normally build in a septic system and garbage dump. Organic materials rot fast out here and metals rust away in no time. So there's not much mess left behind."

Felipe blurted out, "As I see it, the main threat to the environment is from surreptitious hunting and trapping by the laborers on their off time. It's a bad drain on local fish and game populations."

Thomas chimed in, "Obviously the main ecological problem is not from oil exploration or drilling. It comes after the oil is found. There could be possible water pollution from leaking oil barges or pipelines. Air pollution from burning off the wells. Even more important are the roads. They infiltrate the forest and spread havoc by often attracting large-scale agriculture, ranching, lumbering, colonization, and other types of exploitation that this ecosystem cannot handle."

"Well, it's the same old story," sighed Felipe. "Overpopulation! Saving a park like Manú is like trying to cure cancer with an aspirin. As long as the world population increases, we'll have more and more trouble protecting bits of rain forest from people who need farmland or rangeland for food and fiber."

We all fell silent, drinking our Cokes and thinking of this global problem.

I was eager to ask a far different question. Blushing, I said, "Tell us about the camp women. How can you permit them at such a huge operation?"

"If we didn't, we couldn't control the men." The geologist grinned. "They have to have some release. The women have a good life out here. The laborers treat them like queens. They make enough money eventually to return to their hometowns or go to Cuzco or Lima. They buy a little shop and make a better life for themselves. No one is in it for any longer than it takes to make a bundle."

I pondered this unusual life style, finishing my drink. Then the screen door flew open and one of the pilots came in to announce that our helicopters were ready. We all paired off. Felipe and I squeezed ourselves and our gear into a small chopper. The pilot, an Inca lad who looked about fifteen, smiled confidently and whirled us up into the sky.

We followed the brown Manú River, which wound like an anaconda through the endless carpet of trees. Not a sign of civilization. The park appeared roadless, free of airstrips, river ports, towns, and all other signs of human habitation, except four small ranger stations. Eighty percent of the 3.8 million acres of parkland was lowland rain forest transected by the river, while the park's western border stretched into the Andes to almost 12,000 feet.

The Manú River twists and turns through the Amazon rain forest of Peru, one of 1,100 tributaries of the Amazon River.

Now we were landing at Pakitza, a ranger control station at the eastern edge of the park. It lay at least 80 miles from the nearest permanent town, not counting the oil camp. We plunked down through the unbroken canopy and landed in a clearing beside the river. The helicopter pilot grinned good-bye and rattled away to shuttle the rest of our group and gear here.

We were in one of the most remote wilderness areas in the

world. As the last chopper roared off, we were left standing with a mound of tents, packs, and canned goods. A strangely silent jungle afternoon settled over us. Not a leaf stirred in the hot air. Not a bird called.

Felipe broke the heavy stillness with characteristic humor. "Next to the Spanish conquistadors," he boomed, "we're the greatest explorers ever!" He tipped his safari hat at an even more rakish angle, tightened the belt on his khaki hunting shirt, and strode toward the station. Three park rangers hurried down to meet us.

"How times and priorities change!" Felipe laughed delightedly. He admired the rangers in brown uniforms with revolvers, the Peruvian flag with the World Wildlife Fund panda symbol above it, and the well-kept station house. Turning to us, he explained, "In 1966, Major Ian Grimwood came here as a wildlife consultant and completed the master plan for the Manú National Park. World Wildlife Fund of Peru received twenty-five hundred dollars from WWF in Britain to buy the first outboard motor and

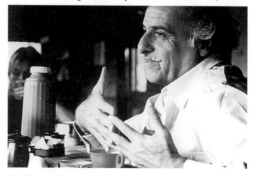

Dedicated Peruvian conservationist, Felipe Benavides, at Manú National Park. He won the J. Paul Getty Award for his work.

build a shelter here. Then on the seventh of March, 1968, President Fernando Belaunde declared it a National Reserve. In 1974, it became a National Park."

Felipe was being modest. I was sure that a man of his wit, stature, imagination, and political fearlessness had probably helped conceive of this enormous park and then fared forth fighting to get it. He kept on talking, as he stared up at the flags. "Meanwhile, World Wildlife Fund, USA, sent funds which helped build and equip the initial guard force. That enabled our government to get through time-consuming processes and accept major responsibility of administration and protection through the Ministry of Agriculture."

Felipe climbed the steps and proudly opened the door of the station. "In 1975, the Peruvian government finally budgeted

Our group at Pakitza ranger station, Manú. R. to L.: Dr. & Mrs. Woodwell, Felipe Benavides, Dr. Thomas Lovejoy, guide, Anne, and rangers.

$250,000 U.S. to run the park, train and support 22 guards," he said. "That's a hell of a long way to come in roughly 12 years!"

After a quick tour of the grounds, the others in our party prudently began setting up tents and unpacking boxes. Despite the tremendous trip, my fear of flying, and the fatigue of heat, I couldn't settle down. I was eager to explore the surrounding forest before dusk. Obligingly, two rangers offered to take me upriver. We eased into a dugout canoe with an outboard motor and knifed our way upstream. The setting sun shone bronze on brooding jungle walls. Here and there a flame-colored flowering tree lit up the dark foliage. A few fingers of palm fronds quivered in the light breeze. My exhaustion seemed to slip away. The only movement was the river itself. Turbulent currents and eddies swirled around jutting trunks and snags. The water was brown and totally opaque. This minor headwater of the Amazon—one of 1,100 tributaries— churned past us at two to four knots. It dropped only a half-inch per mile all the way to the Atlantic, 1,700 miles to the east. At one curve in the river we came upon thousands of sandpipers swirling above a sandbank. Their slim silhouettes in flight made them seem more like bats than birds.

We returned to Pakitza safely before the light failed. As I walked toward the station, a pair of scarlet macaws swerved overhead. The afterglow turned them acrylic red. For a brief instant they winged across the waxing moon, itself a three-quarter-full bud of camellia-white in a blue-black sky. I stopped in my tracks. A wave of reminiscence flooded over me. Back at my cabin, the white-throated sparrows would be singing plaintively from hidden balsam branches and spring peepers would be trilling in the misty marsh. The evening damp and cold would be creeping up from the black lake. How different this world was—dazzling, darkling, scintillating, somber, vibrant, vulnerable.

I found my companions sitting around a hissing lantern at a rustic table, discussing the oil camp. In general, everyone had been agreeably surprised by the minimal environmental impact we'd seen, yet a sense of gloom was with us. To ecologists, oil crews and camps mean that civilization is creeping ever closer to the remaining wildlands. And the spin-offs of civilization often spell disaster in the tropics. By the time we stopped talking, it was very late. I crawled into my tent. Soft flutelike frog sounds came from the

Campsite alongside the Manú River. Anne's orange Mt. Marcy tent from the Adirondacks showed up brightly in the jungle.

impenetrable forest. The camellia-white moon threw strange shadows on the orange nylon walls. It was cool, damp, humid. I slipped into my sleeping bag for comfort. All night, moisture condensed slowly on the walls and dripped silently on my head.

Early next morning we met Adolfo Cuentas, the park administrator, and Bruno Sanguinetti, wildlife representative from Peru's Ministry of Agriculture. They had prepared a 43-foot dugout canoe with a 50 HP engine for our trip through the park. A 50-gallon gas drum and an extra motor were lashed aboard. Our tents, packs, and food were piled in the center and covered with a tarp. The group was seated on the canoe's bottom fore and aft its length. By ten o'clock we were ready. Traveling upriver, we surprised 16 stately *jabirus* (large storks), stalking along a mudbank like so many preoccupied attorneys. Every submerged log and stump seemed to hold turtles sunning and sleeping under a sun sizzling enough to cook them in their shells. Sandbars were crisscrossed with tracks and prints of wading birds and mammals. Flocks of parakeets and tiny parrots flashed over the river constantly. No matter where we looked, wildlife was abundant.

The canoe twisted and turned back on its route, following Manú's meandering curves. In midafternoon we stopped by the trail to Cocha Cashu. Here was another small ranger station and research facility beside a lagoon lake. It was usually cut off from the main channel of the river except during peak flood time. Every so often, one of the river's ox-bow bends broke through its neck and made a new straight course. Then a *cocha* (lagoon) formed, cut off, and was left behind to stagnate and dream—except during floods. The three o'clock sun struck the surface like a laser beam. We were half-blinded by the brassy glare, half drugged by the heat. Unanimously, our party decided to go back to the river, take a swim, and pitch camp. We'd return to Cocha Cashu next dawn.

Trailing the group quietly through high forest, I was impressed by its dimness after the open lagoon. One thin sun shaft fell on a mossy tree trunk. I held out my light meter. It gave a weak flicker. No more than one to five percent of full sunlight ever reaches the floor of a primary rain forest—one which has never been cut or burned in historic times. Its thick canopy, like a lofty greenhouse roof, shuts out the blazing sun, keeps the atmosphere cool and damp, and protects the ground from pounding rains.

We chose a broad white sand beach for our bivouac and soon had a cookfire blazing. Supper was canned ravioli, ripe mangoes, and cups of cocoa laced with pisco, Peru's very special brandy. An ocellated poorwill was wailing as I fell asleep.

At five o'clock it was still dark and completely silent when I crawled from my tent. A slight rustling came from the 15-foot canebrake that edged our sandbar. Dripping dew, I thought. Relieving myself, I slipped back into my sleeping bag for another snooze. Later, I discovered the tracks of a large jaguar only 30 yards from the tent. No doubt the rustling had been this cat prowling by. I knew that jaguars are very curious and do not attack people. How I wished I'd caught its golden eyes in my flashlight beam. Still this visitor made my night at Manú one of my most memorable camping experiences.

As daybreak approached, I heard a distant humming like a generator starting or a high wind blowing through the canopy. It changed note, grew stronger, formed harmonics. Just then Felipe

emerged from his tent, tall and aristocratic, even in rumpled clothes and a new beard. "Howler monkeys!" Felipe exclaimed. "What a nice reveille!"

Back at Cocha Cashu, white dawn mist still clung to the torpid water. The morning was clear, cool, and comfortable. Three of us crept into a shallow shell of a canoe, collectively clutching more than $5,000 worth of camera equipment. The donkeylike bellows of horned screamers resounded from the

Military Macaw in palm at Cocha Cashu.

shores, while overhead the first petulant shrieking of parrots and macaws began. A few wild Muscovy ducks floated on the placid surface. Cormorants, herons, egrets, anhingas, rails, and kingfishers posed on damp branches.

Suddenly we heard a loud splash directly ahead. We peered into the low-hanging trees. Two, three, four, no, _five_ hoatzins stared back! They are peculiar, primitive birds which resemble pheasants, though not related, and which have claws on their wings. A sixth young one was scrambling up onto a branch like a lad about to dive into his favorite swimming hole. Three cameras clicked sideways in unison as the three of us almost overturned the tiny craft. We were very close to these odd birds with their glaring red eyes, bare blue face patches, and crested heads. They reminded me of huge brown cuckoos—until I saw a youngster swim by underwater and then claw his way onto overhanging branches to his nest! Circling Cocha Cashu we must have counted over 30 hoatzins and seen about ten percent of the 1,000 bird species in the park. This watery remnant of the Manú River ranked as my finest birding experience since visiting Corkscrew Swamp Sanctuary in Florida as an Audubon tour leader.

On our way back to the river the morning was climaxed once again by the sight of 25 _huanganas_ (peccaries). They had dashed ahead of us, gaining a few minutes' lead. Yet before we could trace them to the riverbank, the spoor of a jaguar was already superimposed upon their tracks! Had my nocturnal visitor swum the Manú and decided upon pork chops for breakfast?

We continued upriver toward Tayakomé, the interior ranger station. That night we slept at the heart of the park 100 miles from the closest settlement. We were perhaps 30 miles from a tribe of indomitable Amahuacas and two miles from a village of peaceful Machiguengas. Sometime during the night, ghostly sounds of a drum and rattles filtered into my dreams. At first I imagined one of our party had a transistor radio. Then reason told me that the Machiguengas must be having a celebration. Their primitive music added a new dimension to Amazon impressions.

Indeed, their headman, or _cacique_, came to see us next day. He was called Itayano. A black toucan-feather band surrounded his forehead. He explained that he was keeping sober to look after the men, women, and children who often got dead drunk on _masato_ (fermented crude liquor) and lay about the village all day.

The next morning I decided to hike alone into the dry land rain forest, known as _terra firme_, to explore and photograph. "Be careful," Felipe warned me. "The terra firme makes up 90 percent of the Amazon basin, and it's terribly easy to get lost in there.

There's nothing to eat or drink. A person can starve or thirst to death."

No doubt the Machiguengas would have disagreed with Felipe. Being unskilled in foraging for food in Amazonia, I heeded his words. I called out what time I expected to be back and double-checked my compass bearings.

Once inside the forest, a hundred shades of green engulfed me. Wild figs, *Cecropia*, cedrelas, myrtles, *Bignonia*, rosewood, lianas, air plants, ferns, vines, and orchids all grew beneath the 125-foot canopy composed of tall trees like the Brazil nut. Many palms grew in the understory. *Iriartia* had prop roots six feet long; *Astrocaryum*, wicked spines; *Sheelia,* long, arching fishtail fronds. In tiny pools of water trapped at the bases of bromeliads clinging to tree branches, more than 65 species of small plants and animals thrived. Fallen logs were clustered with creamy mushrooms, lichens, rust-red fungi, purple toadstools, yellow slime molds, pale water molds, and other saprophytes. Although the forest seemed dominated by the green producers, it was also an important place for decomposers. In fact, they are one secret of the rain forest's incredibly rich productivity and ultra-rapid recycling of nutrients.

Felipe was right. Of the biomass I saw in the dry land rain forest 99.9 percent was vegetation; 0.9 percent was animal. Putting it another way, for every 5,000 plants, there was one animal individual. Conversely, along waterways: the *igapos* (permanently flooded swamp forest), the *varzea* (annually flooded forest), cochas (lagoons), and rivers, fish and wildlife abounded. Famine vs. Feast.

On the ground hundreds of ants and termites scurried about. Most evident were the big *saubas* (leaf-cutting ants). They are well described by Henry Walter Bates, the famous nineteenth-century English naturalist, who spent years in the Amazon. Columns of these ants were busily hauling bits of leaves to their subterranean galleries. Below a large mound of red earth lay deep shafts in which leaf litter was used as a medium on which to grow fungi. This was the food of ant larvae. Watching them intently, I now saw a slow-moving army ant wander past my boot. Hastily, I stepped back. Nearby, a thin line of fire ants was threading its way up a *Tachigalia* plant (member of the Leguminosae family) to their nests in the leaves' hollow petioles. This symbiotic arrangement insures that the ants have a home while the plant benefits by having them eat up other vegetation which tries to crowd it out. For a moment my imagination multiplied all the ants I could see in a ten-foot radius by the almost 2.5 million square miles of Amazon territory. The mathematics were awesome. Truly ants must outnumber in individuals all other terrestrial animals. Of the 12,000 species in the world, 7,600 kinds of ants have been described scientifically. During my morning trek, two of the striking differences between tropical rain forest and temperate woodlands became evident. Any five acres around my cabin in the Adirondacks would have ten to twelve kinds of trees growing. Here, in the same-sized area, an average of 200 species could be found! Such density means that individual members of any one species are thinly scattered over wide spaces. I never saw a solid stand of any one tree, such as the balsam flats or birch groves up north. This diversity and distribution results in healthier plants.

The other difference was the soil. Where a large tree had been uprooted, I noticed with astonishment that the layer of litter and humus was only a few inches thick. The lower level looked reddish, highly leached, and infertile. The taproots of this fallen forest giant had penetrated down only a couple of feet while laterals had spread out horizontally for at least 25 yards. Mycorrhizal fungi grew all over the roots and in the soil and humus.

Indeed, most nutrients in the tropical rain forest are not found in soil as they are in the U.S. mid-western corn belt. They reside in the vegetation itself. It's not the *soil* that's fertile, it's the *foliage*. That luxuriant, green, exuberant forest is totally deceiving. As Dr. Betty Meggers, famed Amazon anthropologist at the Smithsonian Institution, says, "It's a counterfeit paradise!"

Seventy to ninety percent of the total nutrient supply within the ecosystem is locked up in the foliage. Minerals are recycled directly from dead leaves, branches, and wood right back into living leaves, branches, and trunks. Those weird decomposers, especially the fungi, quickly break down organic materials and pass them into the roots. They do their job in about *six weeks*. To decompose tree litter, it takes one year in temperate deciduous woodlands and seven years in far northern forests. Less than one percent of the nutrients escape during this speedy, thrifty, "rot-to-root" procedure. Deep topsoils never accumulate. The forest survives despite its impoverished soils, not because of them. Their main function is to support, not to nourish. In fact, most of Amazonia is literally a desert covered with trees.

Exactly how many tree species exist in the Amazon basin, nobody knows. About 25,000 have been identified. Perhaps as many more are still undescribed. The entire tropical rain forest performs its greatest service by buffering torrential rains (more than 100 inches per year) from damaging the thin soils. Also by keeping ground temperatures low enough (below 77°F), so that bacterial action and decomposition can proceed as they should. I had plenty to think about on the way back to Tayakomé.

The next day we started back down the Manú practically doubling our speed as we moved with the current. Sunshine, light showers, rainbows, and butterflies played over our huge dugout all day. We were treated to more wildlife diversions. A river otter scuttled down a bank. Five glossy capybaras bathed on a beach but bumbled off like big guinea pigs when they saw us. A bevy of little spectacled caimans (close cousins to crocodiles and alligators) slept upon a hot sandbank. In one clearing, four coppery-colored howler monkeys groomed one another with their prehensile tails curled up tight as watch springs. "Some people call this a Green Hell," exclaimed Thomas with great enthusiasm. "I call it a Green Heaven!"

"Right," chimed in Felipe. "At least ten percent of our planet's species are living right here in the Amazon basin. We're seeing the richest forest fauna and flora in the world."

As the heat of the afternoon peaked, we sprawled out on the canoe bottom. Bruno Sanguinetti, standing tall and looking cool in a thin white shirt, engagingly explained the new forest and wildlife law. It was signed into existence by President Juan Velasco Alvarado on May 13, 1975. For the first time, Peru's natural resources (including animal products and ornamental butterflies) are now declared public domain and protected in varying degrees. "It took three years and all our Peruvian experts on fauna and flora to make this law," said Bruno proudly. "Fortunately, most of the resources in this country are still so wild that they merely need protection, not management or restoration."

"I'm not so sure about that!" snapped the indefatigable Felipe. "Colonization and civilization are spreading faster than you think, my friend. If Manú were opened to roads or airstrips, its vegetation, wildlife, fish, and soils would be destroyed in twenty years. The resources would never recover. We need not only protection, but plenty of research, management, and land use planning."

I sat up straight in the canoe. Felipe must be exaggerating. Twenty years to wipe out this immense tract of rain forest? But my travels were to show me that even *his* estimate was optimistic.

No one talked any more. A sense of uneasiness seized us. Sunset was coming. We all stared up at the skein of clouds turning from cerise to maroon to gray. The river was lit with a saffron sheen. Directly ahead, an almost full moon edged through heaps of cumulus clouds. They were milky marble dappled in slate-black, pearl, pewter, and cream, and shot through with streaks of shiny silver. But the lightning was far away. We continued running downstream by moonlight as our ranger-boatmen skillfully navigated deadfalls and snags. One wrong turn and we could be toppled into the water and swept downriver. To regroup and make an emergency camp, soaking wet and without gear, would have been a formidable task.

Before midnight, we were all safely asleep in our tents at Pakitza. Next day we regretfully prepared to leave Manú. Instead of the three choppers that had delivered us, however, a lone whirly bird arrived for us in the afternoon. The pilot explained tersely that one machine had crashed, another was on an urgent medical run into the jungle, and only his helicopter could be spared. "I'll have to make three or four trips," he reckoned, gauging the pile of camping equipment and our assorted weights. "Well, come on," he motioned imperatively to Thomas and me. "You two are the lightest. We'll fill 'er up with as much gear as possible."

Half an hour later we were dumped unceremoniously on the heliport of the oil camp. It was three o'clock. The delay meant all of us couldn't possibly fly out to Cuzco before dark. That airport had no night facilities. The camp was abuzz with activity. Mechanics hurried about makeshift hangars. Drivers ran bulldozers up into the gigantic Hercules transport and disappeared into its bowels to offload heavy equipment. Workers tugged on lengths of pipe and bunches of couplings. No one paid the slightest attention to us. Thomas and I strolled closer to the plane and watched in fascination.

The muffled clacking of a helicopter grew louder. I glanced up expectantly. "That sure was a fast turnaround flight," I said. "Maybe Felipe and George will be aboard."

But it was a different chopper that landed. Slung from its frame was a stretcher with an injured Peruvian workman strapped in. I edged nearer; Thomas hung back. "Better not get in the way," he warned. "We're really only guests here."

"But maybe I can help," I exclaimed. The man was critically wounded, having fallen backward onto a sharp sapling he had just cut along the trail. The point had rammed into his anus and ripped the large intestine. The man needed surgery and massive doses of antibiotics as soon as possible. But the oil camp had no doctor or nurse. The only hope was to fly him out at once in the Hercules to Cuzco and get him into a hospital before dark. Otherwise, by morning, shock and infection would surely have set in. I walked over to the engineer in charge and asked if anyone would accompany the poor fellow on the flight.

"No," he muttered. "I can't spare anyone here. I'm the only one really who could get away, and I shouldn't leave with all this activity."

A daring plan grew in my mind. "I'll go!" I volunteered. "I recently finished a course to become an emergency medical technician. I can at least watch for shock or hemorrhage. I speak Spanish, too, so I can talk to the patient. I'll stay in Cuzco tonight and meet the others there in the morning after the Twin Otter brings them up."

"I'll go, too," volunteered Thomas.

"The engineer stared at us gratefully, then nodded agreement. "Okay," he said, "but the Hercules is hardly a commercial jetliner, you know."

"It doesn't matter. It'll get us there," I reasoned. "How soon is it leaving?"

"Right away." The engineer shouted more orders. The injured man was carried inside and laid on the floor of the plane. I followed hesitantly. A hundred men gathered around the rear door and huge loading ramp to gaze up at me. I was the only woman there, except for the camp followers.

Inside, I looked around in dismay. The Hercules was totally empty and as large as a barn. There were no windows, benches, or carpeting. The metal floor was smeared with axle grease, motor oil, and clumps of mud. The Peruvian lay impassively on an aluminum stretcher. Then my mind started working. Throwing shyness to the winds, I turned and crisply demanded blankets, ropes, and drinking water. One of the geologists started off to get them. But the Hercules' props were already turning and the giant doors shutting. The pilots were motioning everyone off the field. Only an hour and a half of daylight remained. The flight took over an hour. The door banged closed. Thomas and I were alone with the injured workman without water or a single medical supply.

Kneeling beside the stretcher, I swiftly ran down a mental list: Reassure the patient. Keep him warm. Make him immobile.

Maintain an open airway. Check pulse frequently. I spoke calmly in Spanish to the man and was rewarded with a weak smile. Taking off my light jacket, I covered his chest and loosened his belt. I felt beneath his buttocks for blood. Nothing. His pulse was faint but normal.

Now the transport plane was moving. An incredible vibration filled the hollow chamber. I had an awful vision of the stretcher sliding clear across the floor during the steep angle of takeoff and smashing the laborer against the rear door. Somehow we had to hold it in place. Groping through the oily filth on the floor, I found a recessed ring used for tying down machinery.

"Thomas," I yelled. "Grab a ring on the other side and help hold this stretcher."

I gripped it firmly in my left hand, grabbed the stretcher with my right, and spread my knees to steady my body. How could such an enormous hulk ever become airborne, I wondered. My fear of flying welled up. No way to see outside. Nothing to do but shut my eyes and hang on for dear life.

Miraculously, the Hercules lifted—smoothly, ponderously, without a shudder. The vibrations ceased. The workman, Thomas, and I stayed in one place. I opened my eyes and saw a few overhead lights had come on. I could see my watch. Time for a pulse reading. Take the vital signs.

After half an hour, I was sure the man's condition was stable. I spoke to him comfortingly and then asked Thomas to watch our patient. I got up to find the cockpit. A steel ladder led forward to another level, so I climbed up. Abruptly, I was dazzled by the setting sun spearing straight into the cockpit. Between me and the awful Andes were only two instrument panels, two sheets of Plexiglass, and two Peruvian pilots. They turned to greet me. One set up a jump seat between their chairs; the other placed his headset over my ears. A tango drowned out the motor roar.

The last rays of sun were splendid. They turned the massive snowfields below us to reddish-gold, then backlit the towering, jagged ranges with electric lavender. All at once, I was no longer afraid of these mountains. I was totally transfixed.

"How long to Cuzco?" I managed to ask.

"Too long." The captain frowned. "A headwind is slowing us down. We'll land with only about ten minutes of light to spare."

"Can you radio ahead for an ambulance and doctor?" I urged.

"Already did," answered the copilot. "But that doesn't mean

they'll be there."

"Well, let's hope so. I'd better get back to my patient. Thank you for this magnificent vista."

The laborer was still satisfactory. I stroked his head and told him about Manú to take his mind off the pain. What his chances for recovery were, I didn't know. Surely he was in for a severe infection with the contents of his large bowel loose in the abdominal cavity. I prayed there was a good hospital and competent surgeon at the other end of this flight.

After circling once over Cuzco, the plane landed as neatly as an Andean condor. The rear doors opened and four mechanics jumped in and carried stretcher and man out. The pilots switched off engines and lights. They grabbed their briefcases and appeared ready to leave for home. I searched the grounds for an ambulance. Nothing. "Call, please call, as soon as you get home," I begged them. One gave a thumb's up as they walked away.

Then Thomas and I were sitting alone, with the Peruvian lying supine on his stretcher, upon a cold cement sidewalk outside a closed and darkened airport. The chill night wind whistled down from the mountains and turned our corner eerily. I shivered uncontrollably. Compared to the heat and humidity of the Amazon, this felt like Alaska. Finally, after what seemed like hours, an ambulance arrived. Two attendants carted the workman off. I never knew his name. I never learned what happened to him. All I know is I met him at Manú and said good-bye at Cuzco.

Four years later, most of the exploratory oil camps were gone. The rich promise of petroleum—the "black gold"—had petered out. The pipeline from the upper reaches of the Amazon to the Pacific brought a mere trickle to tankers. City Service's outpost was abandoned. Its trails and airstrip slowly grew back to jungle.

UPDATE

- *Manú National Park has grown to be four-fifths the size of the Adirondack Park, roughly 4,700,000 acres, thanks to the addition of a Biosphere Reserve (UNESCO), the Manú Reserved Zone, and a "Cultural" zone of human settlement. It was declared a World Heritage Site in 1987.*

- The Amerindian tribes are considered a part of the park's natural system, and they are left to use the park as they please as long as their lifestyle does not threaten park objectives.

- The overland journey to Manú now takes only a couple of days, once one has arrived by air or gravel road near its borders and has procured a dugout or boat to go upriver. Six ecotourism companies are said to operate 20-bed lodges in Manú's Reserved and Cultural zones.

- Nevertheless, Manú is being nibbled away on all sides. It is one of the most disturbing potential catastrophes in the making. Here's a list of problems:

  1. In the upper elevations of the park there are 4,000 cattle. The cattle owners burn grasslands regularly to make new grass for them.
  2. Colonization is occurring along the eastern reserve area of eastern Manú. Resettlement is needed to protect the park from illegal squatters.
  3. A North American company has obtained mining rights for gold along a river in eastern Manú. This could possibly attract large numbers of people into the park.
  4. Wildlife poachers enter the park along three rivers in the northwest.
  5. There are illegal <u>and</u> licensed loggers on the eastern and southern boundaries of the park.
  6. The Peruvian Government has appropriated two sections of park for oil prospecting. This violates the Forestry law. No work has yet been done, apparently.
  7. The "Marginal Highway of the Jungle" is planned along the Manú River to connect Urubamba with Madre de Dios areas. This would be a major threat to the National Park, with thousands of squatters settling along the roadway. Efforts have been made to relocate the Highway outside the park. Technical government offices may have proposed an alternative.
  8. Budgets have deteriorated in all Peruvian protected areas. Radios, boats, motors, and field equipment are breaking down. A severe cutback in number of park guards may affect integrity of the park. Likewise, widespread political turmoil has weakened park protection.
  9. On the bright side, several Peruvian conservation organizations (NGOs) have joined under a "Technical Committee for the Defense of Manú." So far, with political endorsement, they have prevented road and canal construction near or in the park.

- These observations came from the World Conservation Monitoring Centre in Cambridge, England. They were written in August 1987 and updated/revised February 1998.

13

MY GREEN HEAVEN

After I got back from Peru, I spent the summer and fall impatiently at my Adirondack cabin, waiting for the long dry season in the Amazon. I was eager to start the second phase of my assignment. However, the cabin needed extensive winterizing. So there was wood to split and stack. The water tank to empty and turn over. The pump to drain. I collected boxes of kindling. Sadly, I nailed plywood sheets over the cabin's lower windows so piles of snow would not break the glass. Now all was in dark below. Little by little, my cabin space shrank in upon itself to hold in the warmth as the cold, rain, and sleet increased.

Nevertheless, it was a time of high anticipation. I steeped myself in books and articles about Amazonia. I fell asleep at night imagining the mighty river, the strange animals I'd see, the new people I'd meet. As always, it would be an adventure just to be aboard the M/S *Lindblad Explorer*. I had traveled on her three times before as staff ecologist for natural history cruises. Somehow, I didn't quite believe that the trim, 250-foot, red-and-white, world-circling ship would actually poke her bows up the Amazon River, three-quarters of a continent inland, to Iquitos, Peru. The 2,300-mile stretch of river between Iquitos and the Atlantic is technically considered an oceanic waterway. It can accommodate boats with drafts of 20 feet year-round.

After closing up the cabin and leaving my woodshed full, I flew to Lima in November. I got out just before the freeze up. Then, I doubled back over the Andes to Iquitos, only 500 miles from the Pacific Ocean. This was the "jump off" port. My first sight of the *Explorer* with her halo of lights glowing in the hot, humid Peruvian night made me catch my breath in admiration. The ship would be my home for a month. I climbed expectantly up the gangway and opened a door to the main deck. A rush of air conditioning and the chatter of 75 passengers washed over me. Everyone was having a pre-midnight snack and getting acquainted as we waited for the ship to cast off her lines and head down the mightiest river on earth.

I shook hands all around and began mentally categorizing the passengers and staff. Some were old friends from other cruises. Others were "regulars"—ardent amateur naturalists and nature photographers who often sailed on the *Explorer*. A few were nervous newcomers, not really sure what they'd gotten into. Most of the passengers were retired couples or widows, well-to-do and well-traveled. Only one couple had scraped and saved for months to afford this luxurious floating nature tour. The staff, of course, swapped work for free passage, meals, and laundry.

One passenger stood out from the rest. He was a striking blond Finn in his thirties, impeccably dressed in tailored slacks, knit sport shirt, and sleek boots. His green eyes were slanted like a Lapp's and had a disconcerting way of constantly flicking around the room. He just didn't look like the "*Lindblad* type." He appeared to be neither bird watcher, photographer, skin diver, nor nature lover. He looked as if he belonged at an elegant bar in some sophisticated European city, not deep in the jungle.

The ship's siren blew. We heard the great engines start to purr beneath us. Fifteen minutes to departure! Everyone hurried on deck and lined the railings. Heavy hawsers dropped with splashes from the moorings, and the gangway was laboriously cranked up tight against the ship's side. A few sleepy but curious Peruvian longshoremen stood on the dock to watch the pretty little vessel depart. Otherwise, no fanfare, no waving, no farewells. At midnight sharp, the bow slowly veered sideways, and an ever-widening slice of black water appeared between ship and dock. I could feel the current catch and pivot the ship. Five minutes later we were headed downstream into the dark jungle night.

Passengers began going into their staterooms or into the bar for a nightcap. I walked forward and climbed to the deck above the bridge. Alone up here, I could be fully aware of the whole river, its smells and moods, undisturbed. Two huge spotlight beams probed across the swirling surface, searching for small fishing boats, dugouts, drifting logs, and uprooted trees. Hundreds of insects had already discovered these lights and formed miniature swirling snowstorms around the glass. Back home, I thought, it would actually be snowing. I inhaled deeply. The air was heavily laden with pungent odors of living and decomposing things, different from anything I'd ever smelled before. This air was alive. For an hour, hair streaming, nostrils flaring, I rode right at the front of the ship, absorbing the Amazon night. Then a spatter of rain began. I turned and groped my way back toward the narrow inner stairway. As the door swung open, a band of light shone out onto the back deck. I glimpsed the red glow of a cigarette and gleam of a well-shined boot propped against the rear deck rail before the door swung shut behind me.

Early next morning the ship anchored off the main channel and we made our first side trip. Daily we left on explorations up tributaries, using rubber, inflatable landing craft called Zodiaks. Six staff members each swung one down from the top deck with a hook, winch, and kingpole, and drove his or her Zodiac to the gangway to onload eager passengers. I helped 12 people into my raft and sat them along the rubber sides. We set off upriver. At sunrise, with mist hanging over the water, it looked like a large, shallow, summery Adirondack lake. As the day cleared, the skies became changeable. Great cumulus clouds built up dramatically, then dissipated. At different quarters of the horizon, black squalls would form, dump heavy loads of rain, and move on. By evening, the red ball of sun would hang in hazy solitude, undisputed, then disappear from a clear sky.

I could see that the Upper Amazon (called the Solimoẽs above Manáus, Brazil, and the Marañon in Peru) is as muddy as a cup of coffee with cream. I nicknamed it the "milk-coffee-river-sea." Everywhere one looked, the water was moving, moving, moving, despite the vast flatness and distance from the Atlantic. I filled a glass and let it settle for half an hour in the bottom of my Zodiak. It changed from cafe-au-lait to the clarity of what one might expect out of a New York City water tap. As wild river water, it was probably purer than most city sources. Even with that sediment, it could be drunk fairly safely. Most water in the Amazon basin is still uncontaminated by man-made pollution except below the large cities and towns. Even the raw sewage of Manáus (over half a million population) and Belém (over a million) is quickly digested and diluted by the enormous liquid mass of this river. Whatever bacteria and viruses might be present are mostly scattered, oxidized, and settled out by the sediments.

We returned to the ship for lunch and a nap in the heat of the day and set forth again that afternoon. The tributaries we traveled were low, since this was the main dry season. Looking upward as I steered the motor, I could see dead branches, grasses, and roots hanging from the high-water mark along the banks. Six months from now, in rainy season, the river level would be 30 to 35 feet above our heads.

The Finn was in my boat. He was wearing the skimpiest of bikinis and a superb tan. He lolled on the rubber bow with his camera exactly as if he were on the French Riviera. All eyes were directed either to him or to the bushes which lined the narrow channel we were threading, where new species of birds and amphibians might lurk. No one bothered to look behind us until an ominous roll of thunder boomed. We all turned and saw a leaden mass of clouds laced with lightning covering half the sky. It seemed to have come out of nowhere and was moving fast. I revved up the motor and began looking for overhanging trees under which we might shelter. There was no chance of getting back to the _Explorer_ before the deluge hit.

As the squall line approached, some older ladies began cowering under beach towels or windbreakers. I should have brought plastic tarps for my passengers. It was a good lesson. Never trust the Amazon. I found a tree, tied up to a stout root, and watched in fascination as the squall raced toward us. The surface of the stream turned from brownish-blue to silvery black. A sheet of rain as solid as cotton pushed over us. And finally a gust of wind buffeted our bodies. The temperature dropped 15 degrees in 10 minutes and an inch of rain fell in the first half-hour. It was my first experience with an Amazon cloudburst. Little did I know that such storms can release 40 times as much water as an average rain in the northeastern United States. Fortunately, most are short-lived. Within an hour the sky and stream looked blue and brown, much as they had before. The main change was that 12 passengers and one staff member were totally sodden and shivering with cold.

"Whoever thought we'd be chilly in the Amazon?" I joked, trying to cheer up my miserable crew. I cruised hastily downstream toward the main river. "Brandy and hot coffee coming up," I shouted encouragingly. A few people smiled. The rest remained glum. The Finn flashed his even white teeth at me, although his flesh was prickled with goose bumps. No wonder, with what he had on.

As we swung into the main Amazon itself, two other Zodiaks neared. Our trio headed for the ship. The placid mirror-mood of the morning had been replaced by a frothy tumble of mud-colored waves. Now we were soaked from spray. I slowed down. At this rate, the *Explorer* lay at least an hour away. I began to think of hypothermia, pneumonia, bronchitis, arthritis, and other ills that might crop up among the passengers from this sudden chilling. Still, there was nothing to do but steer wisely and get us back safely. This was all part of a natural history cruise.

Ahead, some sort of floating building was moored to the bank. Another fishing shack, I thought, until one of the Zodiaks steered toward it. Paulo, our Brazilian interpreter, was piloting that boat. He beckoned imperatively at us to follow him. When all three of the Zodiaks were jostling alongside the shack, Paulo clambered out and disappeared inside the building. Two minutes later he came out of the floating store carrying three quart bottles of what looked like patent cough medicine. A broad grin split his face. "Cashasha, everyone! Good Brazilian firewater. Bye, bye, cold shivers. Drink so you won't get sick."

A bottle was passed around each Zodiak. People sputtered and gasped as the fiery liquid hit their stomachs and bloodstreams. Then they asked for seconds. Before long, three very tipsy boatloads of people were bucking down the Amazon river, laughing and singing. No one became ill—perhaps because of this cashasha remedy. Our story made a hit that night at the evening "recap" before dinner.

As the ship traveled downriver, I began to notice changes. The river widened, deepened, and seemed less closed in by the exuberant rain forest. Whereas the Manú had been a single meandering channel, bordered by dense vegetation, the Upper Amazon was braided and full of channels. Daily the horizon receded and diminished. Islands came and went. Swamps, igapos, canebreaks, and mudbars edged the river. The only thing that never changed was the color of the water.

This far inland it was all muddy, or "white," for torrents came rushing down from the Andes rich with suspended particles of eroded soil and minerals. It is low in bacteria and almost neutral on the acid-alkaline scale (pH 6.6 to 7.0).

Further downstream we would encounter "black" water the color of strong tea. This originates from impoverished sandy forest soils far away from the main river itself. "A black river is a starvation river," say the natives. It is marked by a paucity of fish, insects, and aquatic life. The water is very acidic (pH around 4.0). Clear blue and green waters flow down from the ancient granite highlands of central Brazil and the Guiana region. These are also poor in animal and plant life and have pH values of 5.5 to 6.5. Thus the chemical makeup of Amazonian waters indicates the type of land-scape from which they arise.

White, black, blue, green—all these waters meet, sometimes in fluid patterns like watered silk, and finally mix. Eventually 200 to 500 _billion_ cubic feet of water and 106 _million_ cubic feet of sediment surge out to sea EACH DAY from the Amazon's mouth. Churning, eddying, eroding, sucking, pulsing, whirling, and roiling, they rush inexorably eastward. These turbid, untamed waters drain four-tenths of South America and carry 20 percent of all river water in the world.

One afternoon, our Zodiaks left the _Explorer_ for a fishing spree at Campinhas, a white water lagoon. Several of us were determined to catch piranhas. The ship's good-natured chef had offered to fry them for supper. We sat jigging with simple hand lines and baited hooks. By now, I knew the Finn would be in my boat, scantily clad, snapping pictures of everything, and charming the lot of us. Today was no exception.

Within minutes he had hooked the first piranha. It fell snapping and thrashing into the Zodiak. Twelve pairs of bare feet jerked up. Despite their small size (7 to 17 inches), each of the four species of piranhas has super-sharp teeth. A fish can take a grape-sized chunk of flesh. However, piranhas normally attack only bleeding or thrashing prey. They bite in hunger or defense— as they might do now. We often swam in clear black water tributaries with piranhas and no one was bitten. The Finn dispatched his fish. Feet went back down. Fishing resumed.

In two hours we had enough piranhas for all 75 passengers and six staff members. Delicious! Mysteriously the Finn produced a bottle of cashasha. That was enough firewater to send us singing and shouting back to the ship. From then on, our group felt a special kinship. Many jokes revolved around the Finn's piranha party.

The fish life of Campinhas lagoon was really extraordinary. Hundreds of walking catfish swirled the water with their hard fins. One throw of the round casting net brought up 13 catfish, a black piranha, a wolf characin, and a gorgeous brown-and-yellow _tucu-naré_ (a cichlid).

This abundance of fish life was because of the dry season. Lowering water levels were constricting the aquatic habitats, and their denizens were crowded together as if in a soup pot that has boiled too long. Come rains and higher water, these creatures would scatter out over huge areas and be far more difficult to catch. In fact, many of the large characoids and other major food fishes would head up tributaries to the inundated floodplain forests. There they would feed and fatten on fruits and seeds that fall into the water. Both adults and young fish would find valuable nourishment in these flooded forests.

More than 2,000 fish species have been recorded in the Amazon basin—more than from any other river system on earth. Louis Agassiz, 19th century Swiss-American naturalist, noted that the Amazon contains more fish species than the Atlantic Ocean from pole to pole. Certainly fish is a prized form of protein along the entire waterway. Every town that we visited had a fish market filled daily with fresh catches. I was told that commercial fishing operations between the Río Negro near Manáus and the Amazon, until recently, netted 1,000 pounds per morning. Between 1968 and

Huge catfish and ambitious cat on floating house-dock, Amazon River.

1975, the number of commercial fishing boats on the Amazon jumped from 82 to 748. Because of this increase, fish were being overexploited. They were further decreasing due to heavy logging activities and agricultural changes in the river floodplain forests to grow rice and pasture water buffalo. When these riverbanks are deforested and swampy lowlands are flooded millions of tree fruits and seeds disappear. Fish which eat these food items may die or move away.

On our cruise down the mighty river, in contrast to the Manú, we did not see a single turtle or large caiman. Hunters have been harvesting these animals along major waterways for centuries. The farther downstream we went, the more despondent I felt about the exploitation of the river turtle. In *The Naturalist on the River Amazon*, Bates wrote of the earlier plenitude of turtles. He estimated that in the 1860s, 48 million eggs laid by almost half a million females were harvested *yearly* by natives for food and oil. Hundreds of thousands of adults were killed for meat and shell. Now, not 120 years later, we naturalists aboard *Lindblad Explorer* did not see one turtle along the 2,300 miles of main Amazon channels. As for caimans, the tanning factories in Manáus were reported to have handled five million skins of black caiman annually until 1971.

In 1971, Brazil passed legislation protecting both river turtles and caimans and the principal nesting beaches of turtles. (Only about 10,000 females still use these sites.) But only 50 Amazonian game wardens cover this gigantic area. Poaching continues.

Bates wrote, "Alligators were seen along the coast [banks] almost every step of the way, and the passengers [aboard river boats] amused themselves, from morning until night, by firing at them with rifle and ball."

We took Zodiaks into isolated backwaters one night to search for caimans. We startled a few small specimens but none measured longer than one foot. Quite a contrast to the 20-foot creatures mentioned by Bates.

Manatees were also seemingly nonexistent. They have been coveted by Indians and *caboclos* (mixed-blood Brazilians) for centuries. People used them for meat, hide, lamp oil, and bone tools. In the late 1700s, for example, 8,500 animals were slaughtered at a single hunting station. The meat and oil were exported to Holland and her colonies. Then between 1950 and 1954, the number of hides taken in the state of Amazonas diminished from 38,000 to 5,500.

Both Brazilian and Peruvian laws protect manatees and have declared the animals officially endangered. But insufficient enforcement presents the same problem. Poaching continues.

Shortly before we arrived in Leticia, Columbia's Amazon port, we made a short stop to see a band of Jivaro Amerindians. On the jungle trail to their camp, I found myself walking with Rolf, the Finn. We chatted about the cruise. I was surprised at his enthusiasm. He obviously knew nothing about natural history, seemed to be a terrible photographer, and hated to get his hair wet. Yet he went out bikini-clad, on every field excursion. Then he appeared each evening in the ship's lounge attired in the finest tailored European suits. He always invited everyone at his table for drinks and dutifully asked older ladies to dance. He conversed knowledgeably in five languages on many subjects. When I asked innocently about his profession, he spoke vaguely about "being in finances."

I was intrigued. Somehow he didn't quite ring true. Yet he was most attractive. Why would a good-looking man like this be walking half-naked through the Amazon jungle to see equally half-naked Amerindians?

Then we were at the Jivaro camp, gawking at bare-breasted women, grass-skirted men, red-painted faces, tooth-and-claw necklaces. Cameras clicked and whirled. Jivaro men posed nonchalantly. They sullenly put on a demonstration of their shooting accuracy with eight-foot blowguns and feathered darts.

Jivaro women wear achiote red paint on their faces and grass breast coverings.

"They use curare on the dart tips to kill game," whispered Rolf, pressing softly against me. "It's a nerve poison which kills an animal in just minutes." I looked at him in surprise. How would a Finnish financier know something like that?

In the stilt-legged huts, women suckled babies on the floor and old men slept in hammocks. Outside, kids tagged after passengers, begging for candy and coins. The whole Jivaro settlement had an unreal quality. Later our staff anthropologist told us that this particular band no longer lives from the land and the river. Instead they can live off tourists because enough travelers know of their existence. Thus, these Jivaros can afford to dress up, paint their faces, and hang around camp all day. They survive on the tips and bribes paid them for photographs. Remembering the Guaymí of Panama, I realized that here was another rare and endangered group of humans. I learned later that the number of Amerindian tribes in Brazil has plummeted from roughly 230 to 143 since 1900. The decrease is the result of diseases, persecution, and ecological problems caused by official relocations to unsuitable lands.

The Finn and I wandered through the camp as he took dozens of photographs. Jokingly, I said, "I'd love to have one of those grass skirts to wear around my Adirondack cabin on hot summer days."

"So would I," he replied. "Why not? Let's buy two. In fact, let's buy the whole costume—men's headpiece, the wristbands, women's grass breast covering." He grinned infectiously. "We could wear them to the masquerade party tomorrow night."

So we bargained for and bought the outfits. Then we started back along the trail, looking for achiote bushes. The seeds inside the prickly pods of these plants are used in cooking. They also yield a greasy red pigment that is extremely durable on human skin—much better than lipstick. The next night we went into his cabin and painted each other's faces. The Finn asked me to decorate his back with symbols and signs. Laughing, I applied achiote to Rolf's smooth tan skin and tied a headpiece around his neatly coifed hair. His eyes lingered on me as I worked.

I began to feel self-conscious. "That's enough," I decided. "You look like a tattooed man in the circus. Let's put on our grass clothes now."

Of course, we won the best costume prize—a magnum of champagne. I was giddy with laughter and wine. This was the most fun I'd had in ages. When the party broke up about two o'clock in the morning, Rolf saw me to my cabin door and asked if he could come in for a nightcap.

"Oh, no," I groaned. "I'm so tipsy now I can hardly keep my eyes open. Tomorrow we have a dawn birding trip. I have to be able to run my Zodiak. Another night, Rolf."

He nodded politely and leaned forward just far enough to brush my red-striped cheek with his lips. "See you tomorrow, love," he said softly.

I fell on top of my bunk, grass skirt, achiote, and all. He liked me! The beautiful, mysterious Finnish financier liked me! I tingled from head to foot. Wild visions of traveling around the world flashed through my head. Then cold reason cut in. I didn't want a shipboard romance. They always ended in tears. The two people never saw each other again. Besides, I was here *on assignment* in the Amazon; *not* to party around. The next thing I knew, I was fast asleep. The red dye that came off on the pillowcases did *not* endear me to the ship's Chinese laundrymen.

When the *Explorer* stopped at Leticia, once a notorious Columbian skin- and animal-trade center, I combed the small shops restlessly, looking for contraband. About five years ago, the sale of many kinds of pelts became illegal here. Furthermore, the United States passed its Endangered Species Act, prohibiting the importation of certain animals. Peru was the first Latin American country to ratify this Washington convention. Were these laws being obeyed in Columbia, I wondered? I had to see for myself.

Every shop was jammed with toucan feather necklaces, butterfly wing trays, wooden letter openers adorned with baby alligator heads, crocodile wallets, turtle shell combs, stacks of hides, piles of dried birds, and piranhas mounted on ashtrays. No skins of any large spotted cats were available. Each time I casually asked a shopkeeper for a jaguar skin, he immediately rolled his eyes skyward and righteously proclaimed, "*Esta prohibido, Señorita!*" Even so, somewhere on a colorful side street with houses of prostitution, a tall mulatto sidled up to me and asked, "You want a big yellow one?"

Had I been male, I might have thought he had other merchandise in mind. But it could mean only one thing—jaguar skins! How I wished Felipe Benavides were here. I could just hear him thundering, "If you let one jaguar or ocelot become a coat, shoppers will want more, kill more. Wild animals should not be bartered, exchanged, or sold. There are other ways to make a living." He would have shaken his fist at the mulatto, then softened his explosion with a smile and a winning, "Señor, conservation is not a rich man's hobby. We all benefit from it. What are *you* doing about it?"

Lacking Felipe's flair for extemporaneous speaking, I merely shook my head and walked on. But I felt sure that a black market trade still exists along the Amazon, especially in Columbia, despite the dedication of patrol officers. In the 1960s, before the laws, the annual kill of jaguars and ocelots in Brazil was estimated at about 15,000 for jaguars and 80,000 for ocelots. This has maybe dropped to half. One estimate was that a quarter of the riverboats still carry illegal fauna, either for food or commerce. That's not surprising, given the immensity of the Amazon basin, its inhabitants' meager incomes, and the fact that many European countries have not yet outlawed imports of threatened cats and caimans.

The Finn was walking with me, obviously unconcerned about the animal products we saw for sale. Probably his girl friends wore jaguar coats, carried crocodile bags, and walked around in lizard or snakeskin boots, I thought maliciously. I remembered seeing stunning ocelot coats for sale in elegant shops not far from World Wildlife Fund headquarters in Switzerland. I'd watched stacks of furs and hides, bound for Mexico and then Europe, being loaded at jungle airports in Guatemala, Panama, and other countries. Clearly, multinational legal action is needed to stop the collecting and selling of Amazon wildlife. Morosely, I turned back toward the ship. This part of the trip was becoming deplorable in contrast to the marvelous protected wildlife in Manú National Park.

"Where are you going, my dear?" asked Rolf. "Come on. There's so much more to see."

"No, thanks. This port depresses me. Just look at all the dead animal curios. You stay, Rolf, and enjoy the town. I'm going back to the library on board," I said moodily.

"No way," he announced stubbornly. "Look, Anne, sunset is coming. Let's go up on that hill and watch. We don't sail till 10:00 P.M. We can sample the local beer and have a steak dinner." He coaxed me up a side street, snapping pictures all the while, and then down a quiet path to an overlook above the river. Huge flocks of green parakeets were streaming across the sky. Clouds were turning scarlet and the Amazon rippled in black, orange, and blue. A lone palm made a fantastic framework for photographs. A few dugouts described delicate silhouettes on the river's satiny surface. Gradually I regained my good humor. Leticia was attractive, even if it was a Mafia-like capital of animal contraband in the Amazon.

A little later we sat with two of the ship's officers and a few passengers at a sidewalk cafe. The Columbian beer was cold and delicious. Motor bikes, many carrying two young girls, kept scooting by and a few stopped right beside our table. The girls eyed the men saucily and accosted them in rapid Spanish. The Finn was the only one who clearly understood what they were saying. "They're propositioning us fellows," he laughed. "The brothels are just up the street and they open at 8:00 P.M. Shall we go?" He winked at me.

I stared at him in disbelief. The officers, shy Swedes, looked embarrassed.

"I mean it," insisted the Finn smoothly. "In these countries it's quite permissible to visit such a house, have a drink, look over the merchandise, then stay or leave."

"But they'd never let a woman in." I began, utterly fascinated by the idea. In my line of work I'd never been near a brothel, let alone inside one. I was most curious.

"Of course they will. You're no competition. You're with me." Rolf grinned in his infectious way. "Come on. Let's eat our steaks and go."

And so, along with all the ecology I was seeing on the Amazon, I also had the opportunity to observe the world's oldest profession. I came away surprised, chagrined, elated, and sad. Surprised, because the girls were so young, pretty, clean and courteous. They were far from lewd or sordid. Chagrined, because all my life I had considered prostitution to be evil. In Leticia, I saw the other side of it. These young women provide, for a brief time, human warmth, touch, and attention to the lonely men who work up and down the great rivers. Far from home, illiterate for the most part, beleaguered by heat, disease, and the ever-dangerous waters, men flock to these young women for solace. Elated, because I'd finally seen a side of life I'd never been exposed to. And sad, because there was no other opportunity for these girls to "get ahead in life." Most came from the simplest jungle hamlets and had no education at all. They could marry, have a dozen kids, and live out their lives in the forest; or, they could become prostitutes. There seemed to be little else they might do to survive. Like the camp followers at the oil company site, most only wanted to earn enough money to buy a little shop somewhere and become independent.

As we strolled back to the ship shortly before ten, I looked up at the Finn with new admiration. He was the first man I'd ever met who would dare suggest such a thing. How worldly he was, how cultured, how sure of himself. Perhaps he might be the right kind of partner. Someone like Rolf might understand my professional career and zest for travel. Perhaps he could learn to be concerned about conservation. Surely he would not be jealous or parochial in his life style. I started to think of Rolf in a new light, considering a possible future beyond our idyllic cruise down the Amazon. The next day we entered Brazil. The farther downstream we went the wider grew the floodplain, or *varzea*. Most people lived and farmed here, as it is the only truly fertile land in Amazonia. Although varzea occupies only two percent of the entire basin— twice the area of Holland—it is infinitely more productive than the banks of the Upper Amazon and the endless hinterlands of terra firma which cover 90 percent of this region. Fresh alluvial soils, brought down and deposited on the varzea by annual white water floods, give it a life-sustaining quality. Since one acre may receive as much as four tons of sediments containing precious nutrients, varzea soils can yield two, three, or four times the quantity of crops and cattle as terra firma.

We were due in Manáus the next day. Everyone was excited about visiting this city, now a free port, situated 1,000 miles upriver. In the late 1880s it was sixth richest port on earth because this area was the world's only source of rubber. Manáus once boasted magnificent plantations, resident billionaires, cobblestoned streets, electricity, streetcars, and entire buildings shipped over from Europe and England. Rubber barons were said to be so wealthy that they lighted their cigars with paper money. They sent their dirty laundry to Paris by ship, built chateaus of imported European bricks, and entertained friends at the lavish Teatro do Amazonas. This opera house seated 1,600 and rivaled La Scala.

A few passengers planned to disembark at Manáus and spend some time there, flying to Belém to rejoin the *Explorer* before she headed for Río de Janeiro. A special dressy dinner and dance was planned for the night before our arrival at Manáus.

Rolf (whom I now thought of as "my Finn") asked me to be his date. By coincidence we both wore white. He, in a hand-stitched suit of lightest wool with a black-and-white, polka-dot tie, looked like an early Manáus rubber baron, save for the blond hair and slanted green eyes. I wore a long gown of sheer dimity with puffed sleeves and low neckline. My pigtails were abandoned for an upswept bouffant hairdo, bare feet for high heels. When we walked into the lounge together, a hush fell. The old ladies started whispering. Like it or not, as far as they were concerned I was having a shipboard romance. Dinner was elegant. We sat at the captain's table. The wine master doted. The maitre d' hovered. The dance music was slow and romantic. Glancing at my tall, slim escort, I could think of nothing but our days ahead in Amazonia.

Next morning, I had to take a group of passengers shopping in Manáus, so I didn't see Rolf. When we returned at noon, I went straight in to lunch and didn't go to my cabin until well after 2:00 P.M. A note and a bulky plastic bag were on the bunk. The note read, "Hi, Love. I received a cable from my company. Have some urgent business to attend to. Will try to join you in Belém. Keep the grass skirt. It wouldn't fit in my luggage. Maybe it will remind you of me. Love, Rolf."

I was stunned. Why hadn't he told me in person? What could be so important in Manáus that he couldn't wait? I rushed back downtown to the main tourist hotels. Rolf was not registered at any of them, although one desk clerk remembered a tall blond man had made an overseas call there.

"Where to?" I asked breathlessly.

"Who knows?" he shrugged. "It could have been New York or Berlin or Paris or..."

"Are there any planes out today?"

He scanned the airlines guide. "Yes, flights go to Río, Caracas, Miami, and Bogota."

There wasn't time to go to the airport, as the ship was due to sail at 5:00 P.M. I went back and spent a nerve-racking afternoon in my stateroom, hoping he might come back to the *Explorer* to say good-bye. But when the vessel pulled out into the Río Negro's black waters, the dock was empty. And then the ship curved back into the mainstream of the muddy Amazon again. Manáus simply faded from the horizon as if it had never been there. Just like Rolf.

The night before we reached the mouth of the Amazon a week later, I stood on the top deck one last time. I was wildly impatient to reach Belém, yet nostalgically trying to capture the essence of my month-long trip. I thought of pink freshwater dolphins rolling in the blue waters of the Tapajoz River under a rosy sunrise. The precise smacking of spade-shaped paddles dipped by Amerindians into a jade-green jungle streamlet. Giant *Arum* and *Victoria amazonica* waterlilies in a Rousseau landscape. Black nunbirds, a green araçari, two cream-colored woodpeckers, spangled cotingas, and masked crimson tanagers all feeding together in one giant ceiba tree.

Then I thought of too, too many beautiful, brown-skinned, sloe-eyed children waving from stilt-legged shacks. The sullen Jivaros with their blowguns. The splendid new luxury hotel at Santarem, as plush as any in Acapulco.

Actually it was easier to think of what the Amazon is *not*, than what it is. It's not just a river. It is a vastness. Vastness coupled with brooding peacefulness. This peace has a deceptive quality of foreverness. Perhaps this comes from being the earth's oldest and most complex ecosystem; a 60-million-year-old rain forest; and the mightiest river on earth.

Finally, I thought of Rolf. Who was he? A young, spoiled financier bored with it all, taking exotic tours around the world? Or a man with an unhappy past, trying to forget? Or a secret agent? Or owner of a shipping company trying to copy the *Lindblad* natural history cruises? Why had he taken so many pictures of just about everything? How come he knew about interesting facets of life in Latin America? Perhaps I'd never know. If my Finn didn't meet me in Belém, would I ever see him again?

Meanwhile, the river pushed inexorably to the sea. The *Explorer* would dock in just eight hours. I had better come off cloud nine and think seriously about my *Audubon* assignment. After all, I'd be completely on my own now in Amazonia. Best to forget my fantasies and hopes—they were somewhat out of character anyway for an Adirondack woodswoman. Yet I couldn't stop the stray tears that rolled down my cheeks and blew away into the tropical night.

Some weeks later, after I'd returned to my cabin and settled down to write the *Audubon* article, Rolf telegraphed. I called him back the same day at a New York City hotel on Park Avenue. My heart thumped to hear his cultured resonant voice again.

"I'm here in the city for two-and-a-half more days," he said. "A boring business trip. Come on down and stay with me, Anne."

Hesitating, I murmured, "It's so good to hear from you again, Rolf. It's been a long time since the Amazon."

"Yes, I know," he said placatingly. "I hated to leave like that, with no warning. But, you know, business is business."

"Well, it's quite a long trip from here to the city," I stuttered. "Over 300 miles." (A mental list was forming in my head: dog back in kennel—stop mail—postpone article—lose my momentum writing—drive truck in heavy traffic and air pollution—need map and directions—). Then on impulse, I added, "Can't you come visit me at the cabin, Rolf?"

"No, Anne, unfortunately not. Sorry, but I'm due back in Helsinki Friday morning. A board meeting," he explained.

I thought of my resolve *not* to have a shipboard romance. I thought of the prestige of authoring a 40-page, interesting, well-illustrated (by Loren McIntyre, free-lance photographer for many *National Geographic* articles and books on Latin America) article for *Audubon*. A real plum for a beginning free-lance writer. I considered my fee to be earned. The feast-or-famine aspect of free-lancing meant a constant struggle to stay solvent. I realized that the deadline of this writing assignment was as important to me as Rolf's board meeting was to him.

I heard myself saying, "I don't think it will work out this time, dear. Give me more notice next time you come to the States, and try to stay a little longer."

We exchanged a few pleasantries and endearments, then hung up. I sensed that even if "my Finn" called again on another trip, *my* profession, *my* dog, *my* cabin, and *my* life-style would take precedence from now on.

———————

14

MY GREEN HELL

After leaving my compact little stateroom on the *Explorer* in Belém, I found myself next morning in a spacious suite on the seventeenth floor of the Hotel Excelsior Graõ Pará. I peered out nervously at Belém's skyscraper skyline, silhouetted against the rising sun. Below, a glut of traffic nudged past the proud old mango trees around Plaza Republica.

What had happened to this sleepy jungle port? The population explosion had happened. The Belém-Brasília Highway, BR 101, had been built. The highway was devised to link Brazil's capital, Brasília, and the highly industrialized south to her major Amazon port. Shipping world wide had expanded. Markets in Europe and the Americas were now available. The 1,100-mile paved road made sense commercially and in this context had been a success. But in terms of environmental degradation, it may have been unwise or even disastrous.

Before I could travel out on BR101 to evaluate the ecological situation for my *Audubon* assignment, I needed to find a good Portuguese interpreter-guide-driver. I spent several days in the steamy city searching for one. Finally I decided on Raymond, an elderly North American expatriate, who worked for one of the leading import-export companies. He assured me that he could take time off from his job and would enjoy driving me into the hinterlands.

On Saturday morning, in a rented and dented Volkswagen, Raymond and I started out on BR 101. My mood was glum. How much nicer if I could be sitting beside Rolf instead of this portly, pockmarked man who talked incessantly. Trucks roared past constantly. Service stations, bars, restaurants, and shacks flashed by continuously. I saw tropical woods and imported goods from Belém heading south. Cattle and cars from the states of Goais and Minas

Gerais, and the city of São Paulo, going north. People were clustered everywhere beside the macadam. My guide explained that over 120 small towns had grown up along BR 101 in the 11 years since it opened. More than two million people, many of them *posseros* (squatters), had already settled haphazardly along its flanks. There had been no government control over colonization along the Belém-Brasília Highway as took place on the Transamazônica Highway. I was to find the contrast in settlement patterns and numbers of immigrants along the two roads quite startling.

Even more amazing was the amount of clearing that had taken place during the highway's brief existence. Mile after mile of flat rangeland met my eyes where tall rain forest had once soared. Only scattered patches of trees remained, or, far back on the horizon, thin lines of forest vegetation. Raymond gloatingly told me that five million cattle roamed the ranches which lined BR 101.

We drove nearly 200 miles without stopping. My guide had arranged for me to visit two ranches belonging to friends of his and to see firsthand how beef growing is done in Brazil. The first ranch belonged to a wealthy family from Belém. They used their property chiefly for weekend relaxation. A few cowboys were kept to round up animals and do chores. Land had been cleared by the traditional slash-and-burn system. Grass seed had been sown desultorily, much of it too long after clearing. Sturdy weeds and scrub trees had taken hold of the land before the first grass shoots appeared. Good pasture land lost out. I could tell that the onslaughts of rainy seasons had already caused a lot of erosion. Reddish gashes and gullies gouged many slopes. The ranch owner complained that a once-perennial stream had almost dried up except during the height of wet season.

As I gazed out from the handsome ranch house, I saw a few scraggly patches of forest and some thin cattle scuffing over sun-baked, cement-hard ground. Yet the drinks were strong and the table loaded with delicious food. My hosts were charming and chauvinistic. Everyone chattered and laughed. Four well-groomed horses stood tied by the door for anyone who wished to go riding. The owners were "playing" at ranching. They were not aware of what was happening outside their windows. If I tried to play environmental doctor and warn them of threatening ecological changes taking place, they wouldn't be the least concerned. Or, if they were, they wouldn't believe an American woman.

At the second ranch, owned by two stocky, tanned brothers

from Belém, I found a pleasing contrast. The land had been par-
tially cleared, farmed, and abused by squatters for seven years. Now
the brothers were waging a vigorous battle to reclaim it.

"We've planted kudzu and other leguminous species on the old
cut-over places," explained the younger brother. "We've sowed
capim colonial (*Bracharia mutica*) and para (*Panicum maximum*).
Those two grasses make the best fodder and have deep root systems
which help hold the soil." He guided us through his stables and
stockyard. "Wherever we prepare new pasture land during dry season, we plant those grass seeds immediately. That way they get full
advantage of the ploughed soil and early rains." He pointed toward
a herd of cattle and continued, "We graze our animals lightly and
rotate them often from field to field. Most of our land has regained
green cover after four years. In fact, some patches of kudzu are
ankle deep."

His older brother chimed in enthusiastically. "We're trying to
think ecologically. We leave large stands of forest to shade the cattle, keep the stream banks and hillsides vegetated, and protect our
wildlife. Most people think we're crazy."

A giant brown bull ambled up while he was talking and began
grazing tamely at our feet. Manuel, the younger man, ran his hand
appraisingly over its shiny shoulder and nodded to his brother.
"Not bad, not bad, eh, Joachim? At times, I'd like to move back to
Belém, but when I see results like this it seems worth staying."

Turning back to me, he went on, "Research done at INPA
(*Instituto Nacional Pesquisas Amazonica*, National Institute for
Amazon Research) at Manáus shows that soil permeability drops
dramatically when trees are removed and replaced by grassland. A
primary rain forest can absorb three and a half inches of heavy rain
in seven minutes. An equal acreage of five-year-old pasture can
handle only half an inch in the same time. All the rest becomes
run-off. The cushioning effect of forest canopy is really astound-
ing."

He gave the bull a slap on its rump and turned to show us the
feeding pens. "We don't want to leave it to the laborers and just
check in on weekends. We get 85 inches of rain a year out here.
That could mean our land might lose 45 tons of soil per acre if cut
bare. It is better for us to keep it vegetated. Well-wooded hillsides
lose only half a ton at most."

"But we're not sure how much longer we'll succeed," mused
Joachim, stroking his bushy moustache. "Some ranches along BR

101 are already exhausted five years after removing the jungle. That ranch you saw earlier? We give it one or two more years before it is completely unproductive. Their range capacity has dropped from one head per two and a half acres to one per 25 in the last three years!"

My driver, Raymond, was blessedly quiet all the way back to Belém, so I had time to watch the sad landscape and ponder its ultimate end. Gratefully, I checked into my room and stretched out, homesick for the Adirondacks.

Next day I decided to take a bird's-eye look at the Belém-Brasilía Highway, so I rented a light plane for a few hours. My pilot, Pedro, was a wiry, crewcut, sunburned man who had been flying for over 30 years in the Amazon. "It's changed a lot," he remarked casually as he belted me into his aged plane. "In the old days I flew for hours over virgin jungle. We used to say, if you had engine trouble and landed alive, wild animals would eat you. If you landed dead, they'd still eat you. So what the hell difference did it make? If those engines failed, you were done for."

He propped open the cockpit cover with a short two-by-four so I could take photographs unobstructed by glass or metal. Then we were taxiing bumpily down the field. In a moment we were airborn. He leaned close to my ear and yelled, "Now there's habitation everywhere. See! Emergency strips, radios, pastures to land in if necessary. I give the Amazon basin another 25 years, and it'll all be populated."

Our flight path took us in a great arc south of Belém. The first 20 miles had been cleared of trees and planted in small oval vegetable plots. Farther out we passed neat square fields of black pepper, truck crops, and small pastures. Not until we were 75 miles from the city did we fly over truly untouched lowland rain forest. Then, angling east toward BR 101, we began to see huge tracts of burning trees. Visibility lessened abruptly. Pedro reached up and slammed shut the cockpit cover. I stared with disbelief at the flames licking up forest and shot several frames.

I recalled hearing rumors that in 1974 the Volkswagen Company of Brazil had defoliated, cut, and burned a piece of land roughly 100 by 100 kilometers (3,600 square miles) for cattle ranches. This was over half the size of the Adirondack Park (6,000 square miles). It has been called the largest man-made fire in the world. Satellite photographs from 940 miles out picked up the smoke which rose tens of thousands of feet. This apparently happened in spite of the fact that Volkswagen had signed an agreement, as per Brazilian law, to cut only 50 percent of the area and leave the other half in forest. Although VW claims it abided by this law, it is widely believed it did not.

Pedro was pointing down at the Belém-Brasilía Highway now, circling over ranch land around Paragominas. He shouted, "Four years ago this was wild forest. It sold for 15 to 25 cents an acre. Now it's worth $400 U.S. per acre as improved land without cattle."

"Can I take some more pictures?" I yelled.

"Sure." He reached up and slid back the cockpit cover, propping it with the board. "Ready?" This time he leaned the single-engined plane on its side, allowing me a clear shot of the ground. Absolutely terrified I would fall out, I nevertheless snapped several shots. But my stomach turned upside down and felt queasy.

Pedro leveled off again and shouted, "Next year I'm going to talk some ranchers into hiring me to spray defoliants on their land. Using hand labor, it costs them about $200 to $250 U.S. an acre to cut, burn, and seed. The biggest trees may not catch fire or fall down for years. Using Vietnam defoliants, I could cover 1,500 acres in an hour. It would be much cheaper. All the trees would be down within two to four years."

I turned a horrified look at Pedro, but he didn't notice. He went on shouting companionably. "After the burning, I could come back and sow grass seed by air. It'd be a good pot of money for me."

Nauseated and despondent, I motioned Pedro to head back to Belém. Vietnam defoliants! How widespread was their use down here? Was there no law to protect the environment from this kind of chemical abuse? By the time I arrived back in my hotel room, I was sick to my stomach and sick in my soul.

My thoughts drifted again to the Adirondacks, and a wave of nostalgia swept through my heart. As if from a small plane, I envisioned looking down on my 30 acres of old-growth forest; then the 50,000 acres of state wilderness adjoining my land; beyond that 100,000 more acres of wilderness lands; and on and on. State wilderness and wild forest areas, totaling 2.4 million acres, were protected by that absolutely unique New York constitutional law known as Article 14.

It reads: "The lands of the state, now owned or hereafter acquired, constituting the forest preserve as now fixed by law, shall be forever kept as wild forest land. They shall not be leased, sold, or exchanged, or be taken by any corporation, public or private, nor shall the timber thereon be sold, removed or destroyed."

No way could anybody or any organization get away with burning or spraying "my backyard"—the Adirondack Park! This law has been in effect and enforced for over 100 years.

Three days later, I took off for the famed new Transamazônica Highway, the notorious BR 230. The National Department of Highways (DNER) of the Ministry of Transportation had kindly provided me with a pickup truck and driver to cover the 195-mile section between Altamira and the crossroads of the brand new Cuibá-Santarém-Surinam Highway, BR 163. I was burning with curiosity to travel part of the "Transam" and see what was happening on Brazil's last frontier. It would have been impossible to cover the entire 3,500-mile stretch in the short time I had available. This central and most heavily colonized piece seemed the most interesting. Although the Transamazônica officially starts as a paved road in Zona Bragatina on the Atlantic coast, it petered out to a mud track somewhere near the Peruvian border.

I flew off by commercial jet from Belém to Altamira, a dusty, TV-Western-type town of about 8,000 people. I envisioned endless miles of thick jungle with no eating or sleeping places anywhere. So I had purchased a dozen large bottles of guaraná (Brazil's equivalent of Coca Cola), cheese, crackers, and chocolate. I went to the market for a hammock, mosquito netting, rain tarp, and two lengths of rope. Then I bought a big burlap coffee sack—an acceptable piece of luggage in Brazil—and stuffed everything inside. I was fully prepared to sleep between two trees during this adventure.

At Altamira, the DNER truck was waiting, equipped with two spare tires, an extra 20-gallon gas tank, shovel, and chains. Looked like we were in for a rough ride. To my chagrin, the driver spoke only Portuguese with an unintelligible accent. I began to appreciate Raymond more.

The Transamazônica has been called everything from an "unqualified and victorious success"—to "a road from nothing to nothing"—to "Transmiseriana." The project was sparked off impetuously in 1970 by former president Emilio Garrastazu Medici after a visit to drought-stricken northeastern Brazil. One-fifth of its then 23 million people were close to starvation. Suddenly, colonization of the sparsely settled Amazon basin was seen as a means of easing pressures and famine in northeastern Brazil. The "conquest of Brazil's last frontier" made a strong political rallying point. Other justifications were access to untapped mineral resources, agricultural and ranching developments, new commercial connections to remote towns on southern Amazon tributaries, and, most important, national security. Brazil, after all, borders on all other South American nations except Chile and Ecuador.

Naturally it was hoped that BR 230 would be a tremendous success comparable to BR 101. Other major Amazonian highways were also envisioned, the longest being the Perimetral Norte (Northern Perimeter Road). This was to run north of the river and link towns with the capitals of French Guiana, Surinam, Guyana, Venezuela, and Colombia. Eventually, this 14,000-mile network was to connect Brasília to the capitals of seven other South American countries.

To my surprise, the DNER driver maintained a steady 40 to 50 miles an hour (except when we crossed bridges) along the superbly engineered dirt highway. We soon arrived at the hamlet, Agrovila Carlos Penha. It was one of many much-touted small-scale colonization projects sponsored by the National Institute for Colonization and Agrarian Reform (INCRA) and the Amazon Development Agency (SUDAM).

Unlike the area along the Belém-Brazília Highway, where settlements were allowed to spring up spontaneously, here they were planned and controlled. A 60-mile-wide strip bracketing the highway (a total of 360,000 square miles, or roughly eight times the size of New York State), is federal land. A settlement—*agrovila* (rural hamlet), *agropolis* (rural town), or *ruropolis* (agricultural and commercial center)—was planned or had already been built every ten kilometers along the Transam.

My driver politely asked with sign language if I'd like to stop. "By all means," I nodded enthusiastically. I saw 48 frame houses with outhouses flanking three sides of a large jungle clearing. There was a tiny elementary school, chapel, clinic, small store, soccer field, and large water tank. The agrovila was the basic unit where colonists lived. From here the farmers walked out to their plots of land. Each family was given 250 acres of virgin rain forest, worth about $700. The government was providing transportation, six-month loans for hand tools and crop seeds, and even some simple farming instruction.

Ten kilometers farther on at Agropolis Brazil Novo, we stopped again. About 100 homes were occupied. I saw a larger school, clinic, sawmill, gas station, and the INCRA administrative offices. Stepping into the director's air conditioned office to introduce myself, I felt ludicrous. Old field clothes, boots, banged-up binoculars, and pigtails seemed foolishly out of place beside a stylish young secretary in six-inch-platform shoes, mini skirt, and dangling earrings. She greeted me cordially, however, and made me feel right at home by saying, "We try to keep up city ways out in the country. It is so remote. There is so much work to do. We have to dress well and have discipline, otherwise..." She shrugged helplessly.

Continuing on, we stopped at small roadside stalls for tiny cups of sweet Brazilian coffee. Everywhere I listened to "Transmiseriana" tales. At one place, a couple related, "Our first year here we thought we could grow everything. Two years later we abandoned our farm and set up this little store. We couldn't grow anything." At another shop, an almost-toothless man in his forties grinned wryly as he recounted his experiences. "Bananas were two feet long the first year. Bananas were one foot long the second year. Bananas were six inches long the third year. The fourth year? No bananas."

Only 10 percent of Amazonia's soil is suitable for agriculture. As living proof, instead of the 100,000 immigrants expected by 1975 (half a million by 1980) only 45,000 colonists had arrived by the time I visited. Many had already moved back whence they came, discouraged by the heat, humidity, diseases, insects, poor crops, and isolation. Their farmland was simply abandoned. Soils are just too poor. And as of this writing, almost all small colonization schemes have been discarded by the Brazilian government.

I was chilled by the treatment of the environment. That first day we drove off and on for 12 hours, and it looked like almost every mile of forest was in flames. Each colonist was taking advantage of the dry season to clear some of his 250 acres. By law, half the plot had to be left in forest, or it could be sold. This loophole effectively cancels out the conservation purpose of the forestry law. The cleared half of the land was planted with subsistence crops of manioc, rice, maize, beans, bananas, yams, with a bit of coffee or guaraná on the side. Here again was another trade-off: tall green timber for starchy kitchen crops.

As one astute Brazilian, F. C. Camargo, wrote in 1948, "The felling of the forest {is} destroying gold; and producing manioc meal, rice, and other cereals {is} producing silver."

Camargo didn't mention sugarcane as one of the "silver-producing" crops. He never could have visualized in 1948 that vast fields of cane would be planted along a long highway. We stopped at an enormous plantation and mill where cane was being processed into raw sugar, molasses, and alcohol. I gazed spellbound at the huge juice heaters of bubbling liquid. My nose wrinkled with the heavy, redolent, sweet odors. I watched my driver turn a spigot and catch alcohol in his hand. "This will be mixed with gasoline to make gasohol for our vehicles," our guide explained. "Regular gas is too expensive out here to buy."

The mill was in its second year of operation and doing well. Several hundred acres were under cultivation and more were being planted all the time. Filters, boilers, evaporators, and other machinery steamed and throbbed at the plant. The whole place looked efficient and up-to-date. But I couldn't help casting a speculative eye at the soils. Might this be another story like that of the bananas in the making?

Cane crops normally take large amounts of nutrients from the soil. Permanent soil fertility is usually maintained by heavy applications of fertilizers. However, Amazon soils don't take kindly to them. Chemical fertilizers are nearly useless because they volatize quickly under the hot sun or leach out with the heavy rains. Also they cannot become "fixed" in tropical soils because of the absence of colloids. As for natural fertilizers, the Transamazônica is too recently settled to have manure and compost from domestic animals available for sugar plantations.

By nightfall, after driving through flame and smoke all day, I smelled like a bonfire. We reached Ruropolis President Medici— which was less than a year old. Trucks and buses were continually rolling into the town, dropping off supplies and people. My driver said that at least 100 vehicles passed this stretch of highway every 24 hours. A little farther west toward Peru, however, travel was minimal and the road often impassable during rainy season.

To my astonishment, the ruropolis had a small motel, with swimming pool and dining room, a church, social services center, and several stores. All its electricity came from an old wood-fired train locomotive engine. I left my hammock, tarp, cheese, and crackers in the pickup. Fantasizing about a hot shower and a rare steak, I rented a motel room. Apart from having to kill a six-inch hairy spider on the wall, I was as comfortable, clean and well-fed as anyone at a roadside inn Stateside that night.

15

GORILLAS and JAGUARS

The next morning I strolled around the ruropolis chatting as best I could with its inhabitants and transients. Portuguese was proving to be very difficult to learn. Some kind of cross circuit in my brain kept Spanish popping out. Nevertheless, I could tell that all these people were enthusiastic about being pioneers on the Brazilian frontier. They made me think of how our early Westerners must have felt. It was heartwarming to listen to their dreams and see their dedication. However, my ecological training warned they were in for trouble.

By noontime I was ready to travel on. My driver and I skipped lunch at the motel and drove towards the Cuibá-Santarém-Surinam Highway, BR 163. "We'll find something to eat along the way," I prophesied recklessly. In the short time here, I was reassured that wherever humans went in Amazonia, rudimentary food, shelter, and drink would be available. Sure enough, before we'd been on the road half an hour, we spotted a tiny, open-air café flanked by uncut rain forest. For 60 cents, we had a full-course lunch of steak, rice, and beans with ice-cold guaraná—chilled in a dilapidated kerosene refrigerator. Only the zillions of flies on the plastic tablecloth made our meal less than appetizing.

The Cuibá-Santarém-Surinam Highway had only been opened a few weeks. No settlements had begun along its right-of-way. Consequently, it offered me a perfect comparison with the small-colonization pattern on the Transamazônica and the large-scale ranching scene along the Belém-Brasília highways. The contrast in environmental vigor and health was obvious. Here dense forest hugged the red dirt roadside. Streams and rivers ran clear. The route was straight as a die through rolling hills and vales. It was empty of traffic. This is what BR 101 and BR 230 had once looked like, I imagined.

Now I could clearly understand that simple, low-key, slash-and-burn agriculture is the best of all traditional methods in tropical forested regions. But it must be done by very *small* groups of semi-nomadic people in very *large* tracts of forest. This ancient farming practice almost copies natural tree uprootings with resultant irregular openings in the jungle. If natives cut tiny plots, plant a diverse mixture of crops (which really mimics the forest's diversity), and move on in two to three years, this is the most ecologically sound agricultural system. Nomads usually don't return to their fallow patches for 10 to 100 years. By then, the nearby forest has grown back and healed that pinprick of an opening in its canopy. The microclimate has not changed. Soils have not washed away nor baked hard. The coolness, dampness, shade, species diversity and composition are intact. This type of slash-and-burn subsistence living can be repeated indefinitely, given a small human population and vast acreage.

No sooner had we left the café than we experienced a bizarre event that could only happen in Amazonia. One soon grows accustomed to strange happenings and often learns to shrug at them. But not me. A traveling circus had broken down on the highway. A rough-looking, bearded man was lying on his back under a van, alternately arguing with a beautiful girl in tights and swearing at a gorilla in a small cage. We braked to a stop and tried to help, but the van was too rusty and rundown. Some parts were badly damaged. All we could do was promise to send out a mechanic from Santarém.

My heart went out to the animals, broiling in the midday sun, cooped up behind wire. There was a margay cat, young jaguar, several snakes, jungle fowl, the inevitable monkeys, and that poor African primate. The gorilla was so far from home and doomed to a life without proper food, water, mate, or exercise. I tried to convince the girl to rig up some shade over the caged animals, but she was too upset by the delay. She seemed more concerned about sunburning *her* skin to bother helping those in fur coats. Finally, I offered the creatures some water from our tank and cautioned the man not to neglect them. "Ahhh, they'll be all right," was his tart reply, as he struggled with a wrench. Meanwhile the small jaguar paced incessantly.

I started to remind him that the poor creatures provided *his* food and shelter, when my driver wisely motioned me to leave. We started off again while I grieved for the animals. After a short silence, I pantomimed, "Do you ever see jaguars on the highways?"

"Sometimes at night," he replied in very slow and careful Portuguese, "where there's wild land on both sides of the road. Never where the farmers are."

I fell silent again, thinking of my experience with the jaguar who circled my tent in Manú. I was remembering how large a range one pair of these spotted cats normally needs—at least 100 square miles. Obviously, large mammals like jaguars, pumas, giant river otters, and tapirs, can never survive in small, disjunct sanctuaries. They couldn't encounter enough food, mates, or territory. They'd be little better off than that young jaguar in its cage. Few large mammal populations can maintain themselves on less than 2,000 to 5,000 square miles of land. Some scientists say half-a-million acres. The designing of national parks in Amazonia must take into consideration minimum critical sizes of the largest, most actively-ranging species.

Unfortunately, in the Amazon basin, human populations are becoming rapidly larger and more sedentary. Areas cut and culti-vated are expanding; the forest is retreating. The 50 percent-cut and 50 percent-save forestry law is not working, so most wildlife has little chance to survive.

The Brazilian government has been encouraging large-scale farming and ranching projects. Tracts were averaging 250,000 acres in size. It had announced a new program that will level about 100 million acres (roughly the area of California) for timber. This is one way to back a national debt of $41 billion U.S. Brazil offers fine tax exemptions, or "risk contracts," for multinational corpora-tions moving into the Amazon basin. Moreover, a new thrust called "Polamazonia" is creating fifteen "poles of development" for towns, agriculture, and industry. These poles will level thousands more acres of land.

There seems to be no way for the rain forest to keep its normal climate or reseed itself under such gross changes. On large clear-ings, it may take 100 to 500 years for soils and rain forest to recov-er, *if* they ever do. Once razed in such grandiose style, it is more likely a rain forest cannot ever be restored. These new maxi-pro-grams of exploitation will be far more destructive to the environ-ment than all the small colonists' plots put together.

All this is happening—just as surely as our West was "won." No longer were the questions: will Amazonia be developed? is it morally right to practice such giant environmental manipulations? Rather the questions are: who will do it? and how?

Still one more amazing site we visited on the way to Santarém was a large hydroelectric dam being built on the Cuná Una, a tributary of the Tapajóz River. Somehow, the idea of harnessing the water power of the Amazon basin had never occurred to me. The rivers seemed too wild, too unmanageable, too prone to fluctuation. Yet here was a dam to rival any medium-sized one in the United States. Its turbines and other machinery were manufactured in São Paulo. I wondered if the government would prohibit colonization along its shores. Far too often, when settlers or squatters move in around reservoirs and cut the riparian forest, erosion and siltation begin. The reservoir looses ten to 40 years of its potential life span, and new dams have to be built sooner. The price of energy rises. In the Amazon, reservoirs can have another detrimental effect. Fruit- and seed-eating fish may lose their foraging grounds when river banks are deforested and swampy lowlands flooded. When the trees disappear, so do their fruits and seeds. These valuable, edible, freshwater fish die or move off.

That day we reached Santarém at sunset. We'd travelled three long days on brand new dirt roads, averaging ten to twelve hours of driving per day, without mishap. Once again I gazed out at the sparkling blue Tapajóz and the incredible "milk-coffee-river-sea." Even here, 500 miles from the Atlantic, tides came and went. I could barely glimpse the far shore. Banks of ivory thunderheads towered over the rain forest. They slowly changed colors as the sun sank—old-rose and beige, strawberry and lavender, ice-blue and mauve. The wind felt fresh and cool. How good to be back along this clear river once more.

My driver found a mechanic and alerted him to the breakdown of the circus van. Then I found an airy riverside room in a local inn overlooking the water. The plush new Hotel Tropical seemed far too luxurious and touristy after my Transam adventures. I collapsed on the bed under a filmy mosquito net which billowed gently in the breeze. The assignment was almost over. I'd been too preoccupied to think of anything except producing photos and notes for my article. Now, memories of the *Explorer* and Rolf flooded into my mind. I tossed fitfully. Would I ever sail aboard that ship again? Would I ever see my Finn again? Because of them, Amazonia would always be a bittersweet place.

Sometime late that night, a bit of the timelessness and peace of the vast river seeped into my soul. It was as if the Amazon were saying, "Be patient. Everything works out in time: your problems, my problems."

16

BLACK PEPPER

When I checked back into the Hotel Excelsior Graõ Pará in Belém, it was almost like coming home. By now, everyone knew me; I was the "American *menina* (young lady) who was writing something about the Amazon." The bell boys smiled, winked, and hurried to open doors and elevator. The chambermaid brought fresh flowers to my room. The European manager kindly invited me to join him for dinner. Brazilian cordiality can be wonderful. Here at the oldest and best hotel in Belém, it was a tradition.

After resting and writing up my notes about the Transamazônica Highway, I decided to go to the Zona Bragatina during my few days left on the *Audubon* assignment. This is the last outpost of Amazonian rain forest before the Atlantic Ocean. The Bragatina covers about 10,000 square miles and has been under cultivation since the Portuguese arrived in the 1500s. It has been called "the most disturbed ecosystem in the Americas."

I wanted to compare this long-utilized region with the newly settled lands I had seen along the highways and with the untouched rain forest of Manú National Park. Only then could I really draw conclusions about how much ecological change was occurring in Amazonia. Raymond and I had a melancholy drive in drizzle from Belém out to the Bragatina. He still talked constantly, but in a subdued tone. The landscape was monotonous and desolate. Only five to ten percent of the zone was left in original forest; the rest was mostly *capoeira*, a worthless scrubby woods of second-, third-, and fourth-growth palms, weeds, *Cecropia*, coarse grasses, and small trees. Could the Bragatina be a preview of what might happen alongside the Belém-Brasília and Transam highways?

Wryly, I recalled the predictions of the English naturalist, Alfred Russell Wallace, in *Travels on the Amazon and Río Negro* (published in 1853). He raved, "I fearlessly assert that here the

primeval forest can be converted into rich pasture land, into culti-
vated fields, gardens, and orchards, containing every variety of
produce, with half the labor, and, what is more important, in less
than half the time that would be required at home." Poor Wallace.
If he could have seen the Bragatina, he would have been disillu-
sioned.

One of the biggest shocks for me were black pepper farms. They
represent an incredible trade-off in the Amazon basin. Behemoth
buttressed trees were being swapped for tiny peppercorns—giants
for grains, ancient irreplaceable forest for brief-lived bushes. An
ecosystem which has taken 60 million years to evolve and reach a
steady-state equilibrium is being razed for small, short-lived plants
(usually four years of good production) which yield no calories or
nutrition. Of all the sights I'd seen in Amazonia so far, this trade-
off seemed the most outlandish.

This final excursion showed me that every twist of a grinder,
every dusting of pepper on a salad or soufflé, represented the whack
of an ax, the slash of a machete, the strike of a match, as virgin
tropical rain forest was cut and burned for pepper farms. That day
I decided never again to eat black pepper. This was my small gesture of disapproval towards unwise exploitation of the Amazon
basin. It was my miniscule sacrifice for its conservation.

In the three months of my assignment I had gone from the
euphoria of seeing magnificent conservation in action at Peru's
Manú National Park to depression over unwise development in
Brazil and other countries. Venezuela was pursuing her own
Conquista del Sur, conquest of her south. Peru and Ecuador were
looking east for oil. Columbia had her lingering market in animal
trade and may also find oil. Brazil was busy ramming roads and
ranches into her huge frontier. More than 60 foreign companies
were bidding for forestry, mining, and ranching contracts in that
country alone. Reputedly, 20 percent of Brazilian Amazon land was
spoken for. The whole world seemed to be pressing in on the last
great tropical wilderness—Amazonia.

I read the predictions of many scientists who specialize in tropical rain forests. Dr. Thomas Lovejoy feels that the primary forest is
within a few years of being 80 percent nonexistent. Dr. Ghillean
Prance, Research Director of the New York Botanical Gardens and
an expert botanist, said somberly, "I estimate that 24 percent of the
Amazon basin has already been 'disturbed.' I predict another 24
percent will go—soon. The other half? I *think* we'll live to see that

half saved." Dr. Robert Goodland, co-author with H. S. Irvin of the controversial book, *Amazon Jungle: Green Hell to Red Desert?*, warns that the desert is only decades away.

Already satellite pictures going back ten years (1968-1978) show that 200,000 square miles of the basin have been deforested. It will be well over ten percent by 1980. By then, it is estimated that one percent of Brazil's rain forest—an area roughly the size of Indiana—will disappear each year. Dr. Otto Huber, a scientist with Venezuela's CODESUR, said gloomily, "Anne, I'm convinced we're the last generation to see virgin rain forest in the Amazon."

A major change in overall climate may be underway, according to meteorologists. Fifty percent of the rain in the Amazon basin is generated by water evaporation from the trees themselves and cycled directly back through the forest. If millions of trees are cut, rainfall may be reduced by as much as 30 percent. Humidity may be reduced and more solar heat reflected, especially from fields. This changes air circulation, wind currents, and weather patterns. In time, it may start an irreversible drying trend. What rain does fall will run off faster and cause more floods and siltation of rivers.

I heard one outstanding scientist say, "We don't really know how large an area of rain forest should be preserved in order to maintain its maximum recycling effect which guarantees a wet climate. By the time we find out, it may be too late. It's like trying to stop a supertanker under full speed from hitting something right in front of it. By the time it slows down, the tanker may have traveled ten miles and left the pieces far behind."

.He left me with the revelation that certain tracts of land, like rain forests, need enormous spaces to maintain their own climate and precipitation.

Another worrisome consequence of deforestation and climatic change is the build-up of carbon dioxide in the atmosphere. Tropical forests hold an enormous pool of stored carbon, the largest on earth. Since the 1950s, CO_2 has been increasing in our atmosphere. This is the result of more and more burning of fossil fuels and of forests. If great pulses of this gas are released because of ambitious Amazon development projects, the global environment could lose its ability to absorb and buffer carbon dioxide. Sudden climatic changes may occur, probably as warming trends in *temperate* areas, from this "greenhouse effect."

There's also a great unpredictable danger to species and genetic diversity. If we lose a million species, we will deplete our earth's catalogue of fauna and flora by about one-fifth. What's lost will be lost forever. Among those million tropical living things there might be potentially beneficial medicinal plants, like alkaloids for the treatment of heart disease, curare in anesthetics, and certain plant chemicals in contraceptives. As it is now, 40 to 50 percent of our medicines and most of our food are derived from wild plants. They are direct gifts of the forest. If these disappear, our planet will be less able to support mankind.

According to Dr. Norman Myers, tropical ecologist, we could already be losing two species a week in the Amazon. Quite possibly, he estimates, this rate could escalate to one per hour by the late 1980s or early 1990s—a biological debâcle.

My drive back to Belém was as dismal as my trip out. I had gone from the best (Manú) to the worst (Bragatina), from the Pacific to the Atlantic, in my quest to write fairly about Amazonia. I said goodbye to my driver and wished Raymond well. Then, as I walked disconsolately through the lobby of the Excelsior Graõ Pará, the debonair hotel manager asked to see me.

"I'm so terribly sorry," he began, "but my staff is not always as well-trained and intelligent as I would like."

What was he leading up to?

"While you were away this time," he said apologetically, "a new front desk man came to work. He straightened up everything and sorted through all the old unclaimed mail. He found a cable for you that had been posted under B instead of L. I do hope it wasn't something urgent that you'd been waiting for."

I started to tremble inside. It had to be from the editor of *Audubon*—or from Rolf.

It was from Rolf. It had been sent the day after he disappeared from Manáus. It simply read: "Meeting impossible Belém. Will call you New York after return. Miss you. Love, Rolf."

At least he had tried to leave a message. However, the cable gave no explanation of why he left the ship so abruptly or of who he was. Yet he did plan to see me again. That was heartwarming. Did I want to see him? Was there any future with my Finn? Probably not. Perhaps I should just write it off as an (almost) shipboard romance. After all, doesn't every woman deserve at least one in her life? I thanked the manager warmly and went back to my room to think.

Strangely enough, my melancholia began to lift. I had been from the best to the worst, literally speaking, both ecologically and romantically. Yet, I was determined to be positive. Perhaps, as the Amazon had whispered to me that night in Santarém, things would work out.

First, I could concentrate on what was being done to save this part of Amazonia to avoid writing a biased article. Then I'd decide about Rolf when I got back to the cabin. Perhaps I was a passing fancy on his part. Surely he was more at home with elegantly turned-out women than with muddy-booted ecologists.

I started interviewing a handful of scientists and bureaucrats, asking them about ways in which Amazonia might be developed along sound ecological lines. There were a few organizations and people working for conservation and using techniques which had minimal environmental impact on the delicate rain forest.

The most intriguing office I visited in Santarém was RADAM (Radar Amazon) of the Ministry of Mines and Energy. In 1971 it had begun one of the largest programs ever undertaken to map the earth's natural resources. Using side-looking radar images, full color, infrared, and black-and-white aerial photographs, RADAM was covering 2.5 million square miles of Brazil's "Legal Amazon." At key sites ground survey teams were dropped in by helicopter, usually in places where no non-native person had ever set foot. This huge reconnaissance effort was not without its perils and casualties. At the time I interviewed RADAM officials, 40 persons had been lost in accidents with helicopters and river rafts. Nevertheless, RADAM had been amassing maps and data on geology, geomorphology, vegetation, and soils. Technicians were drawing up integrated, sensitive land use plans of the entire region, including areas for national parks.

Another group doing noteworthy research was the National Institute for Amazon Research (INPA), mentioned earlier. It is one of the few government organizations dedicated to the *nonde*structive utilization of the rain forest. INPA was looking for products that could be harmlessly *extracted*, so that the forest canopy, soils, and nutrient/rainfall recycling would be preserved. There are choice tropical hardwoods, latexes, ornamental plants, dyes, orchids, gums, waxes, barks, roots, nuts, oils, fruits, medicinal plants, seeds, honey and resins which can be harvested without detriment. Some day, even forest leaves may produce methane and alcohol for fuel and leaf proteins as food.

The former director of INPA was Dr. Warwick Kerr, a dynamic scientist and administrator—perhaps the "academic Benavides of Brazil." He was pushing conservation in Amazonia. Over 200 researchers were working at INPA on various aspects of Amazon agronomy, biology, medical science, and technology.

Dr. Kerr had told me reassuringly, "We Brazilians can do a great deal to self-manage our resources in a sound way, but we can't control ecological exploitation and damage by multinational corporations. Sixty percent of Amazon development is now being done by outsiders, 30 percent by southern Brazilian companies, and only ten percent by Amazonians."

"What kind of damage are you referring to?" I asked.

"A good example is a foreign company that is interested in building an aluminum plant on a major tributary of the Amazon. The pollution from mica wastes could destroy the aquatic ecosystem up to 300 miles downstream. What about the poor local caboclos who depend on fish for food?

"Another example is a timber outfit with new tropical chippers capable of rendering an entire forest into bits and pieces. What about leaving trees for firewood for the native residents? You can be sure that most multinational companies will not offset the deficit cost to the environment with any of their profits from the projects. Now I call *that* ecological imperialism!"

A third encouraging effort that I discovered was the Brazilian Institute for Forestry Development (IBDF), working to establish national parks in Brazil. An American international parks consultant, Dr. Gary Wetterberg, had been loaned to the government to assist with a master plan for the Amazon. And just in time. The current status of parks is precarious. Only two areas were officially managed—Pico da Neblina covering 5.5 million acres, and the Amazon (Tapajóz) National Park, 2.5 million. They are still mostly parks on paper.

The future outlook is more encouraging. Brazil could create one of the best-designed systems of natural areas in the world. This work was being directed by the professional skill and mettlesome temperament of Maria Theresa Jorge Padua, now head of Brazil's National Parks Service. At that time she was probably the highest-placed woman in any conservation office in the world that I'd ever met. I thought her black eyes were as fierce and determined as Indira Gandhi's tawny ones.

Maria Theresa had planned that roughly 47 million acres, at a minimum, be set aside for future national parks in the Amazon region. This means that five percent of Brazil's Amazonia would be protected. If all natural resources criteria were followed, the park system could preserve up to 75 percent of the species that exist in the Amazon Basin on a mere five percent of the land!

Strange as it sounds, cities and tourism are being considered as another way of saving Amazon backcountry. Cities must be self-contained—company-town communities—supporting light industry and artisan shops. Food and other life necessities would have to be imported from southern Brazil. Creeping colonization and slums festering into the forest could not be allowed.

As Dr. Myers puts it, "The only long-term solution to saving tropical forests is rapid urbanization with decent standards of living and expanded trade between rich and poor nations. Light industries like making shoes or assembling TV sets are better alternatives than putting chainsaws and matches to the forest."

Utilization of existing fish and wildlife was another strategy under discussion. With proper management there can be game cropping and aquaculture of animals such as the manatee (which is more nutritious than beef), tapir, agouti, nutria, capybara, and turtles (the so-called "cattle of the Amazon"). Fish, the greatest food resource in the Amazon, might continue to feed protein-deficient people, provided that swamp forests would not be destroyed by lumbering or overfished commercially.

Lastly, "agri-mazonia-culture" is a growing new practice on small family farms. Most locals don't even realize how ecologically sound their system is. They grow a potpourri of native crops—rice, beans, corn, squash, manioc, bananas, and coffee—all mixed together on varzea soil. Free-ranging chickens provide insect control and eventually tasty protein. The variety of plants mimics rain forest diversity in miniature. These farmers are not practicing super-tech agriculture to make lots of money. Rather they grow only enough for their own needs, and to maintain a simple, healthy lifestyle.

By the end of these travels, my conclusion was that no matter what type of development takes place, Amazonia should be kept in *as natural a state as possible*. The ultimate goal should not be millions in short-term profits and quick trade-offs for exclusive use of the First World; instead, environmental stability and self-sustainment of Amazon inhabitants.

I left Belém on a Sunday night at 2:00 A.M. It was hot, muggy, rainy. I was tired after this three-month-long assignment. Curiously, I had a light heart. I just could not believe that the Amazon's future is entirely bleak. For one thing, Latin American governments are keenly sensitive to foreign criticism and world opinion. Possibly all the finger pointing in the press, negative as it can be, will force decision makers to pay attention to the environmental warning signs. For another, *Amazon Jungle: Green Hell to Red Desert?* has finally been translated into Portuguese. Its revelations should have beneficial ecological effects. Another reason for my guarded optimism is the increasing number of environmental-minded leaders in Latin America. There is now a Special Secretariat for the Environment (SEMA) in Brasília, who can relate directly to high government levels.

As I boarded the plane, I clutched my burlap coffee sack firmly under my arm. It was too precious to check in as baggage. In it I had stuffed the Jivaro grass skirts that Rolf and I had worn to the ship's masquerade party. There was also a pod of achiote, the hammock I'd taken out on the Transamazônica Highway, a dried piranha, an Amazon pottery red sugar bowl and some fine Brazilian coffee. The great jet slowly gained altitude and turned north over the 200-mile-wide mouth of the Amazon River. I gazed down onto blackness and wondered: will environmental concerns within each nation save Amazonia? Will economics—the soaring costs of roads, petroleum, machinery, and construction—slow down development? Or will Amazonia save herself? Perhaps after 60 million years of adapting the perfect ecosystem for that harsh environment, she has more resiliency than we realize. Her built-in survival mechanisms may minimize the intensity of human exploitation. Certainly we are already seeing many negative feedbacks—erosion, soil compaction, climatic changes, flooding, disease. People have come, people have gone, people are going. Amazonia has already weathered booms and busts in rubber, gold, oil, and colonization. Maybe she'll weather multinational corporate development as well.

Now we were high in the sky and headed for Miami. I lay back in my seat and relaxed. The long trip was over: Manú, the Amazon River, the highways, and the Bragatina. Seven thousand miles. I had seen many places and many moods of Amazonia. A slow smile spread on my lips as I realized what a long way I'd come. My path had started with the miniature microcosm of Lake Atitlán, Guatemala, with its flightless grebes and rustling reeds. It had unfolded and evolved over many assignments to the vast and complex Amazonian rain forest. In coming to know something of the ecology of each place, I had been privileged to glimpse the wonders of the natural world. And sadly I'd witnessed what can happen when wildlife and wildlands are not treated wisely. Truly, we humans *must* be the stewards of our planet.

UPDATE

- My article for <u>Audubon</u> appeared in the November 1979 issue, entitled "Heaven—not Hell."

- As I write this Update on December 26, 1998, the lead editorial in the <u>New York Times</u> memorializes the ten-year anniversary of the murder of Chico Mendes, rubber tapper from Xapuri, Brazil. As the <u>Times</u> points out, he did more than any other person to foster conservation of the Amazon. Tappers were being driven off their land and killed by invading ranchers (982 men murdered in land disputes 1964 to 1988). Mr. Mendes was head of Brazil's National Council of Rubber Tappers and an activist against cutting rain forests in Amazonia. He even lobbied the World Bank. It once financed roads into the forests; it now finances extractive reserves. The idea of setting aside forest land by the government to be managed by local tappers, thereby keeping the ecosystem intact and productive for rubber, nuts, heart-of-palm, etc., was this ecomartyr's vision. Brazil has set aside 7.5 million acres as extractive reserves in the Amazon as of 1999.

- Dr. George Woodwell, the scientist who joined us on the Manú National Park trip, writes: "Amazonian forests are being devoured by greed everywhere that there is not some powerful governmental effort to protect them, and that is locally enforced by forest dwellers. In Acre (state), for instance, the establishment of very large 'Extractive Reserves' has been a great success, because the rubber tappers, supported by students and staff of the University, and by our own staff, have taken an active interest in defending the region from cattle ranchers, loggers, and others. The Amazon Basin is a frontier. There is no law. I see little hope for preservation of the public interest in an intact and working landscape without vigorous governmental support and equally vigorous local interest. Our own efforts in Acre are powerfully effective locally and show it can be done."

Signed,George M. Woodwell, Director,
The Woods Hole Research Center, January 7, 1999.

- Is the Amazon rain forest still burning? A quick scan of figures shows that between 1978–1988, <u>8,158 square miles/year were destroyed</u>. That's the size of New Jersey! Then between 1988–1989 and 1990–1991 deforestation dropped by half, or <u>4,452 square miles/year</u>. Suddenly from 1991 to 1994 the burning became worse by 34 percent. It hit <u>5,958 square miles/year</u>, or roughly the size of the Adirondack Park! 1995 to 1996, deforestation zoomed out of control—<u>11,196 square miles/year</u>. By 1998, the average was again <u>8,158 square miles/year</u>.

- *Professor Sir Ghillean Prance, a noted tropical botanist and Director of the Royal Botanic Gardens at Kew in England, has this to say: "The deforestation rates in Brazil began to decrease markedly from 1989 onwards, and I was encouraged by this. However, 1996 saw a huge rise in the total area deforested. Because of El Niño in 1998 there was an enormous amount of burning in the Amazon. It was alarming to see on satellite images the pall of smoke that covered the region. Even trees 1,000 to 2,000 years old burned in the normally moist forests. The battle to stop deforestation is by no means won, but there are many encouraging signs in Brazil and other Amazon countries. I believe there's a possibility it can be brought under control."*

- *A couple of the encouraging signs for saving some Amazonian rain forest are (1) that the World Bank and the World Wildlife Fund are joining together in a major thrust to save ten percent of all the world's rain forests. (2) The President of Brazil, Fernando Henrique Cardoso, recently pledged to save ten percent of his nation's rain forests (240,000 square miles) as national parks and ecologically protected areas. In the meantime, even this modest project is on shaky ground. Given the enormous budget deficit and falling <u>real</u> (Brazilian currency), government officials have slashed spending in every department, including the $250 million pilot project to save rain forest. If alternative cuts can be found, this environmental money may be restored.*

- *I am reminded of Dr. Thomas Lovejoy's sage prediction given in 1975 in Manú National Park that "the primary forest is within a few years of being 80 percent nonexistent."*

17

CORCOVADO—
DO YOU HEAR the GUNS?

My little horse was prancing lightly over the stars which lay strewn on Corcovado's dark beach. The vaulted sky was mirrored on a thin sheen of seawater over flat black sand. The real sky arched above me, dominated by an enormous moon and towering thunderheads. Thus I rode, astride, between two tropical star-spangled heavens.

On my left, long Pacific combers pounded ragged rock pinnacles and reefs. Not a ship's light, nor a hut's lantern, broke the darkness along this deserted coast on the Osa Peninsula. It was the wildest beach in Costa Rica, and possibly on the entire Pacific side of Central America. On my right, Joaquin sat a stubby mount, silhouetted against the rising moon. As I glanced at his lean torso, slouched sombrero, and slung rifle, the strains of *Do You Hear the Guns, Fernando?* strummed softly in my head. He could have been a young revolutionary guerilla rather than the reliable assistant chief ranger of this remote national park.

Five of us were trotting northward along this wide beach towards an isolated biological field station. We planned to spend the night there and continue early morning on foot to La Llorona Cataract. It was one of Corcovado's spectacles and worth tackling the 24-mile round trip to admire. Two other park guards, unarmed and leading pack animals, followed. One was a rakish, rag-tag older man who had already made himself known to me. His hair sprung out like black coiled springs from under a battered baseball cap. He was dressed in dingy brown polyester pants and shirt, not the trim brown uniform and arm emblem that Joaquin wore.

Last in line, Loren McIntyre, a splendid freelance photographer/writer specializing in Latin America, ambled along on a big bay festooned with camera bags. All were encased in waterproof covers.

I gave my mare a nudge as we neared the Río Llorona. This was

Joaquin, assistant chief ranger of Corcovado National Park, rides beside the sea on way to La Llorona cataract.

the third our group had forded that night—and the largest and most dangerous. We'd timed our ride to cross when the tide was out. Our horses needed to touch bottom so as not to be washed into the sea on the swift, out-rushing currents. Even so, large ocean fish sometimes hunted a short way upriver. The thought of a sawfish or shark slicing into my horse's body was horrifying. She hesitated, then plunged bravely into the river. Water rose to her belly, then to my knees. After several powerful strokes, the horse found her footing and completed the crossing without mishap.

A half-hour later a bulky shadow suddenly charged out from a clump of coconut palms. It raced diagonally across the sand towards Joaquin and me. My mare reared up in fright. Abruptly I found myself flat on my back. The shadow fled on down the shore. My companions rode up. Domingo retrieved the horse. Everyone burst into laughter. Joaquin explained my "assailant" was a giant, feral, boar hog which had been sleeping under the vegetation. He waited for nesting sea turtles and ate their eggs.

I lay still a moment longer, collecting my senses and giving silent thanks that I'd landed on a starry beach rather than a stony one. I began chuckling and climbed shamefaced back in the saddle.

Before midnight we had completed our trek and dismounted wearily before two thatched wooden buildings. One was a kitchen/lab, the other a dormitory. We unpacked the horses, and Domingo led them to a small water tank. Then he hobbled them out to graze for the night. The other guard brought in firewood and quickly had a quaint three-holed woodstove blazing. I made a hot soup for everyone and opened a large tin of sardines. Exhausted, we

swiftly crashed onto hard slat platforms covered with old mosquito netting while a torrent of rain suddenly sluiced down outside.

Now I was waking up to a sunny day with the sound of sandpipers and waves nearby. Joaquin and I walked to the beach and
bathed in the waterfall. La Llorona plummeted over a steep hill-

**La Llorona waterfall flows right out of the rain forest and pitches down a
cliff into the Pacific Ocean.**

side in silvery rivulets right onto the beach. Loren went for his daily ten-kilometer jog along the surf's edge. Giggling like two kids, we dashed first under the cold, clear freshets and let them beat on our heads and faces. I gulped delicious draughts of water. Then we waded into the warm salty waves just a few feet away to swim.

At breakfast, Domingo produced a strong pot of Costa Rican coffee. Gallantly, he poured me a cup. It reminded me of Ramón sweetly preparing my espresso and bringing it to my tent in the Dominican. But then Domingo threw me a flirtatious look and whispered, "Anna, I slept well thanks to the repellent you loaned me, but "*la reina*" (the queen) didn't come to my bed to warm me when it got chilly."

I almost choked on the coffee before letting out a great guffaw. "You are a funny man," I said. "Pshaw! Surely the temperature didn't drop below 80°F all night. La reina was sleeping with '*los angelitos.*'"

After breakfast, Loren prepared his cameras, and we spent a busy morning exploring and photographing sea grottos, watching undulating strings of pelicans glide parallel to the beach without a wingbeat, and climbing the prop roots of huge red mangroves. Loren was in his glory, switching telephoto, wide-angle, and close-up lenses on three different Nikons with three different films.

Later than day, Joaquin and his two men had to hike farther up the coast to check a remote ranger station. I decided to walk with them to sense the moods of the rain forest and watch for wildlife. As we set out on a narrow trail, a light rain filtered down even though it was dry season. (Corcovado receives 220 inches a year, and it may pour for three weeks without pause.)

The forest dimmed to a greenish, watery light. The dampness released pungent odors. Joaquin pointed his machete at a "monkey vine," thick as a ship's hawser, corkscrewing into the treetops. A band of white-faced capuchins came cavorting through the canopy and used the vine as a playground. I was riveted with my binoculars looking up when Joaquin whispered tersely, "*Terciopelo!*"

I glanced down and saw a streak of yellow slide past us. A seven-foot, "velvet-skin," or fer-de-lance, was out hunting. It is a much-feared and highly poisonous snake of the tropics, related to rattlers. But it wasn't hunting us. Nevertheless, from then on, I looked down at the ground as much as up in the trees.

Soon we passed through a patchy growth of "pioneer" trees and scrubby grass. Joaquin identified these as old pasture plots and farmland which squatters had made and then abandoned in 1973. At the time when President Daniel Oduber created Corcovado National Park in October 1975, 100 peasant families already lived here. They had simply wandered onto the peninsula, grabbed the land illegally, cut and burned virgin forest, and planted subsistence crops. They would have stayed until soil erosion and compaction forced them to leave and repeat the process elsewhere—usually every two to three years.

President Oduber's declaration of national park status was critically important for Corcovado. Only five percent of the land had been desecrated. Ninety-five percent was still virgin, uninhabited woodlands. (Prior to that, the tract was owned by a U.S. multinational timber corporation, but it had never been logged.) The Costa Rican government bought out and relocated the squatters at a cost of about two million dollars. This strategy is clearly the most intelligent and benign way to handle the problem of illegal colonization. It gives the fragile tropical soil time to regenerate itself, the natural vegetation to regrow, and the peasants a chance to start a new and better life.

As President Oduber said philosophically, "It may cost two million now, but how much will it cost 50 years from now?"

We reached the other ranger station in a couple of hours. Our shirts were soaked in sweat from the sweltering moist forest. Stepping onto the wind-swept empty beach we felt ten degrees cooler. Again, I was impressed by the wildness of this park. We were the only humans for miles and miles. Corcovado's very isolation is its salvation.

The rangers had work to do at the station, so I started back alone. They'd catch up later. Before entering the forest, I armed myself with a stout walking stick of driftwood. Peccaries and velvet-skins beware! (What I really wished for was a gun.)

Joaquin's parting words held a warning. "If you smell rotten garbage or hear clicking noises, look for a tree to climb, Anna. Big bands of *chanchos del monte* (white-lipped peccaries) roam the park. They have been known to chase, corner, and kill people—infrequently," he added.

What he *didn't* say was that few tropical trees are easy to shinny. Either they are too thick (some were up to ten feet in diameter), too thin, too thorny, too slippery, or too buttressed to climb.

I asked innocently, "Do the pigs make those clicking noises?"

"No," replied Joaquin seriously. "It's their teeth and tusks."

Domingo threw me a wink and a leer. "It's safer here."

"Not with *you* around, *picaro* (rascal)," I retorted. With that I strode resolutely away and walked for an hour without smelling or hearing anything suspicious. A kinkajou scuttled up the midrib of an enormous palm frond. Some spider monkeys swung by overhead. Suddenly, the frightened shriek of an agouti startled me. I scanned the woods for an available trunk. An ecology textbook description flashed through my mind: the tropical rain forest holds over 100 different species of palms and trees on any two-and-a-half acres as compared to a dozen species in northern USA.

Out loud, I said sternly, "None of those 100 around here will save me." I banged my walking stick against a trunk and declared, "If you spend all your time looking for pigs, you won't enjoy the trail. If you spend all your life looking for dangers, you won't enjoy the journey."

The forest fell silent. I went on hiking. Strangely it became a serene place and reminded me of a favorite Adirondack trail through old-growth beech, birch and maple woods. I passed a small, clear streamlet and drank from it, just as I would do in the Adirondack Park. I arrived back at La Llorona to find Loren taking an afternoon nap until the light became more magical. That night the five of us feasted on fresh fried fish, plantains from the forest, and spicy rice, while Loren told exciting stories in good Spanish about his *National Geographic* assignments (totaling 25 articles and books) and his discovery of the most distant source of the Amazon River.

When we left La Llorona field station, we traveled again by night. Again we forded the three rivers at low tide. No wild hogs charged. We arrived at La Sirena safely at 3:00 A.M.

What was left of that night, we slept away in the huge, airy, wall-less, thatched dormitory at La Sirena's main station. But the snores, rustles, and tosses of 20-odd rangers and a handful of scientists and students around me was hardly peaceful. I determined to set up my little orange Mt. Marcy tent next to the ocean and sleep there for the remainder of my stay.

Gradually I met some of the researchers during meals and asked if I might accompany them on fieldwork. One was studying "poison arrow" frogs. Another small group was into mangrove ecology. A third was watching the behavior of tapirs. It seemed impossible that each one of us had flown in from San José, the capitol, to La Sirena, in a Cessna 180 prop plane. No roads reached the park's borders. No landings were possible by sea due to the surf, reefs, and lack of docking facilities. Air was the only way, even if one had already flown thousands of miles to get to Costa Rica. Flying over that massively crumpled-up country of mountains, volcanoes, ridges, and rain forests, one was finally received only by a grass strip and a wind sock.

Loren and I, however, were not here to do research. We'd been sent by *National Geographic* to do an article on "National Parks of Central America." Since Costa Rica has a grand group of parks and since Corcovado is the star of its park system, we started here. The 89,000 acres hold an amazing array of ecosystems ranging from palm tangles, brackish lagoons, mangrove forests, to 21 miles of wild beaches, and dense lowland rain forest. The largest tree in Costa Rica—a 260-foot-tall ceiba—lives here. The park is unique in the world for its incredibly rich biodiversity on such a small area. Its main thrust is not to provide recreation for the casual tourist, rather, protection for the fauna and flora and opportunity for scientific research.

Arranging this assignment had taken pure "chutzpa" on my part. Since being appointed a commissioner to the Adirondack Park Agency in 1976, I had been tied down very tightly by my responsibilities to this six-million-acre park. Every two weeks I had to be at headquarters in Ray Brook for committee meetings with staff. Every month there was a monthly meeting for two or three days with the other commissioners. Foreign travel had become almost impossible to arrange. I was restless. I was bored. I was homesick for Central America. In short, this woodswoman needed to rekindle and reconnect with her other more adventurous world.

There's a quote by Bernard Shaw that I love. "The people who get on in this world are the people who get up and look for the circumstances they want, and, if they can't find them, make them."

Taking heart, I decided to "make" an adventurous and worthwhile trip to Central American wilderness happen and take two to three months off from the A.P.A. that winter.

I recalled attending the first conference on Central American parks held in Costa Rica in 1974 and making many contacts. One spin-off had been a month's consulting job in 1978 at CATIE (Tropical Agriculture Center for Research and Training). I produced a booklet on "Wildlands of Middle America" which permitted me to learn about every park and protected natural area on the

isthmus. Furthermore, in the past year I'd completed an article for
National Geographic on Voyageurs National Park in Minnesota. It
was slated for the big issue on "National Parks of the United
States."

Idea! Why not propose an article on "National Parks of Central
America?" As far as I knew, it had never been done for a major popular magazine. So I did.

The editors liked the proposal. They assigned Loren McIntyre,
a seasoned, long-time, freelance photographer, to the story and
asked me to write it. In 1980 we spent three months during dry season covering twelve landmark national parks in six countries.
Some of these contained fascinating wilderness areas. It became
the most rewarding assignment of my life.

Our timing was excellent. This tiny "upstart" of a country called
Costa Rica had recently accomplished miracles in park planning
and wildland conservation. Roughly ten percent of this West
Virginia-sized nation had or has gone into parkland. There were
over 25 formally decreed, protected units with 300 to 400 National
Park Service employees to care for them. Units ranged from
national parks to national monuments to biological reserves. Never
mind that Costa Rica got started into parks almost 100 years later
than the USA. (Yellowstone was formed in 1872 and was the
world's first national park). Never mind that the few limited
attempts at protecting natural areas happened in the early 1900s
without benefit of a park service or even the term "national park"
in use. Since 1970-71, the dynamic Costa Rican National Park
Service has chalked up success after success. Loren and I owed our
very presence at Corcovado to this fortuitous array of events and a
few very dedicated Costa Ricans.

One such person was the Administrator of Corcovado, María
Elena Mora. At the time I met her, she was the highest placed
woman in conservation in Costa Rica, if not all Central America.
The presence of professional women in outdoor work was a fairly
new phenomenon in Latin America. Costa Rican girls had only
begun taking college courses in conservation of natural resources
1973–75 and then worked in backcountry and wilderness parks
shortly after that. This, too, lagged behind the States, but not by
much. I was only the second woman to major in natural resources
conservation at Cornell in the late 1950s and the first female assistant professor for that department in 1970–71.

"What sort of reception did you get," I inquired of María Elena, "when you first arrived here and faced an all-male staff?"

"It was a 'baptism of fire,'" she admitted. "It took about six months to get their confidence and feel respected as their boss."

At 26, María Elena was a model example of a successful park superintendent. She joined her staff of 22 men in riding patrols with a rifle, clearing trails with a machete, ordering and dispensing food and medicine, and assisting visiting scientists.

Joaquin verified this by saying, "She does everything we men do, and then some."

Yet her soft voice and delicate complexion belie a stalwart constitution, courage, and indifference to convention. I watched María Elena heave the luggage of two departing researchers into the bucket loader of a small tractor and drive it briskly out onto the grass airstrip. The Cessna was due momentarily.

"I'm so excited about my job here that I just can't sit around an office all day and watch others work," she said, grinning at me. She wiped sweat from her face and tossed back her black bobbed hair matter-of-factly while she waited.

Quickly I snapped some special photos of María Elena, apart from Loren's coverage. Later, at my cabin, I proudly added them to my slide lecture on "Women and Wilderness" which I give at colleges and workshops in the Adirondacks and across the country. I was pleased. By chance, I'd discovered one of the first "fierce eco-feminists" in a Latin country.

"How often do you get to fly out to San José, and what do you do there?" I asked curiously.

"About every three or four weeks. I always have business or meetings to attend at the Park Service. Later, I'll take off my uniform, put on a dress, go out to dinner with my parents. Sometimes I see a movie with friends, and maybe I get my hair trimmed. But that's it. After three days I'm so homesick that I'm ready to fly back to Corcovado."

"What's the worst problem you face now in the park?"

"Apart from 'cabin fever' when it pours for two or three weeks and everyone gets the fidgets," she said, "it's gold."

"Gold!" I exclaimed. "What do you mean?"

"Corcovado has many rivers running out of it along the borders. Some have been found to have gold in their beds. Placer-mining has begun on the Río Carate with heavy equipment right outside the park. The noise is awful," she frowned. "The river is full of silt. I'm afraid mining companies are eyeing rivers *inside* the park."

"How can they do that?" I questioned angrily. "Corcovado belongs to the country and its people, not to gold seekers."

María Elena shrugged. "That's true, but my rangers have intercepted men illegally panning for gold here. They believe any gold they find is theirs. Most are armed. My staff and I now carry firearms when we patrol that area."

The Cessna roared in, and María Elena walked out to greet the pilot and say farewell to the scientists.

I spent the next day with a budding entomologist, Darylene. She was a graduate student, studying "long-wing" butterflies of the genus *Heliconius*. She slipped easily through the forest carrying only an insect net, felt-tipped pens, and a sandwich. Looking nymph-like and cool under a huge, dainty, white hat, she dexterously caught a butterfly and marked its wing. "It's my 992nd *Heliconius*," she said triumphantly. "Maybe I'll break 1,000 today. You'll bring me luck." She set free the pretty flyer.

Her research concerns the butterflies' movements, ranges, and pollination of passionflowers. Long-wings sip mainly nectar from these gorgeous jungle flowers. Darylene traipsed behind the slowly flying, bright insect she'd marked and watched it feed. Here and there she put dye on parts of passionflowers.

"Why do you do that?" I asked. "Those blossoms are brilliant enough."

"When the *Heliconius* drinks nectar with its proboscis, the dye transfers to its face and mouth parts. When I catch that individual again, I can tell by its number how far it flew. In a larger context, my research deals with how the flow of pollen becomes the gene flow of plants—as assisted by butterflies."

"Won't it take years to catch enough of the marked insects to prove your point?"

"Oh, no! I've been getting a 50% recapture of my numbered specimens," she related proudly. "It's obvious to me that this genus has an amazing 'memory' and flies long distances to find flowers."

We were silent while she jotted down notes. Then she led the way to a tiny jungle stream with crystal clear water. We sat down for a picnic lunch. Darylene told me further secrets of this butterfly's magical tropical world.

"Passionflowers are usually poisonous. They contain a form of cyanide combined with sugar molecules." She spoke as if reading a murder mystery story. "Since adult *Heliconius* butterflies only eat nectar, they probably ingest very little cyanide. Most likely they store this somehow in their bodies, and it's enough to sicken or kill most butterfly predators. Although the striking colors and gay designs make the butterflies most conspicuous to insect-eating birds, they apparently warn them off instead of acting as an attractive come-on.

"To make the story even more amazing," Darylene went on, "adult female *Heliconius* lay their eggs on young leaves of passionflowers. When the caterpillars hatch, they are already sitting 'at table' and can start munching. They are able to detoxify some cyanide with special enzymes, even though cyanide is the main defense chosen by passionflowers to protect themselves from defoliation by caterpillars."

My mind was swimming. Truly the neotropical world was a maze of connections and relationships.

Just to wow me some more, Darylene told two more little secrets. "These passionflower butterflies have communal roosts where they rest and sleep. And only the females may live to the ripe old age of six months!" She smiled gently. "Really *Heliconius* is the Cadillac of butterflies!"

On my last night in Corcovado, I resolved to take supper to my tent and spend a relaxing evening watching the sun set into the Pacific and the stars come out. First, though, I moved my orange tent back along the beach to a sandier spot. The couple of nights I'd already spent here had been dreadful. Instead of snoring rangers, I heard hundreds, if not thousands, of fiddler crabs creeping around the tent constantly.

Furthermore, stripes of black upended rock strata criss-crossed the shore, alternating with windrows of round cobbles. Patches of smooth black sand were hard to find. I didn't want to be crammed between the high tide mark and a rocky ridge again.

Luckily there was plenty of daylight left before the abrupt tropical plunge into night. I finally found a dry, wide, flat patch of beach and set my tent back up. Then I built a big bonfire of driftwood. A small breeze cooled the air. The sun slid down to the sea in a spectacular blaze of orange, saffron, apricot, gold, and tangerine behind layered purple clouds. The colors reflected in shattered patterns on the deep blue combers riding shorewards with their mantillas of lacy foam.

That evening I slept soundly for 12 hours, knowing my visit to the national park was a success in terms of article material. I could make readers aware of this splendid place and the network of parks in this conservation-minded country.

When I awoke at dawn, the first thing I saw was a huge moon setting in the west and shining silver into my eyes. The second thing was the east turning lime-green as hundreds of birds began to chorus. It sounded like all 850 species found in the park were practicing. The third thing I saw were the large paw marks of a large jaguar five feet from my tent flap and encircling it.

Corcovado had outdone Manú. Funny, I didn't feel bored, restless, or homesick anymore. I couldn't wait to go on to the Darién.

UPDATE

- María Elena Mora went on from Corcovado to become regional supervisor of several national parks in the Guanacaste region of Costa Rica and then sub-director of Costa Rica's National Park Service. Currently she is Director of Conservation Area Arenal. This is the "Heart of Energy for Costa Rica" and covers 250,561 hectares, or 618,885 acres. It includes a large reservoir and seven protected areas around it, plus the major rivers which supply hydro-power.

- There is still a threat facing Corcovado from gold mining in and out of the park, but in fairly low scale. Its bigger problems are other types of mining and illegal hunting of pacas, peccaries, and tapirs.

- Two marvelous additions were made to the national park system in Costa Rica. A 500,000-acre frontier park, La Amistad (Friendship), back-to-back with Panama's La Amistad and Volcán Barú National Parks on its western border. The other is the mysterious, romantic Cocos Islands, 300 miles offshore in the Pacific.

- In 1983, the J. Paul Getty Wildlife Conservation award went to Dr. Mario Boza and Mr. Alvaro Ugalde, former directors of the National Park Service. Their vision and indomitable devotion to saving natural areas in Costa Rica will never be forgotten.

- Today, 1999, Costa Rica has 24 National Parks, nine Biological Reserves, 31 Protected Zones, 11 Forest Reserves, 45 Wildlife Reguges, and 16 other Protected Categories. This is an incredible 23.8% of its national territory (far more than the U.S.A.). The total area is 1,238,142 hectares, or 3,058,211 acres. The National Park Service is now SINAC (National System of Conservation Areas).

- And Domingo? He's probably still wrangling horses in Corcovado and eyeing all the sweet young female graduate students who come to do research.

18

DARIÉN

I'd heard that the Darién combines legendary rainfall, thick cloud cover, dense jungle, jagged ranges, quivering mud flats, dread diseases, and biting insects in season. It had stymied Balboa and other early European explorers. It has thwarted modern highway engineers and cartographers. Yet during my ten-day expedition to Panama's proposed Darién National Park that winter of 1980, the sun blazed, nights turned cool, most rivers ran clear, and only five mosquitoes bit me.

For our *National Geographic* magazine article on "National Parks of Central America," I chose this wildest and largest of parks on the isthmus covered by tropical rain forests, twisting rivers, and rippled by high peaks. This park is definitely *not* made for casual reconnoitering and recreation. Expeditioning is the only way. The only access available to Loren, the photographer, and me was by single engine plane, dugout canoe, and on foot.

Before we flew from Panama City to our jumping-off spot, Yaviza, at the end of the Pan American Highway, I had a bright idea. Why not contact Benjamin Cuevas Montezuma, the ranger from Volcán Barú National Park in western Panama, who had been such a strong and useful assistant to Clyde Smith and me in 1972. I discussed it with Loren and convinced him we would be better off with a third teammate we knew and could trust. While still in Panama City, we arranged with the national park office to borrow him for this assignment.

Benjamin arrived by bus from Davíd, and the three of us flew to Yaviza. That hot afternoon it appeared to be a sleepy, black Panamanian, congested, jungle town where no one smiled at us until we did. Then they were very friendly. We opted to set up our tents by the Tuirá River where it was ten degrees cooler than in town. After supper, we strolled into Yaviza and found everyone was

wide-awake. Juke boxes were blasting from several cantinas. Loren
coaxed us in one. I discovered another side to this hard-working
cameraman. He loved to dance!

The 63-year-old was soon jiving with a pregnant 16-year-old.
Bristan and Fabio, the two black boatmen who had come to meet
us and set a time to depart next day, quickly ran home to get their
wives. They started dancing. Benjamin glanced at me shyly. I shook
my head and said, "I don't know how." Just then Loren gyrated past
us and yelled, "Come on, Anne. Just jiggle."

Before I knew it, Benjamin grabbed my hand and pulled me
onto the floor. We made a hilarious little United Nations—two
white Americans, a Guaymí, four black Panamanians, and a mulatto teenager from Colombia. The on-lookers screamed with laughter as Loren swayed wildly around the room with his partner. We
cooled down with bottles of beer. At ten o'clock we headed back to
the river a little tipsy and still laughing. I couldn't imagine a cra-
zier way to spend my first night in the Darién.

Bristan and Fabio arrived early at our campsite with a 30-foot
wooden dugout and 40 HP motor. We loaded up and cruised to a
riverside gas stop to fill the 50-gallon tank with gas. The two
rangers were highly skilled in navigating these rivers and took no
chances. Our goal was to meet and photograph primitive Choco
and Cuna Amerindians who lived deep inside the proposed national park. They still live and dress in their traditional, natural way.
One objective stated in the Darién National Park's master plan was
that the unique cultural traits and life-styles of these "eco-systems
people" be preserved.

Our destination was Púcuru, a Cuna village two days upriver
from Yaviza and a day's hike from the Colombian border. To start
into the trackless region of rain forest we had to motor through a
section of tidal flats with deep mud banks. Mid-morning I asked to
get out of the dugout for a rest stop. With the first step I started
sinking into fetid, soupy, grayish muck. It almost felt like quick-
sand. In a panic, I threw myself flat on my back upon the treacherous, quaking mud. The hoots and jokes from my canoemates did
not charm or calm me in the least. Loren aimed a camera and took
several "candid" shots. At once they hauled me over the side and
scooped off handfuls of filth. Then the men all politely turned to
the bow while I sat on the gunwhale in the stern and shyly peed
over the stern. Later, I got my revenge. The others had to sit in the
canoe until afternoon, seeing and smelling muddy me. By then we

A Choco family eating supper "upstairs" in their airy chonto palm hut, complete with dog, in the Darién jungle.

reached rocks and clear water upriver where I could get out, swim, and change clothes.

That evening it began to pour as we were still motoring up the Tuirá. Bristan, our senior boatman, dashed to a lone Choco hut perched on ten-foot stilts to beg shelter. Benjamin and Loren hustled piles of photographic and camping gear ashore. Rarely have I been treated to such hospitality. The Choco father smoothed down the ground for our tents beneath the raised chonto palm floor of his hut. The Choco mother made us a three-stick cooking fire. Their eldest daughter lugged in two pails of water. Younger children shooed away dogs, spiders, chickens, and toddlers. Only the grandmother sat back silently on her haunches, slicing up an iguana for stew. While we five adventurers dined on freeze-dried chow mein and French apple compote, I was wondering what to say if she offered us iguana. Maybe we could sidetrack her with a chocolate bar? It was another United Nations night.

Entertainment that evening was each other. The Chocos gaped at cameras, binoculars, blond hair, and stout boots. I tried not to stare at the bare-breasted women whose skin bore strange black designs. Benjamin didn't gawk at anything. Only much later did I realize he didn't understand Cuna or Choco, nor did they understand Guaymí. Moreover, he was used to bare-breasted women.

When the family tired of our company, they climbed up the tiny steps cut in a long log which was wedged from ground to rafters. This was the ramp to their living and sleeping quarters above. The babies were laid on cloths upon the smooth palmstrip floor. The adults slept in hammocks or on the airy floor. There were no walls. When everyone had gone "to bed" except the father, he reached down, pulled up the log, and turned it upside down. Now the steps were useless. It was his way of "locking up for the night."

"Downstairs," we were pleasantly dry.

Before we left next morning, Loren endeared himself by presenting each member of the Choco family with a Polaroid portrait. These color pictures were the first they'd ever seen. Those pictures

Young Choco woman gets her bangs cut before being photographed.

Loren McIntyre poses with two Choco women, towering above them.

would be treasured for years and were the perfect Thank You gift.

Did they realize how beautiful their huge, dark, sloe eyes looked? And their even white teeth and full smiling lips? Each young woman wore plastic dime-store ornaments in her glossy long black hair, worn dogtags and cheap bead necklaces, and a colorful wrap-around piece of material circling her hips. That was all. I noted how full their breasts seemed, how dark the nipples. Could they all be nursing babies?

On the other hand, the men were dressed in cheap Western work clothes. The polyester pants, dull-colored nylon shirts, and plastic belts were dowdy, even ugly. Yet, one or two Chocos had their canines filed to points, and leaves dangled from their ears. All were barefoot.

We headed on for Púcuru. The farther we went upstream, the more turbulent grew the rapids. Bristan balanced sturdily in the bow adroitly maneuvering around foam-flecked boulders with a pole. Fabio adroitly lowered and raised the engine over rocks in response to hand and foot signals from his partner. Finally it became too shallow to pole or motor.

"Come on," shouted Bristan, leaping into the whitewater. "Push!"

From then on, we all hauled and shoved our laden craft (weighing almost two tons) upriver by brute force. Now Benjamin's great strength came into play. Bristan and Fabio were impressed and began chatting with Benjamin in Spanish for the first time on this trip. Until then, they'd ignored him, for they had no bond by race. Now their common bond was as tough and strong park rangers braving the wilderness.

We stayed in bathing suits all day. While we were cooled by the river, our legs were bruised and our backs strained. What a tremendous contrast, I thought, to be sitting in slimy, muddy stinking clothes *inside* the dugout one day, and trudging barefoot, wet, and squeaky clean *outside* the dugout the next.

The Cunas who met us were far more reserved than the Chocos. For awhile it looked like we would not be invited to enter a hut nor permitted to photograph. Would our whole river trip have been useless? Then Loren repeated his Polaroid magic. He soon had the super-shy women and children, wearing hand-embroidered mola blouses, metal nose rings, bobbed hair, and beaded leg bands, clustered around.

"Take me! Take me!" they begged in ragged Spanish.

Their village was extremely clean and orderly with thatched huts of banana and palm leaves. Women were smoking wild pig, a small monkey, catfish, and various birds on a big grill. A few old wooden chairs and a table stood nearby. Unlike the cordial river Chocos, we were not invited to stay overnight with the Cuna in the forest. So we headed back downriver to an abandoned little banana patch and empty ranchito. Here we set up our tents and put Loren's camera gear undercover. I found a tiny glen full of

Dugout heading through rapids on the Tuirá River with Anne, Benjamin, and Fabio, motorist.   *Credit: Loren McIntyre*

In the shallows, the only way upstream was to haul dugout by brute strength with its two tons of equipment.   *Credit: Loren McIntyre*

emerald ferns and moss with a trickle of water springing out. It looked so pure and crystal clear that I filled our canteens immediately and drank without even thinking of using Halazone tablets.

Heading back downstream next morning we decided to explore the Río Balsas, which would take us to another remote part of the Darién. Going with the current was far easier than against it. Now Loren, Benjamin and I lounged like pampered travelers resting against our packs as we sped under huge, leafy rain forest trees. Sun and shadows. Sparkling rapids. We watched for wildlife. There was time to talk. Loren even played a spitting game with the boatmen—and won.

I spent time catching up on my notes. I said to Loren, "It seems to me this park and its objectives are entirely different from Corcovado. There, it is *protection*. Protecting and preserving the biodiversity, the wild gene pools, the wilderness. The main human use is research. Here in the Darién, it is *prevention*. Preventing the still untouched Cuna and Choco tribes from being absorbed and changed by Panamanian culture. Or given diseases they have no resistance against. Also, preventing hoof and mouth disease of livestock from spreading north into Panama, Central America, and possibly the States. As long as dense rain forest forms a natural barrier, the disease will remain in Colombia and other South American countries. But let the Pan American Highway be extended through Panama and connected in Colombia, and we open up a Pandora's box of plagues."

"You're right," he agreed. "Panama needs this park as a barricade to a lot of things. Imagine what would happen to drug trafficking if a paved road linked Colombia with Panama! Not to mention foreign timber companies licking their chops to harvest those old-growth trees we saw upriver. No better defense exists than impregnable rain forest, acting as a veritable isolation ward along the frontier."

"The Darién National Park can also prevent the mixing of South American fauna and flora and insect life with Central American forms. They are both very different," I explained. "Allow them to emigrate easily or hitch rides on vehicles, and a lot of species will get wiped out while others will experience population explosions."

"Well," said Loren pensively, "I hope our article can point this out. It must reach high level government people who make and manage natural areas here and in the rest of Central America."

We soon saw another threat to the proposed park. Coming to the branchoff from the Tuirá to the Balsas, we discovered outsiders—mixed-blood Panamanians and Colombians—carving out new homesteads *within* the park borders. Gallery (water edge) river forest was gone. Big banana patches covered the banks. Small rustic houses with hammocks stood here and there. It was plain to see that landless settlers were slipping in unopposed.

The Darién Province covers 22% of Panama's territory, but held, at that time, only two percent of its population. With the Pan American Highway completed to within 40-odd miles of the Colombian border, squatters, poachers, and smugglers were invading the park on both ends. Slash-and-burn agriculture with resultant wildfires, and erosion, were just beginning to scar the landscape. It reminded me of the Cuchumatanes Mountains in Guatemala and the Transamazônica Highway of Brazil all over again.

Near Tucutí, we cajoled a camping site from a lone colonist couple newly arrived from Panama City. After we'd erected our tents and had supper, we joined them in their open air hut. The river whispered past and stars trembled in the thatch roof fringes. An owl hooted hoarsely from a mango tree. It seemed like pure tranquility.

"How much land do you have here?" I asked the farmer.

"I don't know," he replied simply.

"Well, how much do you intend to cut, burn, and plant?"

"As much as my energy will allow me," he said.

That candid answer is the philosophy of squatters the world over. If I were a landless peasant, it would probably be mine, too. But I'm an ecologist and know how much more rain forest, its plants, and wildlife are worth to people untouched. It was essential that the Darién National Park be formally declared and operating.

Heading on next morning, we noted that the only deciduous trees left alongside the river were too big to chop down. They looked like ceibas, or baobabs, with huge swollen trunks and stubby branches at their tops. Bristan called them "cuipós" (*Cavanillesia platanifolia*). They made beautiful silhouettes against the thunderheads and gave the faraway hills a gray, ghostly appearance.

At a muddy bend in the river a rustic "safari park" with several ranchitos, caged birds, tables, and a young jaguar on a chain met our eyes. Immediately I motioned to Fabio to head for shore. Loren readied his cameras. A jaguar with a collar, chain, and a padlock was better than no jaguar at all. The animal's keeper came down to the dugout and welcomed us. He assured us lunch was available and the jaguar would not eat us.

"May I touch her?" I asked the young Panamanian longingly.

"Sure," he said. "She won't hurt you. I've had that jaguar since she was born by cesarean."

Quietly I approached the spotted cat, noting she looked three-quarters grown and had all her claws. As I came into reach, she immediately started to play. First she grabbed my leg, then climbed up on my back like a kitten. A *big* kitten. Finally she put her jaws on the top of my head and her paws around my neck. Her weight slowly forced me down onto my knees.

Young female jaguar, "Mancha," licks Anne's hand before climbing up on her back and head.

I wanted to play, too. But her canines were lightly abrading my scalp, and her claws were out halfway. I could feel the tremendous power in her jaws and paws. That taut, gorgeous, black-and-gold body was lithe and muscular. *If* she wanted to, she could snap my neck like a straw or rip my jugular like paper. It would be over before my thoughts could form the idea I was dead.

Suddenly I felt afraid. In the same instant I remembered that fear makes its own smell in the human body. It might entice the youngster into rougher behavior. I willed myself to stay still, be calm, and think affectionate thoughts towards the spotted cat.

The keeper ran back and pulled on her chain. He held a scrap of meat in one hand. She whirled towards him, full of life, and hungry. Grabbing the snack, she gulped it down and started licking the keeper's arm. "Mancha! Mancha!" he commanded. "*Suave con la lengua.*" (Mancha, gentle with the tongue.)

The experience of being held by a live jaguar was so impressive that I could barely eat lunch. Loren announced he'd photographed the action. Bristan and Fabio looked at me wide-eyed. Benjamin wore a strained expression.

I've thought back over this incident many times. Had I really been in danger? Or was Mancha just a boisterous kitty? I'll never know. Certainly the jaguar of the Darién topped the ones of Corcovado and Manú. As we left the "safari park" that day, I looked deep into Mancha's eyes and secretly chose the jaguar as my totem in the tropics.

Now I had two. The raven was my secret totem in the Adirondacks. Both symbolized wilderness.

We had soon passed out of the park and were headed down towards Yaviza. The rivers were busy with cargo boats, dugouts, settlers and Amerindians. The heat was intolerable. No breeze, no bugs. A burning sun. I lay prostrate on the canoe bottom. Two parrots chattered overhead. Frogs sang in low, resonant, steady tones from shore. A big leaf from a *Cecropia* dropped flat onto the water. I heard the plunk of a boatman's pole. Dozing, I thought of all the places we hadn't seen: Paya, Yapé, Punusa, Tupisa, Marragantí, Ucurgantí. Would I ever be back?

Thirteen years later I was. The "M/S *Lindblad Explorer*" cruises were over. Instead, the same owner was running Special Expeditions natural history trips aboard "M/S *Polaris.*" I was hired as staff ecologist to work from the Pacific coast of Panama, through the Panama Canal, and up the east coast of Central America to Belize.

Passengers and staff came aboard the brightly-lit M/S *Polaris* west of the Panama Canal on the warm, sultry night of January 28, 1993. Most of us quickly settled into our cabins after a welcome nightcap. Having flown all day to get to Panama City, we were content to float over a perfectly calm sea to the Pearl Islands—fast asleep. We awoke to find the ship anchored off Isla del Rey in the Pacific. The day passed peacefully as M/S *Polaris* island-hopped southward towards the Darién. We snorkeled, beach-combed, bird watched, and practiced the ship's fire drill.

With dawn barely breaking next day, everyone sat staring at the peaks of Darién from several 30-foot-long dugouts. Manned by stout black boatmen, they knifed us across windy, turbid mudflats to the Río Sambú behind Punta Garachiné. Low clouds scudded across the mountaintops and hid the sun. A few sleepy passengers grumbled, "Imagine paying so much for *this*! Getting up at 5:00 A.M., sitting on hard bamboo seats in a tippy canoe, and being splashed." But they soon forgot any discomfort as flocks of yammering blue-headed parrots and orange-chinned parakeets crisscrossed the river.

For my part, I was ecstatic, being in the heart of the Darién National Park. We were going to a new Choco village called La Chunga. As a harpy eagle would fly, it wasn't that far from Púcuro. However, the tallest peak in the whole Darién, Cerro Pirre, rose to 4,960 feet. It was completely shrouded in heavy rain forest and lay between the two villages. It might take weeks or months to traverse those 40 or 50 miles on foot without trails.

As we left the Río Sambú and entered a small tributary, the scene looked like a J.J. Rousseau painting. Roots of giant trees twisted into the green water. The tall aroid (*Montrichardia sp.*), lined the winding banks with its flat green leaves. Delicate white blooms of swamp spider lilies graced the undergrowth. Keel-billed toucans and collared araçaris hopped in the branches. A green-and-rufous kingfisher winged down the stream, chattering noisily.

Two hours after leaving the ship we came to a rustic landing. The dugouts jostled around unloading excited passengers. Scampering down the bank came three little Choco girls. Doe-eyed, slender, bare-breasted, black hair crowned with red hibiscus blossoms, they gently took people's hands and led them up a path.

It was a touching picture. Gray-haired, serious, business executives were being led from their complicated technological world into a simpler, older, healthier setting. Chubby, well dressed, society ladies were about to see other women living harmoniously with their environment, using the simplest of materials. The little girls were irresistible. They grinned, chattered, and pulled. After a quarter of a mile we reached the village where about 150 Chocos lived.

This was what I'd come for. To enter once again this leafy place where indigenous people seem to respect the intricacies of nature

Choco woman with her handmade baskets at market in La Chunga village, Darién National Park.

better than modern urban people do. I hadn't forgotten the impact the Darién had made on me 13 years ago—that night under the Choco hut—the hospitality. I felt at home.

We spread out into the neat, clean area surrounded by thatched huts on stilts. A group of young girls dressed only in gay, wrap-around mini-skirts and adorned with bright red flowers danced sedately to flute and drum music. This was played by Choco men. Older women stood beside rough tables displaying their crafts. There were small bowls and grass baskets in earth colors with intricate designs. Woven hats, painted masks, carved animals. Beautiful rosewood canoe paddles. Everything was made painstakingly by hand with local fibers and woods. It was a breath-taking little market.

Yet the women were as gentle as the little girls. They spoke no Spanish. The passengers spoke no Choco. Nobody bargained or cajoled. Rather a Choco woman faced a woman tourist and held out her palm flat towards her customer. The palm was painted jet black. She raised five fingers, or three. The passenger pulled five, or three, dollars from her handbag. The deal was done. The prices were very reasonable. I watched the scene for awhile, admiring the body designs of the Choco women. They paint their lower faces and naked torsos with precise red and black designs—a sign of beauty. Many have black bands painted around their upper arms. I was also chuckling at the foreign women's body paint. The red lipstick, black mascara, blue eye shadow, bleached hair, the sun block and the sunburn. Was there really a difference?

Meanwhile some of the men played on their flutes and drums, while others stood impassively in the center of the village. They looked as arrogant as stallions. They were naked except for red loincloths which reached well below their knees and were tied around their waists with rough-looking grass or perhaps bark strips. Their skin was smooth and coppery-colored stretched tight over long sinews and rippling muscles. Each man was covered with geometrical designs of black paint and large patches of red. Surely the red came from achiote berries and was the same dye Rolf and I had painted on *our* bodies for the ship's costume party in Amazonia.

Now I joined eagerly in the shopping spree. The handsome baskets would look stunning on my cabin log walls. I could hang a deer mask from my deer antlers. The rosewood paddle would feel magnificent paddling my "birchbark" aluminum canoe. Thus, these crafts—Darién and Adirondack—melded for the first time.

One or two staff members began motioning everyone to start back. The captain had radioed. The tide was falling, they explained. Here on the Pacific it rose and fell between 12 to 18 *feet*; whereas on the Atlantic, only 18 *inches*. We could not afford to delay and get stuck on those tidal mudflats. I was torn to buy more but began strolling slowly towards the foot path. Two women were painting each other's faces in black. Suddenly, I had a great yearning to have the same done.

They understood my desire without words. One pantomimed and smiled. She was saying, "I will make you beautiful. I will paint you like the jaguar!"

I tingled in surprise, nodded my head, and made a "Do it fast!" sign. Five minutes later she finished. I could just see the oldest and slowest passenger disappearing around a bend. Knowing I could outrun him to the last dugout, I hugged the Choco woman, pulled off my earrings and pressed them into her very black palm. "Thank You!" I breathed. The expedition leader glared at me as I jumped into the canoe, but with everyone laughing at my face paint, he didn't say a word.

That afternoon we cruised further down the Darién coast from Punta Garachiné to Punta Caracoles. I was privileged to see most of the Pacific coast portion of the Darién National Park. Thanks to a peaceful ocean, we were seeing sights few passenger ships would dare approach. The land rose steeply to over 3,000 feet along the Sierra del Sappo. There was scarcely a cove or bay in its entire length. The mountains were completely covered with primary tropical rain forest and showed no sign of human habitation, cutting, grazing, logging, or burning.

For those of us who were praying to set foot here, the expedition leader allowed two Zodiaks to try for a landing. They found the slightest indentation in the shore and landed on a steep, black, stony beach. We had to scramble out swiftly to avoid letting waves break over the sterns of the rubber rafts. Both Zodiaks backed out and returned to the ship. We were happily alone in this wild place. Behind the exposed beach lay a freshwater river speckled with colorful stones. Those of us who waded up its bed collecting precious rocks finally reached a divine swimming hole. It was backed by cascades of lavender flowers. Pure mountain water—probably as pure as any on earth—slipped past us. I felt as if this day had brought us to Eden. Yet, as we bathed, the sound of the surf grew heavier. A staff member radioed the ship to send in the Zodiaks. Everyone hastened to the hot black beach to wait. Just in time.

It was a shame to leave this paradise—but—all is not as it appears. In October and November, rains often fall for 15 to 20 days without stopping, and violent storms send huge waves crashing upon this coast.

I and my adventurous shipmates had seen what Balboa saw—practically unchanged. We had witnessed the impenetrable Darién jungle and its counterpart, the mighty Pacific ocean. We could envision Spaniards in armor and leather sweating in the heat, struggling through the forests without maps, radar, marine charts, or radios. We had heard of yellow fever, Chagas disease, malaria and dysentery and the death toll they took. Perhaps we left more silent than in our coming.

That night, at the staff recap of the day's events, I read Keats' immortal lines in his poem, "On First Looking into Chapman's Homer."

> *Then felt I like some watcher of the skies*
> *When a new planet swims into his ken;*

> Or like stout Cortez* when with eagle eyes
> He stared at the Pacific—and all his men
> Looked at each other with a wild surmise—
> Silent, upon a peak in Darién.

(*Keats mistook Cortez for Balboa, the true discoverer of the Pacific, who was hoping for a short route to the East Indies. The poem's description of those awed and silent explorers, however, reflected how we felt.)

Then I explained how Vasco Nuñez de Balboa fled from Hispaniola to the Darién in 1510 to flee creditors. According to historians, Balboa "won the friendship of the Indians, who accompanied him on his epic march across the isthmus. Towards the end of September, 1513, he discovered the Pacific and claimed it and all the shores washed by it for the Spanish crown." (*The New Columbia Encyclopedia*).

Could it have been Chocos who accompanied him? Might some of the red-and-black painted men we photographed at La Chunga carry genes of those early guides?

My painted face led to a lot of good-natured ribbing from passengers, staff, and especially the Swedish officers. I sailed through the Panama Canal and up the east coast of Central America with that jaguar design on my skin. I liked it. While I showered every day, it didn't grow any lighter. I was so busy working, and the passengers playing, that it was forgotten.

Every day brought a new and magical island. First, the San Blas Islands sprinkling the northeastern coast of Panama. We stopped at Achatupu for a stroll through a Cuna village and a dazzling "mola market." Next day it was a fast walk around Big Zapatillo National Park off northwestern Panama. Off the Nicaraguan coast, we went ashore at Little Corn Island for a picnic and to buy dozens of lobsters for dinner. Farther up the coast we anchored off the isolated Cayo Cocorocúma where we were greeted by swirling clouds of frigate birds, masked and brown boobies, and brown pelicans. The nature photographers took hundreds of pictures, for the birds were unafraid of humans. Two peregrine falcons put on the best show. They soared high among the frigates, provoking aerial spats. Their high keening cries followed us back to the ship.

Another remote islet, still in Nicaraguan waters, was Vivorillo Caye. Not a bird in sight; however, the key was surrounded by the clearest seawater yet and an untouched satin-white beach. The snorkelers raved about lemon sharks, white-spotted rays, a nine-foot barracuda, and many colorful reef fishes. My skin took on a deeper tan this faultless day.

Vivarillo Bank seemed a favorite anchorage for shrimpers. Although a staff member in a Zodiak visited five shrimp boats, not one would sell the chef shrimps for supper. That night a full moon rode above a placid sea dotted with lights of trawling shrimp boats.

From here on the weather deteriorated. We proceeded to Islas Cochinas in the Bay Islands of Honduras, and finally Half Moon Caye in Belize, all on squally, dismal days. The trip was almost over.

Now it was our last night aboard with a fancy farewell dinner scheduled. I wanted to wear a white cocktail dress sprinkled with pink roses, white heels, and my hair in a chignon. Looking in the mirror I noted the black design had faded not one iota. So far no person and no animal had objected to my painted face. I had grown fond of it, yet it would never do to leave it on for this special event.

I really *did* try to remove the jaguar design. After soap-and-water and baby oil, I tried milk, Clorox, hydrogen peroxide, and Coke without effect. I spoke to several women friends and asked for their help. They loaned me expensive skin creams, body lotions, and rubbing alcohol. No good. In desperation I sought out the Chinese laundry supervisor. He gave me samples of Tide, Ajax and Comet. Zero.

In desperation, I went into the ship's library. Only an hour left to cocktail time and the staff recap. Quickly I thumbed through botanical and anthropological texts. There it was!

"A black dye comes from the *Genipa americana* tree. It is used by various primitive tribes in the American tropics. The fruits yield a blue-black juice which cannot be removed from human skin by even the most vigorous methods. It lasts about ten days."

Well, I'd tried every vigorous method possible. My face felt raw from scrubbing. On went my white, bell-skirted, cocktail dress and white heels. Up went my hair. Carrying my head high, with whiskers and dots, I stepped into the cocktail lounge and took my place among the staff. When my turn came to speak, I recounted how I got painted and with what. Then I listed all the products used which had not removed the dye. The passengers were in stitches. It made a jolly evening out of a nostalgic farewell dinner.

So, I had to fly home from Belize City via Miami to JFK, and finally Albany, N.Y., traveling with a scarf sheathing my head and lower face. It wasn't until I stepped off the plane into a snowstorm and pulled on my winter parka that I let the light shine on my face. Naturally, the Choco women had wanted my jaguar design to stay on. And so did I, if the truth be known. It lasted for 20 days.

UPDATE

- *Following this and one other Special Expeditions cruise to the Darién, I produced a front-page, Sunday Travel, ecological article for the* Boston Globe *entitled "Wilderness Cruise in Central America." The* National Geographic *article, however, did not fare as well. Due to the political strife throughout the isthmus—Nicaragua, El Salvador, Guatemala, Panama— the article was put on the back burner. Loren's and my editors felt it would be a liability to print an article extolling national parks in these war-torn countries. Readers trying to visit them might get caught in dangerous situations.*

- *The Darién National Park encompasses 3,399,117 acres and is now zoned into: a strictly protected core; a "cultural" zone with two Amerindian populations; a small development zone for ecotourism and environmental education; and an inspection zone 24 miles wide along the Panama/Colombia border. It became a national park in 1980; a World Heritage Site in 1981; and was recognized as a Biosphere Reserve by UNESCO in 1983. Despite these accolades and protections, the threats facing this enormous land-bridge of lowland forest are the most distressing of all Central America's protected wildlands.*

- *Most scientific research, protection, management, and conservation activities were suspended for months in 1998 due to armed groups in the Province of Darién. There were confrontations of (supposedly) Colombian guerillas, paramilitary, common bandits, and the Panamanian police. This caused great insecurity among local inhabitants, park rangers, technicians, and organizations. Many people were displaced or were moved for security reasons. Even though this unstable situation is controlled right now, the unrest and fear remain. Fortunately, ANCON has taken over many responsibilities in managing the park as a result of some of these events.*

- *In 1998, Colombia was declared free of hoof-and-mouth disease (aphthous fever). This prompted new meetings between Panamanian and Colombian officials about continuing construction of the Pan American Highway through the Darién forest. The Panamanian park service and ANCON, plus many other groups, fear that sick animals from* other *South American countries would be transported on the new highway and still carry the disease into Panama, Central America, and possibly Texas.*

- *Likewise, extension of the highway would bring spontaneous colonization, more deforestation, illegal hunting, uncontrolled mining, agriculture and ranching, soil erosion, and disruption of traditional Choco and Cuna lifestyles, probably by diseases.*

- *Natural resources protection on the Colombian side of the border has been largely unsuccessful. There is severe forest destruction, colonist invasion into Panama, and* (probably) drug trafficking.

* Benjamin reminded me when we said goodbye in Panama City that on my first trip
  here to study Volcán Barú in 1971–72, he was not even allowed inside the hotel,
  where Clyde Smith and I stayed, to say goodbye. On our trip to the Darién in 1980,
  he was permitted into the hotel lobby and restaurant to have dinner with Loren and
  me and to say goodbye.

19

HALF MOON CAYE— AN UNCERTAIN PARADISE

I picked my way gingerly along a wet trail through an impenetrable, rank, dense tangle of bushes and short trees. The stench of bird droppings, dirty feathers, and chick carcasses hung on the humid air. Caught beneath an interlocking canopy of sandpaper trees, wild figs, and gumbo-limbos, the atmosphere could not get deodorized by the fresh sea breeze above.

The same leafy canopy intercepted laserlike beams of sun from sanitizing the soil and stabbing away the gloom. Underfoot, hundreds of hermit crabs crept about and an occasional black rat streaked for cover over the dead leaves and spattered excrement. I swiftly decided to put on my sneakers for this walk.

I was reminded of Belize City to which I had flown by jet three days ago. The same sorts of smells and sights pervaded its dusky streets from sewage-choked canals and gutters. Offal and garbage floated near wharves and shore. Odors of the fish market stupefied my nose. Black vultures swaggered everywhere, sublimely indifferent to these fetid stinks. Their lack of an olfactory organ allows them to scavenge with gusto. Praise heaven, I thought, for these natural garbagemen of the bird world.

A hired seaplane had next brought me from Belize City to Half Moon Caye, 60 miles from the mainland. This key is virtually an island wilderness, for it sits the farthest east from Belize and at the edge of the ocean's deep. Off the Atlantic side, the forereef sheers from *three* feet to *three thousand* feet underwater.

Half Moon Caye is an ancient rookery—perhaps the largest in the western Caribbean. It is certainly the largest and oldest of any seabird sanctuary in Belize. Each winter and spring, approximately 500 breeding frigate birds and 3,500 red-footed boobies concentrate here to mate and nest. Sexy-looking male frigates, with ballooning crimson throat sacs, flaunt themselves at black-and-white females. They relinquish their marvelous kitery and flop down awkwardly atop the trees. The boobies sport an unusual white-gold-and-black phase of adult plumage found only here and in Trinidad. Regal! But blue faces, pink-and-blue bills, and salmon-colored feet almost make them look like clowns dressed for a circus.

Suddenly, a shaking of branches overhead startled me and sent rats and crabs scuttling. A "wish willy" waddled pompously up a tree limb, popped through the tree roof, and settled itself lazily beside a booby nest. The three-foot, scaly-tailed lizard barely blinked at the quaking chick within. Fortunately, lizards and birds co-exist gracefully; the former being vegetarians, the latter fish-eaters.

The ascent of this reptile reminded me of the busy, vibrant world above. All is not feces and filth on Half Moon Caye, nor in Belize City. It also reminded me of the magazine assignment I was on to photograph and write about this rookery. Half Moon Caye had been declared a Crown Reserve in 1928 and had been managed by the Belize Audubon Society since then. This small, steadfast group was the nation's only conservation watchdog. Originally, Belize was a United Kingdom crown colony called British Honduras. As such, it had a proper English tradition of small sanctuaries to protect song and sea birds. Then in September 1981, the nation became independent; and, in November 1981, the new National Parks Systems Act was legally formed. Half Moon Caye was its fledgling first unit, becoming a national Natural Monument in March 1982, with its surrounding reefs, sandbars, and mangrove keys. Then—the only marine reserve in Central America!

The six-square-mile monument lies within Lighthouse Reef—one of three atoll-like formations off Belize. The 22- by 4-mile atoll includes the notorious Blue Hole (filmed by Jacques Cousteau) and Half Moon Caye. It is a scuba diver's paradise, a fisherman's delight, a ship captain's terror, and a seabird's haven.

March weather, I found, can be squally and disagreeable. When I flew in that morning, the small seaplane had bucked and shuddered in 25- to 35-knot gusts of wind. Rain showers pelted the island intermittently. Waves were choppy and almost too high for the pilot to attempt a landing. I leaped off a pontoon, and he threw my gear after me haphazardly so as not to risk pounding the plane against the dock.

I was entirely alone and unprepared for foul weather. Spying an abandoned shack near the beach and coconut grove, I dragged my baggage inside to keep dry. The interior was dilapidated but had a rustic platform for a bed. Holes in the roof were letting rain drip inside, so I ripped a square of plywood from the floor and covered up the roof holes over the bed. It worked with a big conch shell holding it down.

With such gray, dismal light and strong winds, I doubted photography would be possible. I wrapped my camera bag in plastic, slid it under the bed, and put on a rain poncho. At least I could locate the rookery and find the bird watching tower described by Belize Audubon Society. It was a rickety structure, the rungs extra slippery with rain. I started to climb towards the platform when a creak and a tremor forced me to look down. I was struck by the gross underworld 25 feet below. No way I wanted to risk falling into that purgatory. The birds would have to wait till tomorrow.

Back at the shack, I thought about finding the lighthouse keepers who were the island's sole inhabitants. Two men and their families manned Half Moon Caye lighthouse, kept half the island tidy (not the rookery half, obviously), and helped an occasional visitor. But it was late afternoon, and I was tired. Instead, I fluffed up my sleeping bag, wrote down some field notes, and prepared a freeze-dry dinner over a tiny camping stove. Slipping into the bag, I thought of Anegada and how different this tropical island seemed. Would it be another tropical paradise? Or not? I fell asleep to the patter of rain on the wooden roof and a northeaster buffeting the side of my shelter. Off and on during the night, ripe coconuts were ripped loose and fell with dull thuds on the wet sand. I would start awake and pray a heavy frond wouldn't land on the shack and flatten it.

Next morning it was still blowing and raining. As I gloomily lit my stove to make coffee and oatmeal, I became aware of impish eyes peeping in at me. A small tyke, brown as allspice and dressed in tattered shorts, smiled shyly. I coaxed him into the makeshift campsite out of the lashing rain and gave him a granola bar. Island bred and born, it was his first such sweet.

"So, what's your name?" I asked.

"Little John," he replied pertly.

"Do you live here all the time?" I inquired.

"Yes, missus," he nodded. "My Pappy he do care fo' de lights. My Mammy she be my teachah."

"I'd like to meet him and your momma," I said. "Let me finish my breakfast, and you can take me to them."

A short while later, the ragamuffin led me triumphantly to one of two neat white cottages beside the lighthouse. Little John was my introduction to the keepers, John and Rudy, and their wives, Felicia and Lydia. I soon discovered what a novelty I was. Weeks or months might pass without any foreign visitors, they told me. The Harbor Master only came out on rare inspection trips. Belizean fishermen came and went in their native sloops. Now here was a lone American woman, in pigtails and jeans, wanting to see birds and tropical fish.

For the next three days, while I waited for the sun to re-appear, I tried to maintain polite, well-balanced visits between the two homes. It was tricky.

At Rudy's, a staunch Seventh-Day Adventist, we would drink hot Ovaltine and breakfast on bread freshly baked by Lydia in a 50-gallon drum oven. At John's, a hard-drinking fisherman, I would nightcap on Belizean rum and sample shark meat caught that afternoon. Always their children clustered around, clean, neat, polite, with big black eyes full of wonder at my binoculars, cameras, face mask, and note books. In them I glimpsed traces of Arawak and Caribe blood, plus English, Spanish and African. Such is the melting pot called Belize.

During this time, I came to appreciate the good care Rudy and John took of the caye's coconut plantation. They raked the clean sand smooth and whitewashed the trunks. They poisoned out black rats with Warfarin in coconut husks and swept up fronds and litter. These palms provided them with coconut oil, milk, and meat at home, plus extra sales to passing fishermen.

Their most vital task was cleaning the cottage cisterns and making sure roof gutters and spouts piped rainwater directly in. The two families depended wholly on collected rain to survive. I discovered there is absolutely no fresh water on the island. Anyone who comes there must bring their own supply—beg—or go thirsty. I had to beg when my canteens were empty.

The sun came out. John and Rudy led me back to the rookery and climbed up with me to the platform. From there we were able to look down over the colorful nursery. Bright light shimmered on orange blossoms and shiny green leaves of this rare natural island forest. The fuzzy white booby chicks, those red gular pouches of the male frigates, and the red-footed adult boobies made a Christmas-like scene.

A spanking sea breeze rustled the canopy where flimsy nests held newly hatched chicks. Those in the shade slept peacefully; those in the sun panted and lay prostrate. The black frigates looked like gangly Halloween cutouts on their nests. Incubating booby parents kept up a constant screeching or bill-clucking. This almost sounded like toads around an Adirondack pond on a warm spring night. Only they were protesting against trespassing lizards (wish willies) and iguanas (bamboo chickens), dive-bombing frigates, restless fledglings, John, Rudy, and me. It was a gay, chatty, feisty bird kindergarten.

"Here come de Billy-hawk!" cried out John, as a magnificent osprey flew low over us with a fish in its talons. "Now de frigate, he goin' rob dat fish." A mid-air collision looked imminent. Chicks cowered. Boobies screeched. Lizards leapt. But the osprey outmaneuvered and got away.

I photographed for over an hour, obtaining fine pictures. John and Rudy went to check the windward shore for any "treasures" brought in by waves or wind.

As I clambered down the tower ladder into the stench and gloom, I reflected that "Paradise" cannot exist without "Purgatory." The natural nutrients from stinking bird excrement and carcasses eventually add to the productivity of the forest, the soil, and insect life. This, in turn, attracts more small birds like northern warblers and vireos. (Perhaps that monotonous songster, the red-eyed vireo that nests near my cabin every summer, actually spends his winters on Half Moon Caye!) These nutrients also enrich the surrounding sea and its fish life and invertebrates. Lastly, scavengers metamorphose filth into food.

Meeting up with Rudy and John, I asked how the rats got onto Half Moon Caye. They explained that everything came via ships and seafaring men. The stowaway rats and mice, the abandoned cats and dogs, everything stranded on this 40-acre islet had to adapt to eating coconuts, eggs, and seabirds, in season. Or, whatever edible floats ashore.

"Dese animals make it real hard fo' de birds to survive. We don' have enough poison or traps to keep up with de rats," said John. "Once a ship anchored here for awhile and dumped ten dogs out. Dey went wild, and we had to shoot de poor things. Dey were climbing trees to eat chicks and sneakin' into our houses for food. Don' know what dey *drank*. Maybe dey filch some my rum!" he chuckled.

"Nuther thing real bad fo' de birds is de hurrycanes," added Rudy. "Hurrycane Fifi damaged lots of coconut palms. Hurrycane Hattie killed lots of boobies. Hurrycane Greta she de worse. Blew for 18 hours. Waves like mountins rolling over de sand and comin' within porch level on de houses."

We walked back to the other half of the island. I saw a sport-fishing boat pulled up at the dock. A bull-chested man with red hair jumped off and bore down towards us. He wore a yellow T-shirt which read, "IF YOU AIN'T A SCUBA DIVER, YOU AIN'T SHIT."

"Dere be Mistuh Larry," beamed John and walked faster.

Rudy explained to me, "He be a dive mastuh, and he bring small groups of friends here to camp and dive. He very nice fellah. He always bring de kids clothin' and candy."

Then I was meeting Larry Smith with his brash shirt and his sunny Texas smile—and my life changed. I watched him exchange warm bear hugs with the two black men. "Hey, John! Hey, Rudy!" he greeted them heartily.

"Hey dere, Mistuh Larry, mon," they chorused. "Welcome! Dis here be Missus Anne," they introduced me. "She fly in here couple days ago in dat noreaster. Takin' pictures in de rookery. She from New York, and she snorkel some."

Larry turned his bright blue eyes upon me appraisingly. "Hey, Anne! Nice to meet you. You are a diver?"

"Well, sort of," I said hesitantly. That slogan on the T-shirt had me intimidated. "I'm really an ecologist, but I have my certification from NAUI. We don't get to dive much in the Adirondacks. It's too cold and dark in our lakes. I'm on a writing assignment alone here and brought my snorkel gear."

"You-all's welcome to join us," offered Larry. "I've got a small, select group of ecology-minded divers from Texas. You'll like them. And I've got compressors and extra tanks aboard. Come on over." He waved us towards the boat graciously.

John, Rudy and I followed the burly man, built like a Santa Gertrudis, and stepped on board. Jimmy Buffet was crooning softly in the background. Six fit, tanned, blond Texans were preparing their gear for a dive. Larry introduced us all around and brought three ice-cold Belikin beers over.

"Why don't you dive with us after lunch, Anne?" he said. "We're going to do The Wall. It's one of the most incredible dives in the Caribbean."

I was eager to go, but felt unqualified to suddenly jump right in. "Could you possibly check me out first, Larry?" I asked. "It's been a while, yet I don't want to hold you back from your guests."

"Sure as shooting," he smiled. "You can buddy with me. My guests are all friends and have been with me before. They know my safety rules."

Before I knew it, I'd wolfed down some canned sardines, put on my bathing suit inside the shack, and was back aboard. Larry fitted me out with tank, regulator, and vest. We waded out from the dock, and he carefully supervised my entry into the sea. We dove out towards the reef for about 20 minutes. He gave me a thumbs-up signal. I'd passed his check!

I'd never have believed an opportunity to dive Belize's famous barrier reef would materialize on this trip. How amazing! The 175-mile-long reef starts south of Cozumel Island off the Yucatan Peninsula and runs to the Sapodilla Cayes in the Gulf of Honduras. It's second in size to the 1,250-mile-long Australian barrier reef. Some serious divers say the continuous stretch off Belize is the most vivid and profuse tropical reef system in the world. Half Moon Caye lies like a jade jewelet attached to this aqua-green-and-ivory strand.

The Wall is an almost vertical cliff of coral. To dive down it is like free-floating past a towering condo complex whose sea dwellers peer out at you from their apartments. I felt like I was pouring through a spectrum of blues. The warm waves which washed over the reef crest and coral heads were a vibrant turquoise. This shaded into cobalt at about 30 feet and slowly deepened to ultramarine at 90. The steep slope plummeted on into an indigo void.

I felt a strange, unreasonable pull drawing me down to the terrible pressured purple of the abyss. With it came panic. I stared around for Larry and found him right by my side. He pointed to his depth gauge and watch, then motioned upwards. Grabbing my hand, he held it calmly, comfortingly. He had sensed my fear. Ninety feet! It was my deepest dive ever. The steady reassuring sound of bubbles from my regulator slowed my breathing. Larry held me safely within that narrow zone where humans can be one with the sea.

When my buddy and I broke into the surface, I let out a jubilant yell. Larry grinned and shouted, "All right!" A bond of trust had been forged on The Wall. Little did I realize that Larry had introduced me to a new world and new ecosystems that day and that I would follow him to many more, exotic, tropical dive sites.

We rested on the three-foot-deep shelf and looked towards the deep blue Caribbean beyond the atoll. There, hard aground, sat a blackened freighter. It had been thrown against the forereef shoals years ago. It hangs there as a reminder of the might and treachery of the ocean. Many other wrecks rested along the barrier reef. Some were from the days of Spanish galleons, others as recent as the late 1970s. Most recent was a freighter loaded with several tons of bagged, agricultural, chemical fertilizer. Once the bags broke open, the fertilizer could do irreparable damage to corals by asphyxiating these sensitive animals. The same is true all along the Belize coastline where large farms, orchards, and ranches are appearing. Many use chemical pesticides, insecticides and fertilizers. These are leached out and into streams and rivers during the hard rainy season. Flowing into the shallow sea offshore, they are a new threat to this fragile barrier reef and its fisheries.

Larry put his facemask back in place, regulator in his mouth, and beckoned. We finned slowly back towards The Wall. Bands of reef fishes swam around lavender sea fans. Butterfly fish and rock beauties vied for the most imaginative black-and-yellow patterns. A pair of French grunts hung motionless under the massive branches of elkhorn coral. Inside the tangle of smaller zigzag branches a group of blue tang and sergeant majors hovered, all looking the same way like little birds in a tree.

A spiny lobster at least five pounds in weight waved cautiously with his red antennae. I tapped on a dead piece of coral, trying to lure him further out of his hole. He stared at us with beady eyes on stalks, then slyly disappeared. Further down, under an enormous brain coral, ten young "bugs" peered out and waved their antennae. A few advanced timidly. One gently touched me with one antenna, trying to figure me out. Evidently they had never seen human divers. I left any possible hunting up to Larry. He made it a firm rule to take only what was needed for dinner aboard each day. No more. Now he shook his head, no, and swam on. I was glad.

Every few feet brought us to new inhabitants along The Wall. Over 220 species of reef fishes have been recorded here. We swam over an eel-grass flat and came upon a mass of crumbled coral. Larry popped to the surface and wrenched his regulator out. "Damn dive boats," he exclaimed angrily. "They anchor anywhere they please, never thinking about the damage those hooks and heavy chains can do to sea life."

"Why doesn't the government put out permanent anchoring

Fishermen and frigate bird at Half Moon Caye, Belize.

blocks with buoys?" I asked.

"It's part of the new plan. I hope it's soon because more and more people are discovering Half Moon Caye," he sighed. "We also need signs and buoys marking the boundaries of the Natural Monument so that fishermen don't poach inside it. There's too much illegal fishing going on. Bagfuls of conch, dozens of lobsters, big tubs of reef fish. It'll become like the Florida Keys or Roatan, Honduras, if conservation isn't practiced here soon."

Our dive group was coming back to the sportfishing boat.

We floated on our backs and sculled lazily in towards the boat. Larry climbed aboard, took off his tank, then leaned down to grab mine. I shrugged it off my back and handed it up. On deck, he clapped me on the shoulder and said, "You did great!" I felt as if I'd gotten an A+ on my Ph.D. orals. Then he began helping the others out of their gear and started filling up the empty tanks.

"Hey, Lar," called one of the blond men. "Shall we set up our campsite before we take another dive?"

"Good idea," Larry said. "I'll stay here and top off these tanks. Turning to me, he asked, "Where are you camped, Anne?"

"Oh, I'm still in that leaky shack over there," I pointed. "It's rained every day since I arrived and the wind was high, so there was no point to put up my tent."

"Well, sake's alive, come on over and join us. We always camp under the palms, high and dry, and use the same fire ring." He frowned. "That's another thing needed here. Designated small camp sites with permanent fire rings. Also a couple of privies back in the bush and garbage trenches. Sometimes the British military uses Half Moon Caye for R and R. Up to 25 men will camp and dive for a few days and bring dozens of tanks, compressors, tons of food, crates of beer bottles.

"I had a talk with them about preserving the beauty and wildness of the island. They're pretty good about cleaning up. But other folks aren't. If it weren't for John and Rudy, the place would be full of garbage and t.p."

That evening we had a cookout at Larry's campsite. The children came, as well as John and Felicia, Rudy and Lydia. Kids of every age and every shade of brown cuddled close together around a huge bonfire. John began telling stories in his sing-song patois. His black eyes glowed in the firelight, and his frizzy hair fluttered in the freshening breeze. He peopled the night with blood-spattered pirates, headless sailors, and ghosts of those wrecked off the reefs of Half Moon Caye. The children began to shiver and sniffle.

Sunset faded. The last of the frigate birds held aloft like kites by the tug of the trade wind settled into their rookery. The stars came out like polished points of obsidian. A rising wind buffeted the palms. I turned to Larry during a lull in John's repertoire. "Tell me how you came to Half Moon Caye."

He related how a diving buddy had been here and raved. So he made a trip in 1977 and "discovered" the island. "My emotions that day were strong," he said. "As my eyes viewed Half Moon Caye for the first time, my impression was everlasting. I could not have imagined a more Polynesian-looking island. The setting sun was gilding these lush palms and turning the rusting old iron lighthouse to magenta. The frigates were soaring against a salmon-and-silver sky. My mind strained to absorb the color, life, and beauty that God had created when carving out this magnificent paradise. 'I will be back many, many times!' was my thought as we dropped anchor."

Everyone was rapt with attention at his words.

"I've made half a dozen trips here now and taught many divers to respect and protect the sea. But there are some things I haven't the power to stop. Like oil exploration taking place on the barrier reef. And the effects that raw sewage from Belize City may be having on this marine ecosystem and its coral. There's even talk of

Asian super trawlers fishing here. You-all know what havoc they can wreak with their half-mile-long nets scraping over the ocean floor. Anything that gets caught ends up dead."

I cringed inwardly. *This* island paradise certainly was not safe and faced far more environmental assaults than did Anegada.

Larry continued. "Yet it's still so hauntingly beautiful. You don't hardly know me, Anne, so you don't know that after a dozen trips, I met and wed Donna. She's a young divemaster from Texas. We held the ceremony aboard a boat in the protected north cove of Half Moon Caye. All these guys were here on that occasion," he said, waving his hand around the circle of friendly faces.

"We were honored by a school of 1,500 to 2,000 dolphins which playfully escorted us towards the beach and seemed to be approving our intentions.

"Two weeks later, on the final evening of our honeymoon here, we witnessed a silver 'moonbow' at night arching over Half Moon Caye," he related with some emotion. "Donna and I gratefully accepted these moving manifestations as God's approval of our marriage."

"Dat right, mon," broke in Rudy, devout man that he was.

Since then, Larry and his wife have come back repeatedly. Some dive trips they worked together; others, one or the other came. To celebrate their first anniversary, they spent a month camped alone on Half Moon Caye.

It was clear that this remarkable, sensitive man was probably more familiar with this island and its reefs than any other diver on earth. Also, that two things mattered most to Larry: diving safety and ocean conservation.

I vowed inwardly to help him. I could write articles that would tell readers about this precious place—birds, fish, lizards, The Wall. And I could share my environmental knowledge and contacts with him to promote ocean conservation. The Divemaster could teach the Woodswoman to be a better diver.

The Woodswoman could help the Divemaster become a well-versed environmentalist.

The bonfire had died down. Kids were asleep. The cookout was over. "Shift in de wedder, mon," predicted John as he rose and picked up two babies in his strong arms.

My tent flap faced east towards the Caribbean. At midnight I lurched awake to hear our tents snapping like artillery fire. The sea was up and booming upon the forereef. By dawn, gusts had reached

40 knots, and black-boweled squalls pounced down on us.

Larry cancelled the day's dive. Pinned down by waves and wind, we sensed how isolated Half Moon Caye really was. No water, radio, phone, food, electricity, or any other services. The nearest decompression chamber was 600 miles away in Miami.

I offered to take the group into the rookery and tell them about the birds. Then we could take a faint shore trail to the far end of the island, about two miles round trip, and beachcomb. It was one area I hadn't been to yet.

The farther we walked, the more upset we all became by the flotsam and jetsam sullying the shores. Legless dolls, plastic bottles of every description, flip-flops (no two ever matching), a Japanese telephone directory, tar balls, an outhouse seat—it was endless. All the throwaway trivia of fancy cruise ships and garbage of Caribbean coastal towns seemed to have washed up on the far end of Half Moon Caye. Even though John and Rudy could double as caretakers for their end of the island, while taking care of the all-important lighthouse, they could not manage this sea litter. In spots it was three feet thick over the once flawless white sand.

John and Rudy could make sure campers and visitors carried their garbage off the island, but they could not control sea currents and careless ship captains. By the time we turned back, my bare feet were absolutely black and heavy with tar.

Bilge pumping of oily water and oil spills were the culprits. There is a constant threat of spills by oil tankers which visit Belize frequently from Aruba and Mexico. Half the United States' imported oil comes via crowded Caribbean shipping channels—one of which lay right off the Belize barrier reef in 6,000 feet of water.

I lagged behind my friends, trying to clean the soles of my feet. The divers took a short-cut back through the rookery. As I reached the first nests, a roar seemed to swell out of the east and rapidly approach the dense forest. I immediately thought of a small tornado or big squall line coming through. Abruptly the roaring became a screaming of high-pitched jet engines. In a flash, I saw two fighter planes streak overhead, right above the nesting birds. They were dull khaki color, low and mean, killing machines.

A great commotion began above me with chicks struggling to jump out of their nests, adults screeching and flying up at these strange aerial predators, a few fledglings falling down onto the fetid forest floor. The gay bird kindergarten was in chaos. I shrieked, too, and shook my fists at the jets. Didn't the pilots know that planes should maintain a 2,000-foot ceiling over nesting colonies? It was part of our master plan for the man-o-war birds' rookery in the Dominican Republic. It was accepted protocol for flamingo nesting areas in the Yucatan, the Bahamas and little Bonaire. On instinct, I raised my camera and fired off a shot.

Unable to do anything to help the frantic birds, I kept on walking and soon came to the dock. Everyone was standing around discussing the sudden crazy flight of the jets. When they saw me, they fell silent. Unaccountably, I ran to Larry and fell sobbing against his chest.

"Why did they do it?" I sobbed over and over. "The chicks, their parents, the frigates are all terrified."

Larry held me firmly. "Settle down now," he said soothingly, as he might to a frightened horse. "The fly-boys were just having a joy ride. They probably don't even know there's a large rookery here. Those pilots come straight from England, and they fly a fleet of Harrier fighter jets kept here for 'protection.' Even though Belize is independent, the United Kingdom still keeps a toe-hold."

"Well, we've got to do something, Larry," I sniffled, trying to compose myself. "Look at all the problems you've described which are threatening this paradise. And now the air force is flying over. How do you know they won't play 'war games' and strafe the island or drop a few dud bombs? Then I exclaimed, "Let's go to Belize City! See government officials and explain what's happening out here!"

Larry was keen to go but felt he should stay with his dive party. "I'll back up your visit with a formal letter," he offered.

"May I use the ship's radio?" I asked, as a wild plan formed in my mind. "The seaplane was due to return the end of this week for me. If I could get it to pick me up tomorrow, I'd have one full day left of my trip to devote to helping Half Moon Caye."

"Go right ahead," agreed Larry enthusiastically. "I'll do the letter after supper and have it ready for you to take along. Maybe my dive group and the lighthouse keepers can add some good points."

By evening the northeaster had passed and stars came out. I lay in my tent and scribbled notes furiously for the meetings next day. Outside the tent flap, Orion, great winter hunter, strode over the palms. Back in the Adirondacks, he'd be hovering over the pines. Instead of the noisy surf in front of me, there'd be a snowy lake. The sea breeze might be a blizzard. Instead of a balmy 75°F, the night temp might be minus 25. I tossed nervously. At 3:00 A.M. I crept outside and walked under the coco palms. Blazing above the southern horizon stood the Southern Cross. A good omen.

At breakfast aboard the sportfishing boat, Larry gave me a four-page, lucid, stunning letter to present to the Permanent Secretary of the Ministry of Natural Resources. His finest line read: "I challenge you, Sir, to disagree with my statement that any more majestic, life-supporting reefs anywhere else in the world can offer anything to compare with what exists within the boundary of your new marine park surrounding Half Moon Caye."

He had signed his name, followed by Master Diver, Gold Instructor, and Coral Reef Instructor. "Superb, Larry!" I beamed. "There's another letter I thought of last night. When I'm back home, I'll write to Prince Philip in England and tell him about the Harrier jets over the rookery."

A stunned silence filled the cabin. "You *know* him?" ventured one of the divers.

"I met him once or twice," I said modestly. "He's President of World Wildlife Fund, International and a Vice-President of the International Union for Conservation of Nature and Natural Resources. Sometimes I attend their meetings." I didn't mention Prince Philip giving me a WWF Gold Medal as Conservationist of the Year Award in 1974 in Switzerland, nor Prince Bernhard, the gold Rolex watch.

"What an idea!" said Larry. "He's probably the symbolic Commander-in-Chief of the British Forces. He can contact the British Air Force leader here."

"Right," I nodded. "It's worth a try. After all, 'a cat can look at a king.'"

An hour later the seaplane arrived. Thirty minutes after that I was off-loading my backpack and other gear in Belize City. Two veritable stanchions of the Belize Audubon Society met me. Driving into town, we discussed strategies, and I updated them on Half Moon Caye. They made some critical phone calls, and off we started for Belmopan, seat of all government agencies and the new capital. En route I got glimpses of the lacey, bric-a-brac woodwork of city homes, the white grillwork of the Court of Law, stately banks, and a lush green park. I decided Belize City had its attractive side, too.

From the Prime Minister, to the heads of the Department of Natural Resources, the National Park Service, and the Forestry Department, we were cordially welcomed. Our litany was the same to each:

"Half Moon Caye is being destroyed. The barrier reef is in danger. Its coral reefs, seagrass beds, and rich fisheries are inextricably linked to your people. One good way is from the sea's sustenance, recreation, and shelter from hurricanes. The other, a bad way, is the land's runoff, sewage, and contaminants, and overfishing. Belizeans have depended on the reefs and the waters since time immemorial. But Half Moon's ailments are symptomatic of an environmental short-circuit which is threatening the whole marine world. Quick, uncontrolled gains from super-fishing methods, hi-tech agriculture, and flashy tourism cannot compensate for the long-term, dependable, sustainable benefits of the barrier reef itself."

The immediate reaction to our outburst was the reassurance that the Belize government wished to utilize its natural resources wisely and not make the same mistakes of other countries. They acknowledged that the present laws and enforcement were not adequately protecting marine resources. Staffing and money were in short supply and so were expert resource personnel.

Months later a personal letter from Prince Philip stated:

"I have made some enquiries about the use of Half Moon Caye and I am satisfied that the military authorities in Belize are fully aware of the status of the National Park and the need for all persons visiting the island to avoid disturbing the wildlife."

Yours sincerely,

Philip

Perhaps the melange of emotions which goaded me into action did a little good. Prince Philip may have stopped the jets. Maybe Larry's letter jolted some bureaucrats. I believe that experiencing one side of Purgatory may lead to regaining Paradise on Half Moon Caye.

 ## UPDATE

- *In 1986, I received word from Belize Audubon Society that marker buoys had been put into position at the northern and western boundaries of Half Moon Caye Natural Monument by the Royal Engineers Dive team of British Forces. They also expressed willingness to install permanent mooring sites for this area.*

- *The New York Zoological Society made seven large signs for the Caye with a map* of the reserve, a quote from the law designating the park, information about the rookery, and the request not to litter.

- Belize Audubon rebuilt the rickety tower and put in a higher platform with sturdy ladder and safety railings for visitors. The Natural Monument was enlarged in 1980 and now covers almost 10,000 acres.

- U.S.A.I.D. sponsored a Phase II Country Environmental Profile of Belize in 1984. It proposed that the barrier reef, small cayes, inner lagoons, Half Moon Caye's coastal edge, and the three outer atolls become a World Heritage Site under UNESCO's World Heritage Program.

- I produced two articles about Half Moon Caye with photos. One was published in Oceans magazine, the other in Animal Kingdom magazine of the New York Zoological Society.

- Larry is currently a Divemaster on a beautiful sailing vessel in Indonesia. He called to wish me Happy New Year in January 1999. Sometime later, this poem came to me:

THE WALL

Free-falling into forests of ghostly blue,
Filled with fluttering fish,
Gliding among branches of black coral,
Carressed with softest surge,
I cease breathing, kicking, sculling,
To camouflage my descent
Down the awesome wall.
A spotted eagle ray wings across my trajectory,
Watching, watching.
A dozen crawfish antennae finger my fins.
One pair of liquid black eyes peers into my face mask,
Probing, probing.
I slide through crevasses of ancient reefs,
Scrutinized by eerie gray eels,
Waft past trunks of tall sponges,
Speckled with questioning fairy shrimps.
Barracuda hovering at my side,
Sharp teeth glinting in the dim light.
Turquoise deepens to royal blue.
Ear drums crackle.
At the edge of the great abyss,
I stop and stare into purple infinity.
Towards Africa 4,000 miles away,
Towards the great plates 28,000 feet below,
Into monstrous upwellings too cold to imagine,
Into hidden currents more powerful than wind.
Hugging the sheer wall,
A speck of bubbling protoplasm,
I surge skyward.

20

SCOTLAND'S STRANGEST LANDLORD

An opalescent yet ominous dawn sky hung over the heaving North Atlantic. Ahead rose a jagged mass of gray rock of the most forlorn, forbidding island I'd ever seen. St. Kilda— prize possession of the National Trust for Scotland. Our chartered yacht, the "M/S *Deramore*," rolled uneasily in dark swells. I was reminded of St. Kilda's reputation for high seas, treacherous anchorages, and vicious storms. The all-time British wind speed record, 198 mph, was taken here in 1980! A mishap at the beginning of this trip would never do. My last assignment had been on a warm tropical sea; now this one was on a cold ocean the color of pewter. Before, I'd walked on a low, coconut-covered islet; here I'd be scrambling up a craggy, grass-covered peak. Also, those red-footed boobies and black frigates nesting atop a lush, dense forest bore little resemblance to these gleaming white gannets clinging to steep spires of rock. In short, St. Kilda Island 110 miles off Scotland was nothing like Half Moon Caye 60 miles off Belize. My risk factor had shot up.

I had been invited by the The National Trust for Scotland and its counterpart, the Scottish Heritage, USA, to write an article about their conservation practices and philosophy. This month-long sojourn would take me to their wildest holdings situated in far-flung corners of the country: St. Kilda, Torridon, and Fair Isle. All told, the Trust owned and operated over 100 properties. It is Scotland's largest *private* voluntary conservation organization. No *national* parks or refuges exist in Scotland, unlike Central America, England, Wales, Canada and the United States. However, the Trust's protected areas are as varied, fascinating, and beautiful as national parks and wildlife reserves elsewhere. Thanks to the Trust about 185,000 acres are well preserved in a nation only the size of Maine (yet with 2,300 miles of coastline). Each year over two million visitors are attracted to its properties. I was to find the Scottish example uplifting, efficient, and heart-warming after my many conservation trials in Third World countries.

I was worrying that landing on Hirta, the main island of St. Kilda, would require great determination and agility. My five ship-mates and I were queasy after the long journey in ten-foot waves. Wisely, the ship's captain anchored in Village Bay, the only pro-tected cove, and waited. When the Trust members and I had recov-ered, we went ashore. The seas had calmed, despite predictions of gale winds. A bright sun was out. Climbing onto the small jetty was easy. We put on day packs filled with sandwiches and sweaters, and walked up the dirt road to a British Forces installation. The Ministry of Defense leases a portion of the main island as a missile-tracking station, and keeps a few army men there. We paid our respects and picked up our guide, Wally Wright. Following the cheerful, burly Trust warden, we began to hike up St. Kilda's high-est peak, Conachair, (1,397 feet).

The island changed character completely under warm sun and light breezes. The odd feeling I'd had about this place vanished. Its slopes lay emerald green and dotted with brown, raggedy sheep. The sea was smooth and smoky blue. The abandoned, black stone houses and huts circling the bay looked quaint, not foreboding. Village Bay was prettily edged with a white sand beach. When we stepped onto Conachair's top, the views were spectacular. Next stop, Labrador, due west.

The entire St. Kilda archipelago surrounded us: Hirta, the largest island where we stood; smaller Soay, the sheep isle; narrow Dun, uninhabited; and Boreray of the great gannet colonies. In addition, five imposing "stacs" (pinnacles) pierced the blue sky. One was over 500 feet tall. Each was covered with white gannets and whitewashed by bird droppings. One quarter (120,000) of the world's population of gannets nested here. Even as we gazed down on the whirling flocks of seabirds, wisps of banner clouds were con-densing off the rocky tips of the stacs. No wonder that seamen say, "St. Kilda makes its own weather."

Tendrils of mist also curled up around our group as we edged carefully along the 1,200-foot perpendicular cliffs of Hirta. By holding Wally's stout arm most firmly, I peered over and saw verti-cal condominiums of birdlife. Shags sat closest to the sea, then guillemots, next razorbills, followed by kittiwakes, puffins, and finally fulmars near the cliff tops. This organized arrangement reminded me of The Wall off Half Moon Caye with its thousands of marine denizens. The only difference was the cacophony of noise. Thousands of birds squeaked, shrilled, squawked, and screamed. Thousands more whirred past on the updrafts like dragonflies. Wally said proudly, "St. Kilda is home to over a million birds!"

It was time for lunch so we spread out just below the summit, facing south into the strong May sunshine, and listened to Trust naturalist, Donald. Waving a sandwich in one hand, he pointed down and said, "St. Kilda is actually an ancient volcano's remains. Its islands and stacs are solidified remnants of liquid rock which fed a huge oval cauldron of lava. That's why they're in a kind of circle. The center of the cauldron became Conachair, and then parts of the circle eroded away. The basic rock is gabbro."

"Why are there sheep here?" Joyce asked. She was a Trust board member, loved animals, and lived on a large farm.

"The former inhabitants, St. Kildans, brought them in by boat. They're blackface on Boreray and Soay sheep on Hirta. No one tends them now, so they roam wild. That's why they look so tattered."

We fell silent. Far below the surf was softly purring. Seals brayed from caves and grottos in the rocks. A fulmar swooped down over us in a threat display. Down slope, I heard a snipe drumming. Finished eating, I lay back on the grassy hill and thought of how circumstances had brought me here. Once again, it was the serendipity of a conference.

One spring day in 1978 I joined the other ten commissioners at the Adirondack Park Agency in Ray Brook for our monthly meeting. Before each session, there was time allowed for our remarks and news. The Chair began by saying he had received word from The National Trust for Scotland inviting an APA representative to their First International Conference on Conservation in early May. Although he'd love to go, said the Chair, he had other obligations that month. He wondered if I would consider taking his place since I was the only ecologist on the board.

Scotland! I'd never been there nor thought of going. Yet in those days I only had one book published, *Woodswoman*. The New York publisher took care of sales and distribution, so it didn't demand much effort on my part. May was black fly season. Good time to escape them. I agreed to go. Thus began my love for

Scotland and my love affair with The National Trust for Scotland.

The conference was inspiring, serious, sincere. Our field trips were enlightening, educational, fun. I came away with a dozen new ways to look at preserving wildlife and wildlands.

Two years later, the same Trust officers planned their second international conference. They wrote and asked if they could hold it in the Adirondacks in concert with the Adirondack Park Agency. I was given considerable responsibility to set up the field trips and general program. The Scots loved our Adirondack Mountains. We exchanged valuable ideas on the management of mountains and lakes. They said the High Peaks reminded them of the Highlands. The following summer two mountain rangers exchanged places between Scotland and New York to gain new experience.

This intellectual exposure and admiration for what the Trust had accomplished gradually gave me a new idea.

Why not do an article about the wild places belonging to the Trust in Scotland? It would be along the same lines as my article on national parks of Central America. I queried *International Wildlife* magazine of the National Wildlife Federation and received the assignment. Thus I came to be here atop Hirta, gazing over the ancient volcanic rim of St. Kilda.

It all goes to reinforce my belief that when you work in conservation of wildlife and wildlands, you throw a pebble in a pond, it makes a ring, then ripples, and each one moves out further and further to touch distant shores.

That afternoon my Scottish companions and I spent two pleasant hours poking around the 140-year-old "black houses" and "cleits" around the bay. The St. Kildans lived in houses with everything stained black from smoke and soot inside. On an island with no trees and little driftwood, everything had to be built of boulders, using turf for roofs. There was no glass, no electricity, no refrigerators, no propane gas, no hot showers. I marveled at how raw native ingenuity and stamina allows humans to adapt and survive in the harshest of environments.

I turned to Joyce and exclaimed, "Can you imagine being a woman here a hundred years ago? Wearing long black wool skirts all the time, trying to bathe, and cooking practically in the dark. Using these cleits (well-ventilated stone igloos) for refrigerators. I'll bet they hardly ever left the island if it meant sailing in a small wooden boat 110 miles west through the Outer and Inner

Hebrides!"

"Oh, I don't know," said Joyce, looking around one black house and its small gray cleit. "Actually they had quite a few resources," she pointed out, practical farm woman that she was. "There was plenty of fresh water year-round running down in small streams from Conachair. Peat lies everywhere. All they had to do was cut out the turves and store them to dry in the cleits. Peat makes a fairly warm fire indoors. The sheep gave them warm cloth and fibers for diapers. I suppose St. Kildans ate lamb and mutton in addition to ocean fish and seabirds. They could dry birds and fish and hang them in the cleits."

Wally joined our conversation saying, "Aye, puffins were used for feathers in bedding and as meat. Young fulmars were rendered for oil used in cooking and lighting. Gannets provided food and eggs. In 1697, one observer estimated that the 180 islanders consumed 16,000 eggs and 22,600 birds per year! Sir Julian Huxley wrote that, "St. Kildans were 'bird people.'"

Donald added, "Surely they grew potatoes, corn and barley in sheltered little fields facing south. Grass could be cut for hay to feed sheep in winter."

I shook my head sadly. "But to think they never ate an orange, drank an espresso, or licked an ice cream cone."

"I'd have loved to have a puffin quilt for my stone bed," joked Joyce. Everyone laughed.

St. Kilda has been inhabited off and on since 2,000 B.C. However, the islanders of the last few centuries were the most intriguing. They were tenants of the Chief of Clan McLeod from the Isle of Skye. They had to pay rent and did so by trading in birds. St. Kildans were superb fowlers, adept at climbing the steep, slippery stacs barefoot. They took seabirds as if their lives depended on it, as indeed they did. Once a summer, the Chief sent a boat to trade salt, tweed, sheep for eggs, feathers, bird meat.

After the Industrial Revolution, life on the British mainland became more comfortable, complex, and materialistic. The St. Kildans, however, remained almost medieval, isolated, and stubbornly withdrawn. With only birds as money, their society could not survive. Soils were failing. Diseases took their toll of youngsters, especially newborns. The worst incidence of infant mortality in Scotland existed on St. Kilda due to the practice of cutting the baby's umbilical cord with an unsterile rough knife and then rubbing fulmar oil on its belly button. The oil was stored in a dried gannet stomach. Tetanus killed many babies, though no one knew why then.

The British government found it increasingly difficult to handle this "uncivilized" artifact of society. In 1930, the total evacuation of the island took place at the request of the last 36 living St. Kildans. They resigned their heritage to ghosts and seabirds. The uninhabited archipelago was bequeathed to The National Trust for Scotland in 1957.

Nowadays, the only people found here are volunteer summer work parties organized by the Trust to restore and maintain the old village, the small garrison, researchers, and occasional visiting naturalists like our group.

Under cloudless skies, some of us decided to wander down to St. Kilda's only scallop of beach. As we walked, a St. Kilda wren gave its piercing trill. It sounded much louder than the winter wren at my cabin. Might it be competing against seabirds and surf noise? I had remembered to bring my acid rain kit to Scotland, being deeply involved in this environmental problem in the Adirondacks. On the way, I took the pHs of one stream and a tiny catchment basis. They were 4.5 and 5.1, respectively. Acid rain must be falling on St. Kilda, just like the Adirondacks. This pH was far lower than the rocks and soil would normally produce. No one believed me, unfortunately, for the phenomenon was not yet widely recognized in Scotland.

The beach scene seemed right out of Belize—turquoise water on white sand. The sun glared hotly. Donald yelled, "Dare you to go swimming!" I poked my hand in the nearest wave. It felt about 55°F—the average spring temp for a first swim at my cabin. "You're on!" I shouted back. The whole group ran to the water's edge peeling off shirts and pants. No one had brought a bathing suit for *this* trip. Underwear and T-shirts would have to do. By taking a racing leap into the surf and running until we fell underwater, everyone managed a swim of sorts. It was like a concussion on our bare skins. Bracing! Without the passing North Atlantic Drift (Gulf Stream), however, the water would have been much colder.

While we were thawing on warm sand in hot sun, a young commanding officer from the base strode down to invite Wally and me for a Zodiak inspection cruise around the islands. "You can get to do this fewer than a dozen times a year," he emphasized, "when the sea becomes calm as a pond."

Fortunately, the "Deramore" captain decided to accompany us with the ship, as much for safety's sake as to bird watch.

That Zodiak ride should go down in naval annals. While circling Hirta and Soay, we dashed through *three* sea tunnels carved by the sea into rock headlands. Waves hissed against stark, slippery black walls. Spray foamed coldly on our faces. In one, we almost hit our heads on the ceiling when a swell lifted the craft. The turbulence in those dark passages was awesome. Wally claimed that the last tunnel had never before been maneuvered through by boat!

Then we bounced across four miles of open ocean to Stac Lee and Boreray. The inflatable rubber raft bounced so hard that I was almost catapulted into the sea. At the stac, we could practically touch its vertical sides. Nesting gannets stared down at us unafraid or fluttered overhead like big snowflakes. A once-in-a-life-time vision...

Steaming back to the mainland by ship and then driving north towards the Highlands by jeep, I had plenty of time to think about Scotland and the Trust. Already I'd seen tremendous differences in land uses, planning and protection here as compared to North and Central America, the Caribbean, Amazonia, and even the Adirondacks. Basically, Scotland has been inhabited for 5,000 years. Almost all land lies in private hands. The countryside has endured more clearing, burning, logging, oak debarking for tanneries, charcoal making for iron smelters, and grazing than most places in the New World. These uses and abuses of land, especially the large scale introduction of sheep in 1740, denuded much of Scotland and bankrupted its soils. Once this bonny country was 90% forested. Today only 12 to 15% has trees (few of them native).

There are no vast natural wilderness areas left, as in Brazil and Canada. Scotland has, therefore, a radically altered landscape and wildlife. When the N.T.S. was created in 1931, no organization existed which could accept or acquire property, then preserve and hold it for the benefit of the public. The tiny Trust started because of three men's vision. They were true idealistic conservationists with a shoestring budget of $2,000. They wanted to preserve the "best of what had gone before."

Many people were interested in saving their countryside. The fledgling Trust accepted gifts of everything from formal gardens, tiny houses, and old mills to sprawling mountain estates, islands, and castles. Eventually the Trust acquired Robert Louis Stevenson's cottage known as "The White House," John Muir's boyhood home, and Robert Burns' "wee cottage." It was soon known as Scotland's "strangest landlord."

Today, the Trust's budget is more than 20 million pounds ($33 million U.S.), membership over 230,000, and there are 120 properties.

Lea McNally, ranger and deerstalker, for The National Trust of Scotland— with a daisy in his mouth.

I met Jamie Stormonth Darling, the Trust's former first director, at Trust headquarters en route to Torridon. A traditional Scotsman, he was dressed in a crisply-pleated kilt, starched white shirt, woolen jacket, tie, the obligatory woolen stockings with a small dagger attached, and a sporan. He had a friendly grin, impeccable manners, and warm hazel eyes. I could see how he had built the Trust from nothing to "the best." He told me, "We now moderate idealism with good housekeeping. We conserve, as well as provide recreation, education, employment, and enjoyment."

I spent two marvelous days with Lea McNally, ranger and warden for Torridon. He had met me with his jeep and jumped out holding a daisy between his teeth! Short, tan, and wiry, Lea was a deerstalker, authority on red deer, and author. He regaled me with stories and information on the long drive to Torridon. At Torridon I felt close to true wilderness. It's one of the last areas in Great Britain where one can walk all day without seeing a soul and get at least five miles away from a paved road. Among those savage, red sandstone mountains, I could safely drink wild water, listen to a great silence, and breathe in pure air—three precious commodities in our technological world. It was easy to see why Scotland is called "the Lung of Europe."

"What's a deerstalker exactly?" I asked Lea later at supper.

"It's a game manager," he said. "Since wildlife in Great Britain and much of Europe is owned and cared for by individual landowners, game managers are essential. We're well respected professionals. We census herds, check range conditions, determine quotas to hunt, harvest excess animals, and carry the carcasses out for home use."

Lea gave me a quick glance and said shyly, "In my 32 years as a deerstalker, I've killed close to 3,000 stags and hinds. Mind you, I'm not proud of it, but it's a job to be done. Only misfit or injured deer are culled—cleanly, quickly, and often mercifully." He drew in a deep breath. "A deerstalker's objective is always to produce a healthy herd in balance with its habitat on that owner's land."

"That's almost the same as we were taught in wildlife biology class," I said, "except that American game belongs to the public and is managed by the states and federal government."

Lea's thoughtful commentary continued as we wound around mountains and down glens. I understood even more the tremendous changes which have impoverished the Highlands. All the major predators—wolf, lynx, brown bear, and boar—have been killed off or the woodlands burned to remove their refuges. Sheep, goats, and cattle have nibbled down vegetation and kept young trees from growing tall. Once Lea stopped alongside a peat bog and dug in the soil. Soon he uncovered an ancient stump with roots of the original Caledonian forest.

"Imagine," he said to me, "when Caledonian pines covered the flanks of these mountains. Birch and rowan grew in boggy places, and the land was green, moist, and full of wildlife. But too much wood was cut for fuel, building materials, and smelting iron ore. Then the great sporting estates of the Victorian era managed land for red deer and red grouse exclusively. Owners deliberately burned down forests. Now we're being "coniferized" with plantations of exotics like Sitka spruce. There's a poverty of fauna and flora within them." He shook his head mournfully. "The combination of teeth and fire over centuries here has been inexorable. All we have left now are heather, stones, and beautiful views."

Next morning I scrambled after Lea's springy steps in a landscape that looked like a gigantic alpine rock garden. He stopped often to look for red deer in that treeless terrain, but they had moved higher in the hot weather. He carried a 20-power spotting scope, canteen, knapsack, and had the pockets of his loden green knickers crammed with snacks. He explained that the red Torridon

Lea and Anne take an all-day hike through the Torridon Mountains. Lea is spotting deer with a 20-power scope.

sandstone was 800 million years old. I stared at the cliffs which looked like layers of potato chips and were just as friable.

Our hike took us to Coire Mhic Fhearchair, a deep glacial indentation between two 3,000-foot peaks. A limpid loch lay at the bottom, gouged out by glaciers, now fed by snow and springs. With a broad smile, Lea took off his pack and boots. Then he perched on a rock and hung his bare feet in the water. "Aye, that feels good," he said.

I took out my pocket thermometer. It showed the air was 82°F. I stuck it in the water, and it dropped to 56. "Well, Lea, it's warm enough for a swim." And I told him about our dip at St. Kilda.

This time I had a bathing suit with me, hoping there'd be a tarn or loch along our route. I changed and swam a few yards out to a flat rock. Scrambling onto it, I laid on the warm surface and relaxed. Here was an enchanting scene. Pipits were singing like larks. Burns (small streams) splashed musically down the peaks. White bogbean was blooming around the lochside. The silvery shape of a trout swam by. Small insects hovered shimmering in the still warm air. A golden eagle soared far, far above us.

A splash resounded against the stark cliffs as Lea did a belly flop into the water. He scrambled onto the rock with a shiver and

A bracing dip in remote Loch Mhic Fhearchair of Torridon. Water temperature was about 50–55°F.

informed me this was the second time in 13 years he had found it warm enough to swim!

"What a wild, grand, savage place," he exclaimed. "No wonder Queen Victoria loved the Highlands so. She kept her *Highland Journals* from 1848 to 1867. They were published in 1877 and are one of the happiest books ever written. She called the Highlands "fine and wild" and wrote that 'Hardly anyone ever comes here.'"

"I agree," I replied contentedly. "Nice this way."

After lunch, we walked the three or four miles back to a road and drove to Torridon ranger station where Lea and his wife had a house. After a rich Scottish dinner of salmon, potatoes, turnips and a marvelous pudding smothered in real cream, I took my backpack out to camp. That evening I lay in my tent, reveling in the burgundy-and-electric blue sunset mirrored on the still waters of sea loch Torridon. Around two o'clock, a sudden strong wind set my tent to snapping, much as it had done at Half Moon Caye. I crawled out with my sleeping pad and bag to snuggle down behind a rock in the heather. It was quieter and warmer. When Lea came to collect me and start the drive back to Trust headquarters, he found a sleepy, hungry, tousled camper. For the first time in my camping career, I hadn't been able to build a small cook fire, make espresso, or braid my hair into pigtails in those gusts.

Back in Edinburgh, I met more key Trust executives at head-quarters. Jamie introduced me to a marquess, an earl, a lord and a lady all in one morning. It was apparent that one of the great advantages the Scottish organization had over other groups in America and Third World countries is the backing of peerage. The Queen Mother is the patron of N.T.S. Trust executives are able to seek high-level advice and support judiciously. Unfortunately, dedicated royalty who believe in protection of natural resources just don't exist in Peru, the Dominican Republic, Panama, or New York state.

For my last wilderness fling, I flew to Fair Isle. Because of its remote position between the Orkneys and Shetlands, this tiny islet is a haven for travelling birds. Over 300 species have been seen and 237 of which have been caught and banded. Formerly, Dr. Waterston, a leading Scottish ornithologist, owned Fair Isle and ran the Fair Isle Bird Observatory and Trust. Its purpose was to train young ornithologists, study bird migration, and monitor the surrounding sea for oil pollution and sea food abundance.

In 1954, N.T.S. was able to accept Fair Isle from Dr. Waterston. Many members feared it was "mad" to buy isolated spots like this and St. Kilda. Others pointed out the tremendous social responsibility of shouldering "60 impecunious tenants living on the knife's edge." Bravely, the Trust took over the island and started an imaginative program of improvements which eased living conditions without spoiling the landscape. More importantly this change kept young people from leaving.

While there, I saw the small airstrip where light planes now could land and an improved pier for the twice-weekly mailboat. Electricity was available from generators and windmill—with lines buried. Telephones, too. Some cottages had washing machines, little greenhouses, and even TVs. I met younger local women dressed in designer jeans, plus the famous handknit Fair Isle sweaters. Modernization has stopped depopulation, unlike on St. Kilda. But, it cannot stop the furious winter storms and huge seas. Sometimes waves 60 feet high build up, and salt spray covers the entire two-by-four-mile island. Fair Isle is still the most isolated *inhabited* island in Great Britain.

A young, native Fair Islander offered to accompany me to the northern end of the island where most birds nested. Annie was delightfully straightforward and pleasant. With her apple-red cheeks, blue eyes, straight nose and coarse blond hair, she could have been the descendent of a Viking. Indeed they came to Fair Island as early as 900 A.D. As we walked, skylarks and pipits pirouetted around the sky singing.

"Is it terribly lonely here in winter?" I asked, looking at the gray sea, gray sky, and gray rocks.

"No," she said thoughtfully. "We all do things together here. No one goes their separate way. There's always a lot to do, and people need help with certain chores. If a newcomer doesn't pitch in, we just wait. A few winters will toughen them up; teach them to be neighborly."

The island rose gently as we approached its north end. The sea cliffs were smothered in pink thrift. From the northwest point we could see Foula, Shetland and Orkney far away. The sun was breaking through. The temp rose to 60°F—warm for Fair Island.

"This half of Fair Island is wild," said Annie. "There are moors, sandstone cliffs, stacs, and skerries. It's our commons and where we collect drinking and domestic water. The southern half is where all the houses, gardens, and pastures lie to catch full sun."

As we walked through the heather, pairs of skuas attacked us. Both Great Skuas and Arctic Skuas were dive-bombing and trying to hit our heads. They were dark, streamlined, and determined. One actually ticked my scalp with its talons. A sinister, powerful opponent. With each swoop, the bird gave a high mewling purr like a hungry cat. I turned to Annie. "Let's run!"

"They'll stop in a minute, once we're past their nests," she exclaimed. "For now just put your arm straight up in a threatening position."

It worked. When we reached the very edge of the cliffs, Annie and I crawled on our bellies and peeked over. Hundreds of puffins were nesting just below us in lavender beds of moss campion. Curious, almost tame, they didn't fly off. I was able to fill my lens with puffins, shot after shot. A whole roll of puffins!

Annie told me that over 20,000 puffins raise their young on Fair Isle. "Look below how nicely the weather's cleared," she pointed. The sea lay smooth and softly blue. Twelve fishing boats were heading out. From this height we looked out at a thousand seabirds floating on the surface like specks of pepper sprinkled on soup.

On the last evening at Fair Isle, I couldn't sleep. I sat on the porch of my little guesthouse, staring out at Sheep Rock where hundreds more seabirds twittered. They were as restless as I. Night never came. Poised so close to the Arctic Circle, Fair Isle's skies stay luminescent all June. The light was like mother-of-pearl—pinkish, bluish, lavender. Great fair weather clouds slid overhead, looking like purple Viking ships and calling up the adventuress in me.

But my trip was almost over. No more wild islands or highlands. I'd seen a spectrum of conservation areas that rivaled any place I'd ever been before. I'd briefly entered an arena of action to preserve properties that surpassed anything else I had experienced.

Why was this different?

It was because the Scots believed that preservation of these special lands and enjoyment of them by all the people was of paramount importance. They were willing to expand, evolve, form new partnerships, and integrate youth into their activities. They also understood that land is finite, populations are increasing, and fewer and fewer treasured properties exist. The National Trust for Scotland also has the advantage of being non-political, independent, and venturesome. As the late Sir Frank Fraser Darling, Scottish pioneer of nature conservation, wrote: "I would say that the Trust now leads the world in the wholeness of its approach to environmental management."

Then I wondered why it was that the Adirondack Park, one-fifth the size of Scotland, didn't have the same level of unified belief and caring as here. Why there always seemed to be a certain resistance to efforts of the Adirondack Park Agency and the Department of Environmental Conservation (the two state bodies in charge of the park) to preserve more land. Perhaps we could learn from the Scots.

I went back inside and stretched out under a down quilt. As the murmur of seabirds finally lulled me to sleep, I vowed to use my skills as a writer and lecturer to tell people about The National Trust for Scotland and its philosophy.

Back at N.T.S. headquarters, I said goodbye to Jamie Darling. Tears filled my eyes as I hugged his square shoulders. "It's been so inspiring, so exciting," I began. "I don't know how you do what you do so well."

Hazel eyes atwinkle, Jamie grasped my hands in a farewell gesture and said, "Why, lass, conservation is simply the game of being brave, charming, and perseverant."

UPDATE

- St. Kilda was designated as a World Heritage Site by UNESCO in 1986, and is Scotland's only W.H.S. based on natural features. This is perhaps the highest award any ecosystem or protected area can receive worldwide. Over one million birds breed and nest there, including the world's largest gannet colony of 60,000 pairs. The St. Kilda World Heritage Site may be extended to include surrounding marine environment. The use of St. Kilda as a strategic military base has virtually ceased by British Forces.

- Further conservation work has continued, however, by St. Kilda Work Parties and Archeological Discoveries. These summer volunteer groups maintain and improve the old historical hamlet of black houses and cliets around Village Bay under the supervision of a Trust Archivist. Today, The Scottish Natural Heritage is the Tenant and Manager of St. Kilda. It keeps strong links with The National Trust for Scotland.

- An imminent and serious threat of pollution from oil exploration presently exists. Companies are working not far from St. Kilda along Scotland's west coast of the Atlantic. How ironic: in 1956–1957 The Trust was advised there was no need to accept Lord Bute's bequest of St. Kilda, because "no foreseeable threat to its bird life and marine habitats existed being so far out to sea." As Sir Jamie Darling wrote: NO PLACE IS SAFE ANYMORE. This is a valuable lesson for us all to learn. Threats also includes a general increase in shipping traffic, with all types of cargo, including oil. An oil spill near St. Kila could be disastrous.

- As for Torridon, the growing enthusiasm for the outdoors and outdoor recreation coupled with the popular demand for the "right to roam" anywhere in Scotland are jeopardizing fragile natural areas, wildlife, and wilderness. These views must quickly be democratically handled and revalued to keep some places "ever wild" and protect sensitive wildlife. Climbers, hikers, campers, mountain bikers, and all-terrain vehicle users contribute to the problem when their numbers exceed the carrying capacity of the land.

- On September 27, 1988, Prime Minister Margaret Thatcher spoke to the Royal Geographical Society. She finally recognized acid rain as a serious pollution problem in the U.K. and elsewhere. I wrote her in October, complimented her , and requested a copy of her remarks. With letter, I included a copy of my National Geographic article on acid rain, dated December, 1980.

- Jamie Stormonth Darling was knighted for his exceptional efforts with the Trust and bears the title, "Sir Darling."

Anne and Sir Jamie Stormonth Darling, Director General, of The National
Trust for Scotland at Edinburgh headquarters.

Afterthoughts

So what's the upshot of all my consulting work and writing assignments? Is there a lesson to be learned from these various experiences? Is there a successful way to perform conservation work? Definitely.

Looking over the different approaches, funding sources, and organizations involved, I find there is a "best way" and a "worst way" to follow. I've categorized them from one to five stars: the least effective being one star and the most effective being five.

★ METHOD: working by yourself (with a few local assistants)
Funding: very small grants and your own money
Liaison: no collaborating institution or NGO, some generous private persons in foreign countries
Example: Quetzal Reserve, Guatemala; Half Moon Caye, Belize (partly)
Benefits: practical grass-roots approach, creating your own project and scientific papers
Drawbacks: almost impossible to achieve today; need collaborative institutions, NGOs, and colleagues

★★ METHOD: working by yourself and/or with small team, small college or NGOs
Funding: small diverse research funds and/or grants, usually insufficient
Liaison: small college, NGO, or organization in foreign country/USA
Example: Anegada ecological survey, BVI
Benefits: independence in field; no huge master plan or reports needed; write scientific papers
Drawbacks: insufficient funds; possible poor coordination and timing; reports often delayed; seldom publish scientific papers on project with others

★★★ METHOD: working through IUCN as consultant (now called The World Conservation Union in Switzerland), or other similar independent large agency
Funding: adequate funds for travel, field work, reports, fees
Liaison: has global network with 6,000 scientists, many government groups, etc.
Example: Volcán Barú National Park, Panama
Benefits: good contacts, considerable clout, addresses environmental conservation <u>and</u> sustainable development
Drawbacks: slow in processing and paying due to size and structure

★★★ METHOD: working alone as free-lance writer/photographer on assignment to well-known natural history magazines
Funding: funding for travel and fee for article may, or may not, be adequate
Liaison: no direct collaborating organization in foreign country; many helpful, generous persons and groups available; press contacts
Example: Audubon Magazine – Amazonia assignment; Half Moon Caye story
Benefits: prestigious; exciting work; meet great people; professional pride
Drawbacks: may not reach large audience; too little payment for risks involved; no recovery policy if kidnapped or injured

★★★ METHOD: working as guest lecturer on natural history cruises; or lecturing in foreign countries
Funding: pay inadequate; travel paid; free room/board
Liaison: mainly with passengers and audiences
Example: Lindblad Travel Inc. and Special Expeditions Inc. cruises
Benefits: excellent experiences; great people and contacts; adventures
*Drawbacks:*poor pay; relatively small numbers reached; may, or may not, convince decision-makers, C.E.O.s, politicians aboard; in/out, short appearances; shipboard mentality; no follow-up

★★★★METHOD: working as consultant to multi-national corporation, possibly collaborating with foreign governments
Funding: good fees, travel logistics, backup in field
Liaison: usually excellent coordination with team mem-

bers, foreign officials and workers, corporate heads
Example: Parque Nacional del Este, Dominican Republic
Benefits: good clout, fast results, accessible vehicles and
equipment, excellent master plans
Drawbacks: usually a hierarchy of officials to work
through; corporate finances and government commit-
ments may change abruptly due to business or political
reversals or recessions

★★★★★METHOD: working for top-rate major magazines as free-
lance writer on environmental articles
Funding: excellent funding for travel, field work, plus high
fees
Liaison: access to almost every group, government offices,
well-known persons in foreign country; press contacts;
Letters of Introduction supplied
Example: National Geographic articles on "Quetzal,
Fabulous Bird of Maya Land," and "National Parks of
Central America"
Benefits: Anything for the article; provides photographer,
film, developing, some field gear; prestige and clout; far-
reaching educational value and exposure as each
issue/article reaches 25 million readers; prestige
Drawbacks: may be considerable risks involved, or discom-
forts; no recovery policy if kidnapped; author must be pre-
pared to provide detailed notes, data, names, addresses for
Research Dept. of N.G. to check article before published
(takes six weeks)

★★★★★METHOD: working as consultant or writer for large, private, independent organization committed to conservation of natural/cultural resources
Funding: usually adequate travel funding and fees
Liaison: other similar organizations in country; royalty;
some government connections
Example: The National Trust for Scotland
Benefits: dedicated employees and officers; fast results;
great help in field; many spin-offs; good educational value
to members
Drawbacks: possible change of priorities and policies if top
officers change

Probably most readers have been as astonished as I by my UPDATES. So many changes—most of them deleterious—have taken place in the 20 to 30 years I've been working for wildlife and protected natural areas. It doesn't matter if it's the largest national park in South America, or the tiniest nature sanctuary in the Caribbean, every place is vulnerable. Nature has no defenses against modern high technology, man-made pollution of air and water, and human population explosions. As Sir Jamie Darling would say, "NO PLACE IS SAFE ANYMORE."

If some readers think I'm exaggerating about the critical state of our planet, I beg you to PAY ATTENTION. Pay attention to my UPDATES. Pay attention to global warming, to corals dying in oceans 'round the world, to the increase in infectious diseases, to the thinning ozone layer. Pay attention to whether we can replant trees and regreen Central America in time before the next Hurricane Mitch strikes, or another natural catastrophe.

Please listen to the prudent warnings of two extraordinary thinkers and leaders. Dr. Edward O. Wilson—winner of two Pulitzer prizes, University Professor at Harvard, and one of the most important scientists of this century warns us of a mass extinction of plants and animals. The process is proceeding at a much faster pace than at any other time over the past 4.5 billion years on earth. One in eight plants is threatened with extinction today— precious plants that provide us with food, fibers, shelters, and medicines. His estimate is that we are losing 50 species per day worldwide. That means that 20% of the ten million living forms of life may disappear in the next 30 years.

The second great visionary today, in my opinion, is His All Holiness, Bartholomew I, leader of the world's 300 million Eastern Orthodox Christians. He is called the "Green Patriarch" and is an outspoken advocate of conservation. During his month-long tour of USA in October 1997, he proclaimed the following:

> **"For humans to cause species to become extinct and to destroy the biological diversity of God's creation; for humans to degrade the integrity of the Earth by causing changes in its climate, by stripping the Earth of its natural forests or destroying its wetlands; for humans to contaminate the Earth's waters, its land, its air, and its life with poisonous substances—these are sins."**

Further warnings must come from both the community of scientists and the religious community in order to get them across to the people before we kill ourselves.

In case you are now feeling helpless, overwrought, or paralyzed by such gloomy predictions—stop! Or, if you think there's no way you could do what I've done—wrong! <u>Anyone, any place, any time can do something to save the natural resources of our earth.</u>
Consider these simple acts:

1. Pick half a mile, or two, or three, of roadway and keep it clean. In New York State individuals and groups get their names and the length of road they conserve displayed on signs. (You could also put up some bluebird boxes along the way.)

2. Give donations or volunteer your time and effort to your favorite conservation group. There are hundreds. Consult in the library *The 1999 Conservation Directory* published annually by the National Wildlife Federation. Or you can purchase it by sending $55 to N.W.F., 1400 Sixteenth Street, N.W., Washington, DC, 20036-2266; or order it at 1-800-432-6564. It's the "bible" of conservationists.

3. Do as the "Friends of Lake Atitlán," Guatemala, do every Easter Week. They provide free garbage pickup for vacation home owners by boat or car. Big plastic garbage bags are given to all who cooperate. Later, Friends recycle everything at local garbage collection centers. They are also starting to replant/restore the watershed of the lake with reeds and trees.

<u>Yes, anyone, any place, any time can do something to save the natural resources, and the beauty, of our earth.</u>